Livy's Written Rome

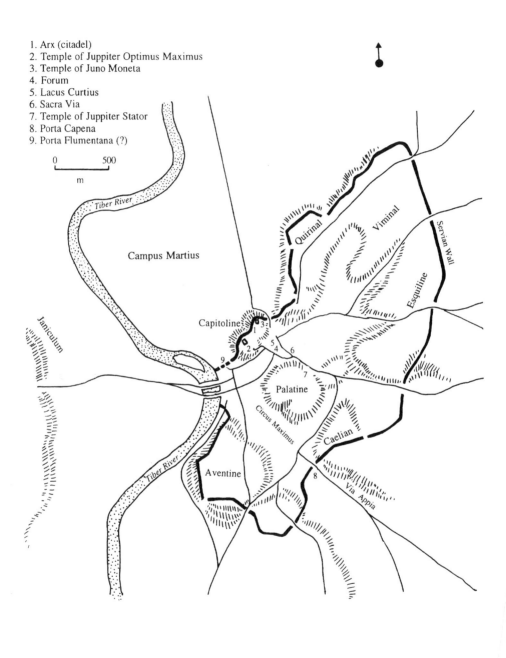

1. Arx (citadel)
2. Temple of Juppiter Optimus Maximus
3. Temple of Juno Moneta
4. Forum
5. Lacus Curtius
6. Sacra Via
7. Temple of Juppiter Stator
8. Porta Capena
9. Porta Flumentana (?)

0   500
     m

Tiber River

Campus Martius

Janiculum

Capitoline

Quirinal

Viminal

Servian Wall

Esquiline

Palatine

Circus Maximus

Caelian

Tiber River

Aventine

Via Appia

Livy's
Written Rome

Mary Jaeger

Ann Arbor

THE UNIVERSITY OF MICHIGAN PRESS

First paperback edition 2009
Copyright © by the University of Michigan 1997
All rights reserved
Published in the United States of America by
The University of Michigan Press
Manufactured in the United States of America
⊗ Printed on acid-free paper

2012   2011   2010   2009   5   4   3   2

A CIP catalog record for this book is available from the British Library.

Library of Congress Cataloging-in-Publication Data

Jaeger, Mary, 1960–
    Livy's written Rome / Mary Jaeger.
        p.   cm.
    Includes bibliographical references and index.
    ISBN 0-472-10789-5 (alk. paper)
    1. Rome—History—Republic, 265–30 B.C.   2. Livy. Ad urbe
condita.   I. Title.
DG241.J34   1997
937'.02—dc21   97-21070
                                                                     CIP

ISBN-13: 978-0-472-03361-4 (pbk : alk. paper)
ISBN-10: 0-472-03361-1 (pbk : alk. paper)

For my mother and father

Acknowledgments

I owe many debts of gratitude to people and institutions who have contributed support to this project. My first and greatest are to my teacher Tom Habinek and my colleague and mentor John Nicols. This book would not exist without their encouragement and inspiration. Philippe Buc, Christina Kraus, John Nicols, and Malcolm Wilson read the entire manuscript at various stages of completion and offered invaluable advice. Marlene Flory and Sharon James read and made useful suggestions on individual chapters, as did my colleague Ben Pascal, whose ability to spot verbiage shortened the manuscript considerably. I have profited a great deal from discussing Livy, memory, and space with Sarolta Takács. William Loy of the University of Oregon Geography Department offered generous encouragement and advice to the amateur cartographer. Jim Marks eased the burden of checking references and compiling the bibliography, and Ann Applegarth gave valuable assistance at various stages of the manuscript's production. The anonymous readers for the University of Michigan Press have vastly improved this book, with their criticisms and suggestions. I am grateful to all of these people for their help. The faults and errors of the final product remain my own.

A University of Oregon summer stipend supported three months of uninterrupted research in 1993. A Harvard Mellon Faculty Fellowship in the Humanities for the 1993–94 academic year made possible a year of research pleasantly interrupted by interdisciplinary discussion with fellow Mellons Paige Baty, Chris Bongie, Jennifer Fleischner, Dagmar Herzog, and Edward Wheatley. The Harvard Classics Department extended gracious hospitality, and I am especially grateful to Ernst Badian and Cynthia Damon, who included me in their Livy seminar.

Finally, I would like to thank my editor, Ellen Bauerle, for her constant encouragement and support.

Contents

Abbreviations

Abbreviations of ancient authors and their works are in general those listed in *The Oxford Latin Dictionary,* ed. P.G.W. Glare, (Oxford, 1968–82), and *A Greek–English Lexicon,* ed. H.G. Liddell, R. Scott, and H. Stuart-Jones (Oxford, 1968).

AJA	*American Journal of Archaeology*
AJP	*American Journal of Philology*
ANRW	*Aufstieg und Niedergang der römischen Welt.* Ed. H. Temporini and W. Haase. New York, 1972–.
BICS	*Bulletin of the Institute of Classical Studies of the University of London*
CA	*Classical Antiquity*
CIL	*Corpus Inscriptionum Latinarum.* Berlin, 1863–.
CJ	*The Classical Journal*
CP	*Classical Philology*
CQ	*Classical Quarterly*
CW	*The Classical World*
G&R	*Greece and Rome*
HRR	Peter, H. *Historicorum Romanorum Reliquiae.* 2 vols. Stuttgart, 1967.
HSCP	*Harvard Studies in Classical Philology*
ILLRP	Degrassi, A. *Inscriptiones Latinae Liberae Rei Publicae.* 2 vols. Florence, 1957, 1963.
ILS	Dessau, H. *Inscriptiones Latinae Selectae.* 3 vols. Berlin, 1892–1916. Reprint, Chicago, 1979.
JRA	*Journal of Roman Archaeology*
JRS	*Journal of Roman Studies*
LCM	*Liverpool Classical Monthly*
LEC	*Les Études Classiques*

Lewis and Short	Lewis, C.T., and C. Short. *A Latin Dictionary.* 2d ed. Oxford, 1975.
LTUR	*Lexicon Topographicum Urbis Romae.* Ed. Eva Margareta Steinby. Rome, 1993.
MAAR	*Memoirs of the American Academy in Rome*
MD	*Materiali e discussioni per l'analisi dei testi classici*
MH	*Museum Helveticum*
Ogilvie	Ogilvie, R.M. *A Commentary on Livy: Books 1–5.* Oxford, 1970.
OLD	*The Oxford Latin Dictionary.* Ed. P.G.W. Glare. Oxford, 1968–82.
PBSR	*Papers of the British School at Rome*
PCPS	*Proceedings of the Cambridge Philological Society*
RE	*Paulys Real-Encyclopädie der klassischen Altertumswissenschaft.*
REA	*Revue des Études Anciennes*
REL	*Revue des Études Latines*
RhM	*Rheinisches Museum*
RHR	*Revue de l'Histoire des Religions*
TAPA	*Transactions and Proceedings of the American Philological Association*
TLL	*Thesaurus Linguae Latinae*
W-M	Weissenborn, W., and H.J. Müller. *Titi Livi ab urbe condita libri.* Berlin, 1880–1911.
Xenia	*Xenia. Konstanzer Althistorische Vorträge und Forschungen.* Ed. Wolfgang Schuller. Vol. 31. *Livius. Aspekte seines Werkes.* Konstanz, 1993.

Introduction

In the last surviving book of his history of Rome, the *Ab Urbe Condita*, Livy describes how the proconsul L. Aemilius Paullus, after defeating the Macedonian king Perseus at Pydna, traveled through Greece, visiting sites famous in history and literature (45.27.5–28.6). Livy says that these places are more impressive to hear of than to see, since report *(fama)* has increased their renown.[1] His account of the tour fosters a sense of Roman ascendancy in a Greece whose greatness belongs clearly to the past. Paullus made his way first through Thessaly to Delphi, site of the renowned oracle *(inclutum oraculum)*, where he requisitioned for his own use two columns originally intended to hold statues of the Macedonian king.[2] Then he went on to Lebadea, to Chalcis, and to Aulis, with its harbor, famous *(inclutum)* for once *(quondam)* harboring Agamemnon's fleet of a thousand ships. Here the proconsul visited the Temple of Artemis, where Iphigenia was said to have died. Moving on, he came to Attica, "where a prophet of ancient times *[uates antiquus]* is worshiped as a god, and where there is an old *[uestustum]* sanctuary, pleasant for

---

1. "It was now almost autumn; Paullus decided to use the early part of the season to travel around Greece, and to visit those places that, made famous by reputation, have been believed to be greater by hearsay than they are when one makes their acquaintance by sight" *[autumni fere tempus erat; cuius temporis initio ad circumeundam Graeciam, uisendaque <quae> nobilitata fama maiora auribus accepta sunt quam oculis noscuntur, uti statuit]* (45.27.5). All citations from Books 41–45 are from *Titi Livi Ab Urbe Condita, Libri XLI–XLV*, ed. J. Briscoe (Stuttgart, 1986). On Livy's use of *fama, fabula,* and the distinction between hearing and seeing in ancient historiography, see G. Miles, *Reconstructing Early Rome* (Ithaca, 1995), 14–20. For a reassessment of Paullus' philhellenism, see W. Reiter, *Aemilius Paullus: Conquerer of Greece* (New York, 1988). On Paullus' appropriation of Hellenic culture, see E.S. Gruen, *Culture and National Identity in Republican Rome* (Ithaca, 1992), 141–45, 245–48.

2. The base of the column at Delphi still exists. The inscription (*ILLRP* 323) reads *L. Aimilius L.f. imperator de rege Perse / Macedonibusque cepet.* On the monument, see Gruen, *Culture and National Identity,* 141–45. On the use of *spolia,* see A. Kuttner, "Some New Grounds for Narrative," in *Narrative and Event in Ancient Art,* ed. Peter J. Holliday (Cambridge, 1993), 204.

the springs and rills all around."[3] His next stop was Athens, a city replete with ancient tradition *(uetusta fama)* but still, Livy concedes, one with many sights worth seeing: the Acropolis, the harbors and long walls, monuments of great generals, and statues of gods and men remarkable for artwork of all kinds.[4] After sacrificing to Minerva on the Acropolis, Paullus went on to Corinth, a city that was lovely then, before its destruction *(urbs erat tunc praeclara ante excidium)*. From Corinth he moved on to Sicyon, to Argos, and to Epidaurus with its Temple of Aesculapius, a place that Livy describes from the perspective of the narrative present: now it bears only the traces of its plundered offerings, but when Paullus saw it, it was richly adorned with the offerings themselves *(nunc uestigiis reuolsorum donorum, tum donis diues erat)*. Paullus went next to Sparta, which was memorable *(memorabilis)* rather for its severity and its customs than for the splendor of its buildings.[5]

On the last and climactic stop of the tour an attraction finally lived up to its fame: Paullus entered the Temple of Jupiter at Olympia and looked on Phidias' chryselephantine statue of the god. According to the Greek historian Polybius, who is probably Livy's source for this travelogue, Paullus, greatly impressed, said that Phidias alone appeared to have made a likeness (μεμιμῆσθαι) of the Zeus of Homer.[6] (Plutarch tells us that the remark was famous.)[7] Paullus went on to add that, although his expectations had been high, the reality of the statue far exceeded them. Livy agrees that the statue did not disappoint: he says that Paullus was deeply

---

3. Briscoe prints: < . . . . *Oropum> Atticae uentum est, ubi pro deo uates antiquus colitur, templumque vestustum est fontibus riuisque circa amoenum* (45.27.10).

4. *Athenas inde, plenas quidem et ipsas uetustae famae, multa tamen uisenda habentes, arcem, portus, muros, Piraeum urbi iungentes, naualia, <monumenta> magnorum imperatorum, simulacra deorum hominumque, omni genere et materiae et artium insignia* (45.27.11).

5. *Inde Lacedaemonem adit, non operum magnificentia sed disciplina institutisque memorabiliem † ac silentiam †* (45.28.4). Cf. Thucydides' observation that buildings and ruins do not necessarily give a precise measure of a city's former greatness (1.10.1–4).

6. On Polybius' version of Paullus' tour, see F.W. Walbank, *A Historical Commentary on Polybius*, 3 vols. (Oxford, 1957–79), 3:432–33; A. Klotz, *Livius und seine Vorgänger* (Leipzig and Berlin, 1941; reprint, Amsterdam, 1964), 21; H. Nissen, *Kritische Untersuchungen über die Quellen der vierten und fünften Dekade des Livius* (Berlin, 1863), 274–76; and, more recently, J. Briscoe, "Livy and Polybius," *Xenia* 31 (1993): 39–52, with references to earlier work. Briscoe makes several good cautionary points about comparing the two authors. On Polybius and the rise and fall of Macedonian power, see J. de Romilly, *The Rise and Fall of States according to Greek Authors* (Ann Arbor, 1977), 8–9.

7. "Much spoken of" [πολυθρύλητον] (Plutarch *Aem.* 28.2); see also Walbank, *A Historical Commentary on Polybius,* 3:433.

moved, as if he were gazing on Jupiter himself *(Iouem uelut praesentem intuens motus animo est)*. And so, adds Livy, Paullus ordered a particularly honorific offering to be prepared, just as if he were about to sacrifice on the Capitoline: *itaque haud secus quam si in Capitolio immolaturus esset, sacrificium amplius solito apparari iussit* (45.28.5).

Livy's version of the tour omits the famous remark about Phidias and Homer and replaces the reference to Greek art and poetry with one to the Capitoline Hill, so that, in contrast to the sculptor, Phidias, who is credited with lending concrete reality to the Zeus represented in the lines of Homer, the proconsul Paullus imposes a distinctly Roman stamp on the god. Paullus travels to the famous Greek towns, starting with Delphi, the center of the Greek world; but when he concludes his trip, he honors Jupiter by acting as if he were at the religious and military center of Rome.[8] Time may have increased the renown of these tourist attractions, but by placing consistent emphasis on their role as reminders of a lost and greater past, Livy's version of the tour indicates how far Greece has declined. Olympia, the one place where reality lives up to expectation, most clearly reflects the new world order: the pantheon conceived by the Greek poet has given way to the one that occupies the site of Rome.[9] Paullus' other actions after Pydna convey clearly a sense of Roman ascendancy, and Livy's description of his trip asserts that Rome is now the cultural center of the world. The narrative, therefore, reflects some fundamental convictions about the organization of space: Rome is the center of the empire it rules, and the Capitoline, the fixed center of Roman religion and home of the gods who are the source of Rome's supremacy, is the center of Rome.

The ex-consul M. Servilius voices these convictions a few chapters later, when he argues in support of Paullus' request for a triumph:

Maiores uestri omnium magnarum rerum et principia exorsi a dis sunt, et finem statuerunt. consul proficiscens praetorue paludatis lictoribus in prouinciam et ad bellum uota in Capitolio nuncupat:

---

8. While the Polybian account is fragmentary, it contains the remark about Homer, which Livy so conspicuously omits. In addition, Polybius says that Paullus took note of the solidity of Sicyon's fortifications and the strength of Argos, whereas Livy simply calls them *nobiles urbes*. On Aemilius Paullus' display of Roman cultural supremacy, see Gruen, *Culture and National Identity*, 245–48.

9. This comes out clearly in Camillus' famous speech against the proposed move to Veii (5.51–54).

uictor perpetrato bello eodem in Capitolium triumphans ad eosdem deos quibus uota nuncupauit merita dona portans redit. (45.39.10–11)

[Your ancestors took the gods for their point of departure in all great undertakings, and it was with the gods that they brought them to a close. When a consul or a praetor, with his lictors in their military cloaks, sets out for his province and for war, he makes his vows on the Capitoline; and when he has been victorious in that war, he returns in triumph to the Capitoline, bringing gifts that are their due to the same gods to whom he made his vows.][10]

Servilius' speech and Paullus' tour appear in the last surviving book of the *Ab Urbe Condita,* yet the worldview they reflect at this moment of Roman triumph is entirely consistent with the one promoted by the history from the beginning. Although Romulus founds his original settlement on the Palatine, the Capitoline is where he dedicates the first temple, the shrine of Jupiter Feretrius (1.10.7). Here he deposits spoils taken from an enemy general killed in single combat, thus making the place the religious center of the city in its military capacity. By the end of Book 1 the discovery of the human head during the construction of the Temple of Jupiter confirms that Capitoline is truly "head" and center of Rome (1.55.5); Roman generals set out for their provinces after making vows on the Capitoline—disaster befalls the city when they fail to do so early in the Second Punic War (21.63.5–15)—and they return from the field with spoils to dedicate there (e.g., 25.39.17, 42.49.16). In the large cycle of the first pentad, which takes the *Ab Urbe Condita* from the destruction of Troy to that of Rome, the Capitoline alone remains intact and provides topographical continuity during the transition to the rebuilt city of Book 6.[11] For Livy, space, time, Roman national memory, and the cultural practices that reinforce national identity all start from this center, move outward, and then return, as action oscillates annually between events at home and in the field, and as the city expands, collapses, and

---

10. There are problems with the text, but Servilius' point is still clear. For the text printed here (Madvig's) see Briscoe, *Titi Livi Ab Urbe Condita, Libri XLI–XLV,* p. 383. In his main text, Briscoe prints: *uictor perpetrato < . . . > eodem in Capitolium triumphans ad eosdem deos quibus uota nuncupauit merita † bonaque pr. trans † redit.*

11. See chap. 3. On cycles of history, see Miles, *Reconstructing Early Rome,* 75–109, an earlier version of which appeared as "The Cycle of Roman History in Livy's First Pentad," *AJP* 107 (1986): 1–33.

grows back stronger than before in Books 1–6. The Capitoline, then, is both the center of Roman space and a Janus-like beginning and ending point for temporal cycles.[12]

This model does more than reflect political and religious Romanocentrism: it plays an important role in organizing the narrative.[13] Faced with the real events of the past—a mass of particulars that, as it has been said, "do not offer themselves as stories"[14]—the historian must either supply

---

12. On the Capitoline as the beginning and end of temporal cycles, see also the description of the consul's departure at 42.49.16. A.M. Feldherr ("Spectacle and Society in Livy's History" [Ph.D. diss., University of California, Berkeley, 1991], 5–7) points out that by evoking anxieties for the future (will this consul return in triumph?) as well as memories of past consuls, the sight "provides a direct link to the progress of the state through time."

The present study can be read as complementary to Feldherr's, which focuses on the use of ritual and spectacle in Livy, including its effect on the reader. While, like Feldherr, I am interested in the visual, I am concerned more with the way references to the physical city and its monuments interact with the organization of the narrative, and less with the impact of appearances on events.

13. The idea of the "shape" of Roman history has begun to receive attention. C. Nicolet (*Space, Geography, and Politics in the Early Roman Empire* [Ann Arbor, 1991]) calls for geographical readings of authors who are not writing geography per se—poets and especially historians. He suggests "a sort of spatial and temporal spiral," beginning with Rome's expansion in increasingly distant defensive and offensive wars. According to Nicolet (8–9), in the Augustan Age geography begins to *influence* history. Nicolet sees Livy's growing interest as a result of contemporary interest in the subject. (As evidence, he points to Agrippa's map on the Porticus Vipsania [100–101].) On contemporary geographical knowledge and exploration, see Nicolet's discussion (57–94). His sympathetic discussion of Livy is in sharp contrast to the views of the critics who call Livy an indifferent geographer at best on the grounds that he did not travel much and includes few geographical excursuses in his work. On Livy and geography, with examples of errors, see P.G. Walsh, *Livy, His Historical Aims and Methods* (Cambridge, 1961), 153–57; M.R. Girod, "La Géographie de Tite-Live," *ANRW* II.30.2 (1982): 1190–1229. Girod (1192–93) defends Livy by pointing out that this appearance of indifference is partly the result of accident, since the epitomies of the later, lost Books 103 and 104 refer to descriptions of Gaul and Germany. Girod also points out that Livy was writing Romanocentric, not universal, history. Therefore, what did not matter to Rome would have been irrelevant digression, while Italian geography was something that Livy would have expected his audience to know. Judging Livy as a geographer is complicated by the lack of evidence for his life and travels. He was familiar with the area around his native Patavium. He lived in Rome at some point, but there is little evidence to tell how long; he claims to have seen the tomb of Scipio Africanus at Liternum. E. Badian ("Livy and Augustus," *Xenia* 31 [1993]: 31 n. 12) underscores the dearth of evidence for Livy's travels.

14. H. White (*The Content of the Form: Narrative Discourse and Historical Representation* [Baltimore, 1987], 4) writes: "Narrative becomes a problem only when we wish to give to real events the form of story. It is because real events do not offer themselves as stories that their narrativization is so difficult." See also S. Bann, "Analysing the Discourse of History," *Dalhousie Review* 64, no.2 (1984): 376–400. An interesting study of the way literary experience influences the perception and interpretation of events is P. Fussell's *The Great War and Modern Memory* (Oxford, 1975). Although Fussell's subject is modern, his

from his imagination or find in his sources patterns that make these events elicit a sympathetic response from his audience. The reader of Livy's preface, for example, comprehends Rome's entire past in the organic and medical metaphors of growth, disease, and decline, as well as in the architectural metaphor of the construction and collapse of a massive edifice.[15] In addition, while adopting the chronological framework of his annalistic predecessors, Livy organizes sections of the history around such central themes as the power struggles between different segments of Roman society, and presents particular episodes as dramas divided into discrete acts.[16] Finally, the books, pentads, and decades of his narrative correspond to historical epochs.[17] A Romanocentric worldview is, then, one of several ordering devices, some traditional and some unique, that give shape to Livy's narrative and distinguish significant particulars within it. Combined, these devices place a distinctive stamp on

discussion is useful for anyone interested in literary convention and historical events (especially pertinent are chaps. 3, "Adversary Proceedings"; 4, "Myth, Ritual, and Romance"; and 5, "Oh What a Literary War").

15. On the body/state analogy, see J. Béranger, *Recherches sur l'aspect idéologique du Principat* (Basel, 1953), 223–30. For Livy's use of medical terms, see E. Dutoit, "Tite-Live s'est-il intéressé à la médicine?" *MH* 5 (1948): 116–23. Livy mixes architectural and organic metaphors twice, first when he describes Rome's decay (Pref. 9): *labente deinde paulatim disciplina uelut desidentes primo mores* [sc. the reader] *sequatur animo, deinde ut magis magisque lapsi sint, tum ire coeperint praecipites, donec ad haec tempora quibus nec uitia nostra nec remedia pati possumus peruentum est.* He does so a second time (Pref. 10) when he points out that the healthful *(salubre)* thing about studying history is looking at evidence set out on a record/monument *(monumentum).*

While these images are immediately clear to the reader of the preface, the loss of the last two-thirds of the history prevents us from knowing whether or not Livy organized the entire history around them. On the effects of this loss, see J. Henderson, "Livy and the Invention of History," in *History as Text,* ed. Averil Cameron (London, 1989), 64–85, esp. 76–83.

16. On patterns of strife, see J. Lipovsky, *A Historiographical Study of Livy: Books VI–X* (New York, 1981); on the organization of particular episodes, see Ogilvie. On Livy's use of the dramatic reversal, see E. Burck, *Die Erzählungskunst des T. Livius* (Berlin, 1934; Reprint, Berlin and Zurich, 1964), 210–17.

17. E.g., Book 1 starts with the fall of Troy and ends with the expulsion of the kings; Books 1–5 end with the fall of Rome to the Gauls. On cycles, see Miles, *Reconstructing Early Rome,* 75–109, 110–36. On Livy's organization of his text, see P.A. Stadter, "The Structure of Livy's History," *Historia* 21 (1972): 287–307; T.J. Luce, "Design and Structure in Livy: 5.32–55," *TAPA* 102 (1971): 265–302; and esp. idem, *Livy: The Composition of His History* (Princeton, 1977). Luce (*Livy,* 3–32) catalogs the various ways of dividing the *Ab Urbe Condita* that have been suggested by previous authors. On the location of particular episodes at the "edge" or "center" of a book, see C.S. Kraus, "No Second Troy: Topoi and Refoundation in Livy, Book V," *TAPA* 124 (1994): 282–83.

Livy's version of the received tradition. Scholars have long appreciated Livy's skill at arranging material as a facet of his style; more recently they have come to realize that it is one way in which Livy conveys his conception of historical change and that his masterful organization of a long and heterogenous narrative demonstrates his sophistication as both artist and historian.[18]

In writing history *ab urbe condita,* Livy describes both the Roman world extending through space and the life of the city extending through time.[19] As it recounts the events of Rome's early history, Book 1 introduces the major topographical features of the city proper: the Tiber, the Aventine, the Palatine, the Capitoline, and the Forum.[20] Then, the opening passages of Book 2 link the expulsion of the Tarquins to the origin of the Campus Martius and the creation of Tiber Island.[21] After the destruction of the city in Book 5, Camillus' great speech weaves topographical references into a coherent and significant landscape that the Romans find they cannot abandon. In the first half of Book 6, the Capitoline represents the city by synecdoche when it becomes the spatial and rhetorical center of a debate concerning political supremacy in a reborn and outward-looking Rome. The city's physical changes correspond to institutional changes and are, at the same time, historical events in their own right. Thus they both provide material for the narrative and give it its shape.

This book examines Livy's use of the Roman world, particularly the city Rome, as one of his primary organizing devices. It argues that a great deal of evidence for Livy's complexity and sophistication as a thinker lies in his presentation of Roman history as a story of space and memory, of the landscape and its acquisition of meaning, and of the

18. On historical order, development, and change, see esp. Luce, *Livy,* 230–97; Miles, *Reconstructing Early Rome,* 75–109.

19. On the time/space analogy, see Kraus, "No Second Troy," 267–70.

20. E.g., Tiber: 1.3.8, 1.4.4; Aventine: 1.3.9, 1.6.4; Palatine: 1.5.1, 1.6.4, 1.7.3; Capitoline: 1.10.5; the future Forum: 1.12.1. On the development of the landscape in Book 1, see M. Griffe, "L'Espace de Rome dans le Livre I de l'Histoire de Tite-Live," in *Arts et Légendes d'Espaces: Figures du Voyage et rhétoriques du Monde,* Communications Réunies et Présentées par Christian Jacob et Frank Lestringant (Paris, 1981), 111–22.

21. 2.5.2–4. The Tiber Island was created from the Tarquins' grain crop, which was cut from the Campus Martius and thrown into the river. Other constructive destruction in Book 2 includes Valerius Publicola relocating the site of his new house from a "regal" to a "republican" location (2.7.5–12) and, in the next year, the destruction of the Pons Sublicius to defend the city from the Etruscan army on the Janiculum (2.10.1–10).

monuments that attempt to preserve that meaning. Accordingly, this book is concerned with the representation of space, monuments, and memory in the *Ab Urbe Condita* and also, in converse, with the idea of the *Ab Urbe Condita* as a spatial entity, a monument, and a lengthy act of remembering. In claiming that Livy writes originally and profoundly about the past by writing originally and profoundly about space, monuments, and memory, this study joins a body of recent critical work on Livy that reconsiders previous assumptions about Livy's methods, goals, and merit as a historian. In particular, these are the assumptions made by source criticism *(Quellenforschung)*, which seeks to identify what writers Livy followed in each part of his history.[22] This is not to deny the usefulness of source criticism to Livian studies but to move beyond seeing it as an end in itself. For example, in recent years the study of the rhetorical devices that ancient historians use when they criticize other historians or when they write about themselves, their goals, their sources, and their methods has emerged as a promising subfield of historiographical studies in general.[23] Consequently the question has arisen as to whether or not the metaphor of the historian *following* his sources is apt. The image of Livy lost in the records of Roman history and dogging the tracks of the annalist Valerius Antius in one direction before turning aside to follow Claudius Quadrigarius in another has given way to one of Livy as a Roman Daedalus constructing a monument from the rubble of the ages and leaving broken edges visible as reminders that any coherent account of the past is, at best, contrived from ruins.[24]

---

22. The main figures among the source critics are H. Nissen (see *Kritische Untersuchungen*) and A. Klotz (see *Livius und seine Vorgänger*). E. Burck began the argument for Livy's control of his material and his text; T.J. Luce and subsequent critics have carried it further. For work in the years between Burck's *Die Erzählungskunst* and Luce's *Livy*, see W. Kissel, "Livius 1933–1978: Eine Gesamtbibliographie," *ANRW* II.30.2 (1982): 899–997; J.E. Phillips, "Current Research in Livy's First Decade, 1959–1979," *ANRW* II.30.2 (1982): 998–1057. Miles (*Reconstructing Early Rome*, 1–7) extends Livy's control of his text to include the self-conscious display of its contradictions.

23. See, e.g., A.J. Woodman, *Rhetoric in Classical Historiography* (London, 1988); J.L. Moles, "Livy's Preface," *PCPS*, n.s., 39 (1993): 141–68; idem, "Truth and Untruth in Herodotus and Thucydides," in *Lies and Fiction in the Ancient World*, ed. C. Gill and T.P. Wiseman (Austin, Tex., 1993), 88–121.

24. See in particular the excellent chapter titled "History and Memory," in Miles, *Reconstructing Early Rome*, 8–74. In much of the theory of monuments and history that underlies this study, I am in agreement with Miles. His focus, however, is on Livy's rhetorical use of the seeing/hearing dichotomy, not on matters of space.

Livy's account of Aemilius Paullus' tour reflects what is probably a universal tendency to view one's own city as the center of the world.[25] The *Ab Urbe Condita* (Christina Kraus and others note that the title has spatial as well as temporal significance) is nothing if not Romanocentric. In an ethnocentric view of the world, places and peoples are interesting or uninteresting to the degree to which they are connected to or impinge on this center. They are also interesting if they occupy the other feature of a whole, the edge.[26] Livy's narrative journey through Roman history, a long and circuitous trip, takes author and reader through a model of Roman space that emphasizes its center, Rome, and periphery, the various frontiers. In addition, Livy organizes particular episodes around other spaces that emphasize center and edge: the city with its outer walls and inner citadel; the camp with its central meeting place and peripheral fortifications.[27] Various degrees of distance, familiarity, and importance between center and edge can be expressed by a series of concentric circles representing boundaries—for example, those of the city, of Italy, of the territory under Roman control, and then of the known world.

25. This model has received much recent attention. See A. Vasaly, *Representations: Images of the World In Ciceronian Oratory* (Berkeley and Los Angeles, 1993), 133; Kraus, "No Second Troy," 281. On ethnocentricsm in general, see Y. Tuan, *Topophilia: A Study of Environmental Perception, Attitudes, and Values* (Englewood Cliffs, N.J., 1974), 30–44.

26. For Romans in the late first century B.C., the known world was circular; they called it the *orbis terrarum*. Roman ethnocentrism reached its logical extreme in the idea that the *urbs* was not just the center of the *orbis terrarum* but was identical with the *orbis terrarum* itself, an idea that was particularly important in the Augustan Age, as is suggested by the popularity of the collocation *urbs et orbis*. See E. Bréguet, "*Urbi et Orbi:* Un cliché et un thème," in *Hommages à Marcel Renard*, ed. J. Bibauw (Brussels, 1969), 1:140–52; Nicolet, *Space, Geography, and Politics,* 31–34; J. Romm, *The Edges of the Earth in Ancient Thought* (Princeton, 1992), 46–48.

27. In some cases the center of the space/narrative analogue is not topographical but a charismatic and powerful man radiating authority to those around him. For it is easy and natural to superimpose such a simple and versatile model onto other categories. For example, the Stoic philosopher Hierocles (writing a hundred years after Livy's death) arranged human relationships in a series of concentric circles. A man is the center point, his intimates and family occupy the inner rings, and less intimate connections take up the outer orbits. The wise man, according to Hierocles, seeks to bring those who occupy the outer orbits closer to the inside, to draw them nearer to himself by treating them as if they were close connections (Stobaeus 4.671.7–673). As A.A. Long and D.N. Sedley point out (*The Hellenistic Philosophers*, 2 vols. [Cambridge, 1987], 1:349–350), a similar model appears in Seneca's letters (*Ep.* 12.6–9). Seneca arranges a person's lifetime in a series of concentric circles, with a day occupying one of the inner rings, a month the ring around it, a year the ring around that. On his description, see T. Habinek, "Seneca's Circles: *Ep.* 12.6–9," *CA* 1 (1982): 66–69. For more discussion of this model, see chapter 5.

In addition, a spatial model of personal identity requires both a fixed and solid center (something of one's own that establishes identity positively) and sufficiently impermeable boundaries (something that establishes identity negatively by separating a person from others). A nation requires public centers, whether they are places, leaders, or ideals, as well as boundaries, both physical and cultural, that distinguish it from other nations.[28] It relies on public institutions and public monuments to preserve this identity over time. On the one hand, Livy's representation of Rome focuses on the city center—especially the Forum, where factions argue about the nature of the city, and on Arx and Capitoline, which epitomize Rome in its religious and military capacities. On the other hand, it directs attention to the edge of the republican city, the city walls with their gates, through which good and evil influences enter and leave.[29]

What follows will concentrate on episodes in the *Ab Urbe Condita* that involve monuments (in Latin *monumenta,* "reminders") commemorating important persons or events. These are monuments that Livy has located precisely by reference to a permanent landmark, such as a hill, a gate, or the Forum. Such precision has a universalizing function: a reader at Rome could see the *monumenta* or, if not the *monumenta* themselves, the places where they once were; a reader who was not in the city or had never seen it could imagine them in a generic urban setting, near the citadel or Forum and therefore at the city center, or near a gate and therefore at the periphery. I have narrowed this study further to focus on reminders that for various reasons fail to point unambiguously back to a particular person or event. With one exception (see chap. 2), they are *monumenta* that Livy represents as lost, decayed, or broken and that the text restores. Such ruins can bear a great deal of interpretive weight for two reasons. First, Rome itself is the product of a lost city, Troy, whose destruction still resonates in Livy's history, particularly in the first pentad.[30] This raises the possibility that instances of loss and ruin at Rome throughout the *Ab Urbe Condita* have thematic significance. If the

28. A good example of cultural boundaries reinforcing physical ones is Rome's religious development during the reign of Numa: *Et cum ipsi se homines in regis uelut unici exempli mores formarent, tum finitimi etiam populi, qui antea castra non urbem positam in medio ad sollicitandam omnium pacem crediderant, in eam uerecundiam adducti sunt, ut ciuitatem totam in cultum uersam deorum uiolari ducerent nefas* (1.21.2).

29. On topographical boundaries and narrative, see D. Konstan, "Narrative and Ideology in Livy: Book I." *CA* 5 (1986): 198–215, esp. 198–201.

30. Kraus ("No Second Troy," 270–82) argues that the references to the Trojan War, first in the victory over Veii and then in the Gallic sack of Rome, assimilate the destruction of

destruction of Troy released regenerative forces that founded Rome, and if Rome's own Troy-like destruction in Book 5 caused the city to grow back stronger in Book 6, then even piecemeal destruction, disintegration, and loss merits examination to see what alternate Rome it might generate.[31] Second, the main thrust of Livy's narrative is forward and outward; Rome's accumulation of land, buildings, and spoils provides evidence for an account of increasing wealth and power. The references to deteriorating monuments offer a narrative that runs counter to this litany of accumulation. The mention of renamed places, destroyed buildings, and lost spoils reveals that the present is not simply the sum of the past, that the past is different for what it had as well as for what it did not have.[32] Livy's reader contemplates the evidence for Rome's irretrievable loss, much as Aemilius Paullus viewed the famous sites of Greece.

The *monumenta* restored by the author perform the same dual function of reminding and advising that other *monumenta* do, but their messages are more complex. While intact *monumenta* point back to exempla and draw moral lessons from them, these reminders draw attention to themselves as well and convey a second set of lessons. When monuments fail and the text restores them, reminders of stories give way to stories about reminders. By drawing attention to the author's reconstructive activity, the restored monuments commemorate his recollection of that past. Here Livy's history becomes didactic on two levels: while the contents of the narrative teach lessons about the past, the narrative related by the lost and restored monuments conveys lessons about ways of remembering the past through the present. In addition, destroyed monuments draw attention to the fallibility of memory and the traditional ways of preserving it, because they indicate that the loss of the past is permanent, and because they hinder access to the past with all its original lessons.[33] Consequently, they emphasize the arbitrary and insecure

---

both these cities to that of Troy. Rome, in contrast, rebuilt along new lines, marks a successful departure from Troy, a repetition with a difference. On this theme in the *Aeneid,* see D. Quint, *Epic and Empire* (Princeton, 1993), 50–96.

31. On the *altera Roma* theme, see P. Ceausescu, "*Altera Roma:* Histoire d'une folie politique," *Historia* 25 (1976): 79–108; Kraus, "No Second Troy," 278–82.

32. For discussion of the dynamism of decay in modern contexts, see D. Lowenthal, "Past Time, Present Place: Landscape and Memory," *Geographical Review* 65 (1975): 1–36; idem, *The Past Is a Foreign Country* (Cambridge, 1985), esp. 125–82 (chap. 4, "The Look of Age").

33. On Livy's use of variants as rhetorical gestures drawing attention to this fallibility, see Miles, *Reconstructing Early Rome,* 55–67. On destruction as commemoration in a modern context, see J.E. Young, *The Texture of Memory: Holocaust Memorials and Meaning* (New Haven, 1993), 27–48.

nature of lessons drawn from such an imperfectly recollected past. This artificial landscape, not a mirror of the city but a handful of the mirror's broken shards, reminds the reader that a coherent account of real past events is not a reproduction but a reconstruction.

In his preface Livy says that it will be a pleasure for him "to have taken thought for the memory of the deeds of the foremost people on earth" [*rerum gestarum memoriae principis terrarum populi . . . consuluisse*] (Pref. 3). We can understand this expression, as we can many expressions in the preface, to be a double entendre. Here the meaning of "the memory of the deeds of the foremost people on earth" slips between the objective and the subjective: Livy writes for the memory of Rome's achievements as well as for the ability of Romans to remember their past.[34] The lesson of the history, then, is about both the contents of the past and the importance of remembering the record.

This book aims to be representative, not exhaustive. After briefly discussing the idea of the *monumentum* (chap. 1), it examines four episodes in which Livy's narrative maps the plot of a story onto the Roman landscape, then commemorates the particular enactment of the plot in a monument. These plots are simple, constructed around movement between spatial polar opposites, like the movement to and fro between starting positions that characterizes a battle narrative or the movement between low and high that represents the rise and fall of an assault on a citadel.[35] Such movements generate metaphors: for example, the movement between low and high that characterizes an assault on a citadel can also represent a politician's rise and fall. As plots they convey particular lessons when Livy superimposes them on the unique features of the Roman landscape at critical moments in Roman history.

---

34. On the "slippage" of other words in the preface, see Moles, "Livy's Preface," 142.

35. Kraus ("No Second Troy") observes that Livy's text, like Livy's city, grows "by fitting together *locus* after narrative *locus*." According to Kraus (270), "These commonplaces are narrative paradigms with which to construct stories that are both familiar and new. By using them as building blocks which can be indefinitely recombined, the historian can make connections via repetition and allusion. The reader, who recognizes the motifs, understands not only the story being told but also its relationship to past history." Kraus discusses this topic more extensively in a forthcoming study of formulaic elements in Livy. The spatial plots I am talking about are even more abstract than the literary commonplaces to which Kraus refers. (Kraus' exemplary topos is the capture of a city.) They are simply repeated movements, the stuff of which commonplaces (like the capture of a city) can be made.

The first case study (chap. 2) examines the relationship between an abstract plot, its setting, and its monuments, through a close reading of Livy's account of the battle over the Sabine women. The second (chap. 3) contrasts Livy's account of the political career of M. Manlius Capitolinus, hero and demagogue, with that of M. Furius Camillus, hero and exile: by using the Capitoline as the focal point for the events that bridge the gap between Books 5 and 6, Livy shows how one place becomes an ambiguous reminder as it acquires conflicting associations over time. A close reading of the story of Lucius Marcius, who averts a military catastrophe in Spain during the Second Punic War (chap. 4), shows how memory and reminders provide lifesaving boundaries for national identity in a time of crisis. Chapter 5 presents a detailed study of a problematic narrative that stems from problematic reminders: the account of the so-called trials of the Scipios and of Scipio Africanus' withdrawal from Rome. In addition to treating critical moments in Rome's history as events shaped by and shaping space, these episodes raise issues about the relationships between *monumenta* and the nature of Roman memory and between *monumenta* and the nature of Roman identity. The conclusion returns to Livy's preface and asks a series of questions. Livy's history, it suggests, is an extended representation of space that creates and maintains a sense of crisis. Where is the author and what role does he play in this crisis, and where and who is his ideal reader? How are the relative positions of author and reader crucial to the well-being of the state?

In the decades after Actium, as Romans tried to forget a century of civil war, and as the city underwent a comprehensive program of ideologically motivated construction and reconstruction, Livy produced his own morally charged model of Roman space.[36] Like the Augustan building program, it was massive, comprehensive, and coherent; and like the Augustan program, it reshaped Roman space in a way that aimed to guide the perception, thoughts, and movements of those who entered

---

36. On the dating of Livy's work, see T.J. Luce, "The Dating of Livy's First Decade," *TAPA* 96 (1965): 209–40. The bibliography on the Augustan building program is enormous, but for general treatment, see F.W. Shipley, "Chronology of the Building Operations in Rome from the Death of Caesar to the Death of Augustus," *MAAR* 9 (1931): 7–60; idem, *Agrippa's Building Activities in Rome* (St. Louis, 1933); F. Coarelli, "Public Building in Rome between the Second Punic War and Sulla," *PBSR* 45 (1977): 1–23; P. Gros, *Aurea Templa: Recherches sur l'architecture religieuse de Rome à l'époque d'Auguste* (Rome, 1976); idem, *Architecture et société à Rome et en Italie centro-méridionale aux deux derniers siècles de la République* (Brussels, 1978); P. Zanker, *The Power of Images in the Age of Augustus,* trans. A. Shapiro (Ann Arbor, 1988).

it.[37] The chapters that follow will show how, in constructing his written city, Livy constructed a reader who made national memory personal by receiving Livy's interpretation of the past, not just as images in the mind's eye, but as a heightened and altered awareness of the space around him or her, of his or her own movements through that space, and of the change in perspective this movement produced. This reader's sense of space contributes to Livy's definition of Roman historical memory and, in consequence, to his definition of Roman identity.

---

37. For a discussion of the way in which the Augustan development of the Campus Martius guided the sight and movement of anyone entering Rome from the north, see D. Favro, "Reading the Augustan City," in *Narrative and Event in Ancient Art,* ed. Peter J. Holliday (Cambridge, 1993), 230–57. In his chapter titled "Foundation and Ideology" in *Reconstructing Early Rome* (137–78), Miles points out the strain placed on republican values by the transformation of the city into the capitol of an empire and notes the moral idealization of the countryside that was the result.

Chapter 1

The History as a Monument

The idea of the *monumentum* is a particularly useful tool for studying space and memory in a literary text, because its meaning embraces space and memory in a complex way.[1] Varro's definition of the word provides a convenient starting point for an analysis of *monumenta* in their spatial and cognitive aspects.

> Meminisse a memoria, quom in id quod remansit in mente rursus mouetur; quae a manendo ut Manimoria potest esse dicta. Itaque Salii quod cantant: Mamuri Veturi, significant memoriam . . . ; ab eodem Monere, quod is qui monet, proinde ac sit memoria; sic Monimenta quae in sepulcris, et ideo secundum uiam, quo praetereuntis admoneant et se fuisse et illos esse mortalis. Ab eo cetera quae scripta ac facta memoriae causa Monimenta dicta. (Varro *De lingua latina* 6.49)[2]

> [*Meminisse,* "to remember," comes from *memoria,* "memory," since there is once again movement back to that which has stayed in the mind; this may have been derived from *manere,* "to remain," like *manimoria.* And thus the Salii when they sing "O Mamurius Veturius" signify a *memoria,* "memory." . . . From the same word comes *monere,* "remind," because he who reminds is just like memory; so are derived *monimenta,*[3] "memorials," which are in burial places and for that reason are situated along the road, so that they

---

1. For a full discussion, see H. Häusle, *Das Denkmal als Garant des Nachruhms: Eine Studie zu einem Motiv in lateinischer Inschriften. Zetemata* no. 75 (Munich, 1980). See esp. "*Monumentum* und *Memoria*" (29–40) and "Das Denkmal und sein Leser" (41–63).

2. For the text printed here, see L. Spengel and A. Spengel, eds., *M. Terenti Varronis de lingua latina libri* (New York, 1885; reprint, 1979).

3. The spelling *monimentum* is less common than *monumentum,* which I shall use except when quoting Latin passages that use the alternate form. On the orthography, see *TLL* 8.1461.

can remind those who are passing by that they themselves existed and that the passersby are mortal. From this use other things that are written or produced for the sake of memory are called *monimenta*, "reminders."]

According to Varro's definition, *monumenta* occupy a middle ground. They remind people here and now of events and persons that are remote in space and time. They stand between—between their maker and their viewer; between an exploit, *res gesta*, and the viewer or reader whom the commemorated exploit inspires.[4] By naming the person who has died, sometimes even by speaking in the first person for the dead, Varro's exemplary grave marker preserves a particular fact about the past: that the person it commemorates existed (*sic Monimenta quae in sepulcris, et ideo secundum uiam, quo praetereuntis admoneant et se fuisse et illos esse mortalis;* notice the conflation of the two subjects in . . . *admoneant . . . se fuisse*—the *monumenta* speak both for and as the person commemorated). In addition, the *monumentum* points out a truth pertinent to every passerby: that he or she is mortal too.[5] Thus it recalls the past and provides information to the present.

Both of these functions can become more complex. In pointing to the past, a *monumentum* like Varro's grave marker can recall not only its dedicatee but someone else as well, perhaps the person who dedicated it. This multiplicity of reference expands when, pointing to two or more persons, the *monumentum* also commemorates a relationship like parenthood, for example, or marriage. The second, admonitory, function is inherently complex, for the universal truth communicated by a monument contains an implied challenge, one that extends the force of the *monumentum* into the future (e.g., "Claudia was mortal and so are you. This monument praises her because she was a dutiful wife; you should be dutiful too, if you want to be remembered in a positive way;" or "L. Cor-

---

4. See T.P. Wiseman, "Monuments and the Roman Annalists," in *Past Perspectives: Studies in Greek and Roman Historical Writing*, ed. I.S. Moxon, J.D. Smart, and A.J. Woodman (Cambridge, 1986), 87–100. He points out that the physical *monumentum* stands between the *res gestae* and their literary celebration, so that two layers, the monumental and the literary, come between event and reader.

5. I take *se fuisse* absolutely (as does the entry for *monumentum* in Lewis and Short) instead of with *mortalis*. If *se fuisse* is taken with *mortalis*, the monument would make the redundant point that a dead person is mortal, which hardly needs to be made by a tomb, instead of reminding the viewer that the dead person existed, one purpose of a tomb.

nelius Scipio was aedile, consul, and censor. Therefore his *elogium* is worthy company for those of his ancestors; try to top his *cursus honorum*").[6] As Cicero said, a *monumentum* ought to have more regard for the memory of posterity than for favor in the present.[7] The word *monumentum,* then, denotes a reminder, but one that also exhorts. Present temporally as well as spatially, Janus-like in pointing back to the past and forward into the future, from the viewer's perspective *monumenta* link together all of time.

Because a *monumentum* presupposes an audience to remind, Latin writers generally use the word for reminders that are exposed to the public view.[8] These range from buildings to place-names; from items made for the purpose, like inscriptions and statues, to acquired marks, like scars and mutilations; and from published versions of speeches to trophies and spoils.[9] As enduring material tokens of the past, *monumenta* exist in physical space (or as toponyms, they distinguish a place from its surroundings) and themselves produce hybrid places where natural space and time intersect with what might be called "monumental space." When a person moving through natural space encounters a *monumentum,* his or her thoughts move back through this monumental space to the person, place, or event that the *monumentum* commemorates, and the *monumentum* projects them forward into the future.[10] Varro's exemplary *monumenta* are "in burial places" *(in sepulcris)* and "along the road" *(secundum uiam).* Their purpose is to inform "the passersby" about death. The person who pauses before the

---

6. For these particular inscriptions, see *CIL* 1.2.1211 (= *ILS* 8403) and *ILLRP* 310.

7. *Quae monumenti ratio sit, nomine ipso admoneor: ad memoriam magis spectare debet posteritatis quam ad praesentis temporis gratiam* (*Nonius* 32.17).

8. Vergil's minotaur hidden in the labyrinth (*Veneris monumentum nefandae, Aen.* 6.24–27) is an exception that proves the rule. Daedalus constructed the impenetrable and inescapable labyrinth precisely to hide the offspring that preserved the evidence of Pasiphae's shameful passion. The labyrinth itself is an enormous reminder built to counter and block the unforgettable product of bestiality.

9. For usage, see *TLL* 8.1460–66. The following catalog is intended not to be exhaustive but simply to illustrate the range of items called *monumenta* and of the writers and contexts in which they appear: temples, Livy 1.12.6, 1.55.1, 2.40.12; poems, Cat. 95 and Hor. *Carm.* 3.30.1; *elogia,* Cato *Orig.* (*HRR* 83.10); statues, Plaut. *Curc.* 140, 441, and Cato *Orig.* (*HRR* 83.10); places, Livy 1.13.5, 26.41.11; place-names, Livy 1.48.7, 4.16.1; mutilations, Verg. *Aen.* 6.512; published versions of speeches, Cic. *De off.* 3.4.3; shields, Livy 25.39.17.

10. On spatial representations of time in Latin, see M. Bettini, *Anthropology and Roman Culture,* trans. J. Van Sickle (Baltimore, 1991), 113–93.

monumentum experiences a sympathetic death before resuming his or her journey and life.[11] Then, by moving past the stones, the passerby participates in the monumentalization of the dead person, for his or her presence at the tomb juxtaposes life and death, moving viewer and static reminder, the flow of time passing and the detritus left behind. The overlap of monumental and natural space means that location—that of the *monumentum* itself as well as that of the person it reminds—influences the meaning and impact of this cognitive journey. Thus the *monumentum* controls and directs the viewer's thoughts as they move from the present to the past, then back to the present and into the future.

Finally, to look on a *monumentum* is to experience a psychological distance between oneself and the *monumentum,* the consciousness of being separate from, contrasted with, or measured against it. Varro's passerby, reminded of his mortality, has a heightened awareness that he is alive and has challenges to meet. In sum, we can assume of all *monumenta* some common characteristics: an absent person or thing commemorated; a present audience reminded; a memory or an exhortation that is socially relevant; and a meaning determined jointly by the reminder, its physical context, and the circumstances of each viewer. An encounter with a *monumentum,* then, is more than just looking on one; the experience is essentially spatial and dynamic, one in which the viewer's point of departure, path, and destination all play a part.

Livy's history offers us an opportunity to consider space and monuments in one author's lengthy, if incompletely preserved, work, a coherent and continuous representation of reality. The *Ab Urbe Condita* presents the reader with a written Rome, one that refers to the world outside yet, through its own organization, controls the reader's perception of that objective world.[12] This is particularly evident in Livy's portrayal of the

---

11. On the passerby, see R. Lattimore's fundamental *Themes of Greek and Latin Epitaphs* (Urbana, 1942), 230–37. The elegists, of course, exploit this topos through sepulchral poems addressed to the reader as passerby *(uiator).* See, e.g., Prop. 1.21, 1.22, 2.11; Ovid *Trist.* 3.3.

On grave monuments and memory and on remembering and forgetting as sympathetic experiences, see H.H. Davis, "Epitaphs and the Memory," *CQ* 53 (1958): 169–76.

12. It has become increasingly clear that modern standards of precision are inappropriate for evaluating Roman geographical writing, which scholars now tend to explain in terms of ancient readers' expectations and the limits of ancient geographical knowledge and terminology. As a result, attempts to match literary descriptions to places in the objective world have given way, in many cases, to the study of the conventions that guide such writing. N. Horsfall ("Illusion and Reality in Latin Topographical Writing," *G&R* 32, no. 2

city proper. The hills, river, and plains of the city impose their own shape on the narrative of events, even as the record of those events fills the landscape with significance. The narrative produces a schematized urban topography, one that is all the more meaningful for its abstraction.

While memory, landscape, and narrative have a long-standing association in the idea of the *monumentum,* they also meet in the *ars memoriae,* the mnemonic system preserved in the Roman rhetorical handbooks.[13] This technique for recollecting the substance of a speech entails first memorizing a series of places (loci) to create a mental topography and then stocking them with a series of images *(imagines)* that signify each point of the speech to be remembered. The sequence of places can be a real landscape, which the orator memorizes, or an imaginary one, which he creates and then memorizes. As the orator delivers his speech, he mentally traverses this landscape, recalling each point he wants to make when he reaches the image that represents it. The *imagines* that fill the loci should be striking *(imagines agentes,* according to the author of the *Ad Herennium,* at 3.37) and made even more memorable by ornament or disfigurement. They should also be relevant to the topic to be remembered—an anchor, says Quintilian (*Inst.* 11.2.19), to signify a

---

[1985]: 199) has observed that "no expectation existed in Augustan Rome that the geographical information contained in a work of literature should be precise." Horsfall (203) also says that "it would never do to underestimate at least in Livy the subversive influence of the demands of dramatic narrative and of the necessity of achieving a correct moral balance upon topographical exactitude." T.P. Wiseman (*Clio's Cosmetics* [Leicester, 1979], 43) points out Livy's sacrifice of topographical exactitude in the story of Manlius Capitolinus for the sake of dramatic effect. A particularly useful discussion of the use of conventions in topographical writing can be found in R. Thomas, *Lands and Peoples in Roman Poetry: The Ethnographical Tradition* (Cambridge, 1982). When applied to the study of Livy's *Ab Urbe Condita,* these developments suggest not that we ignore the objective world but that we consider Livy's use of the urban landscape and its monuments less as a set of references to that world and more as a carefully designed stage setting, as it were, for a historical drama.

13. Since others have described it fully, I shall only sketch it here. The ancient sources are *Ad Herennium* 3.16–40; Cic. *De orat.* 2.86.351–87.360; Quint. *Inst.* 11.2.1–52. For modern discussion, see F. Yates, *The Art of Memory* (Chicago, 1966), 1–26; H. Blum, *Antike Mnemotechnik* (Hildesheim and New York, 1969); E.W. Leach, *The Rhetoric of Space: Literary and Artistic Representations of Landscape in Republican and Augustan Rome* (Princeton, 1988), 75–79; Vasaly, *Representations,* 100–102. J.F. Miller ("Ovidian Allusion and the Vocabulary of Memory," *MD* 30 [1993]: 153–64) discusses Ovid's use of words like *memini,* "I remember," and *recordor,* "I recall," as markers signaling acts of poetic allusion. Such markers generate a text between the first text and the one to which it alludes. In a similar manner, Livy's references to monuments create a metaphorical place between the text and the physical city.

naval matter, or a weapon for military affairs. This mnemonic technique may lie behind the practice of vivid representation *(enargeia)* in Latin literature, for it is but a small leap from the rhetorical *ars memoriae* to the orator's use of familiar and significant place-names in his speeches or his creation of a compelling imaginary topography as a means of leading his listeners' minds through his argument.[14] The use of mental mapping in rhetoric may have moved from the realm of mnemotechnics to that of persuasion and then, because of the pervasiveness of rhetorical training in the classical period, from oratory to other genres of literature. Landscape and monuments together comprise a versatile sign system, one that an orator, poet, or historian can use either to guide his audience's perception of a place it actually sees or to conjure up a vivid and memorable image of a place as a setting for action.[15]

Several features of the *ars memoriae* suggest it as a likely model for Livy's conception of Rome's past. First, as Christina Kraus has pointed out, Livy uses the metaphor of traversing space to describe both his tasks of research and composition and the reader's act of reading: the author is among a crowd of writers (Pref. 3); his audience hastens to contemporary material (Pref. 4); events in the past are obscure, like things seen from a distance (6.1.2); the historian takes a byway (9.17.1); he begins to drown in his work (31.1.5); at one point he claims that Greek matters have led him off course (35.40.1).[16] We can extend the parallel: Livy divides his enormous project into manageable units by breaking it into pentads and decades, just as the author of the *Ad Herennium* recommends dividing the loci into manageable segments by placing a distinguishing mark on every fifth locus (3.31). Moreover, the series of loci has to be simplified, so that the speaker can remember it and reconstruct it in his mind. In an analogous way, Livy's Rome does not contain all the real city's monuments and significant places. Rome is too large and its space too complex

---

14. Both Leach (*The Rhetoric of Space,* 78) and Vasaly (*Representations,* 100–102) make this point.

15. Vasaly's *Representations* is the most thorough study of references to topographical features and monuments in Latin literature. On memory and place, see esp. 89–104. On Livy's rhetorical use of one place, see M. Jaeger, "*Custodia Fidelis Memoriae:* Livy's Story of M. Manlius Capitolinus," *Latomus* 52, no. 2 (1993): 350–63. On the manipulation of landscape and topography, see Zanker, *The Power of Images.*

16. Kraus ("No Second Troy," 268–69) points out the metaphor of the byway and observes apropos of 31.1.5 that the image is not coincidental, since the Macedonian wars, the topic introduced at 31.1, are moving Rome's interests overseas.

to "represent fully."[17] Instead, Livy represents it selectively, by referring repeatedly to the places he considers important. In doing so, he draws a schematic, easily comprehensible and easily memorable portrait of the city. Finally, according to the author of the *Ad Herennium* (3.30–31), the orator who has remembered his loci well can repeat what he has committed to them by starting from any locus he pleases and proceeding in any direction, just as Livy's account of events moves in annalistic fashion from events in the city to events abroad and back again.

Extending the parallel still further, we can say that remembering the history of the city entails both memorizing the loci themselves, in this case the city's schematized topography, and remembering the *imagines,* the particular monuments that prompt one's recollection of specific events. One can reconstruct Rome's past either by contemplating the physical urban landscape or by picturing it in the mind's eye. In addition, the loci, here the hills, river, and plains of the urban landscape, can be used again and again, just as waxed tablets can be reused when what was written on them has been erased. While the specific facts of Roman history reside in specific monuments, patterns of thought, which are also part of a people's collective memory, consist of movement in the landscape between them. To remember a sequence of events, one must recollect the right way to move through this remembered landscape. Thus, remembering the city involves learning how to picture the urban landscape and how to move through it by particular routes, a technique demonstrated by episodes in the *Ab Urbe Condita* and practiced by the reader through the very act of reading.

The remembered landscape brings together historiography and the trained memory in a suggestive way, for the sense of sight is crucial both to the *ars memoriae* and to the inquiry expected of the historian. Whether the orator's loci are places he has seen or places he has imagined, he views them in his mind's eye as he delivers his speech. When he uses topography rhetorically, either by referring to the visible or by cre-

---

17. J. Fentress and C. Wickham (*Social Memory* [Oxford and Cambridge, Mass., 1992], 32) argue: "There is always a tendency towards simplification and schematization in memory. Conceptualization means that memory is stored in some 'conceptual' form, as concepts are easier to remember than full representations. The simplification that results from conceptualization can be drastic. Spatial relations in a visual image are apt to be modified so as to make temporal or logical relations of consequence appear more clearly. Occasionally, the spatial arrangement of the figures in the images is even reconstructed so as to manifest relations of cause and effect that were not originally present."

ating an imaginary landscape, he relies on his audience's visual imagination.[18] At the same time, the standards for evidence that Livy received from earlier historians placed vision at the top of the hierarchy of the senses: informed firsthand observation provided the best evidence, according to Polybius (12.4c–d, 24); interviews of witnesses and written accounts, as information that came through the ears, were less reliable.[19] The ideal historian, according to Polybius, actually travels and gains personal experience of warfare and politics. If he cannot experience in person the events he reports, at least he knows how a soldier carries out his duties (12.25.g–h).[20]

In the case of the city and its monuments, the element of autopsy moves from the realm of research to that of representation much as the mental mapping of the *ars memoriae* moves from the realm of mnemotechnics to that of persuasion. The ideal historian witnesses events in person and, through the use of specific details, transmits to his reader the impression of being present at events. To a certain degree the ancient historian shares the orator's purpose in referring to the concrete details of the physical world: both aim to achieve *enargeia,* vivid representation, or *subiectio sub oculis,* putting a picture in the mind's eye.[21] And the goal of this vivid representation is to move the reader or listener emotionally *(mouere).* Livy achieves this verisimilitude in part through references to specific landmarks and monuments.[22] Yet his references to monuments place them in new relationships with one another or juxtapose monuments that are otherwise unrelated, thus producing new, compound reminders and a tension between objective reality and the reality

---

18. According to Cicero (*De orat.* 2.87), the Greek Simonides, whom the Latin sources credit with having invented the art of memory, first discovered that vision is the strongest of the senses. See Yates, *The Art of Memory,* 4.

19. On ancient standards for evidence, see C.W. Fornara, *The Nature of History in Ancient Greece and Rome* (Berkeley and Los Angeles, 1983), 47–90. On vision in Livy's predecessors, with discussion of these passages see Miles, *Reconstructing Early Rome,* 9–14; in Polybius, J. Davidson, "The Gaze in Polybius' Histories," *JRS* 81 (1991): 10–24; in Cicero, Vasaly, *Representations,* 89–104; in Livy, Feldherr, "Spectacle and Society," 3–7.

20. As Miles points out (*Reconstructing Early Rome,* 19), Polybius' criticism of Timaeus is invaluable for understanding Livy's "conspicuous and repeated difficulties." On this criticism, see K. Sacks, *Polybius on the Writing of History,* Classical Studies 24 (Berkeley and Los Angeles, 1981), 21–95.

21. On the potency of images, Feldherr ("Spectacle and Society," 308) says, "spectacle is such a powerful tool in Livy's text that in some cases it can substitute for, or even generate, reality."

22. Vasaly (*Representations,* 26–39, esp. 29–30) discusses the ability of places, especially those that bear traces *(vestigia)* of the past, to move *(movere)* people.

created by the text. The new reminders point back to complex relationships between stories and produce vantage points from which the reader can see a new reconstruction of the past. While vision aids the orator's recollection, while it helps both orator and historian persuade an audience, for the historian and his reader it is but a step toward intellectual insight and understanding.

The famous sentence in Livy's preface acknowledges this.

Hoc illud est praecipue in cognitione rerum salubre ac frugiferum, omnis te exempli documenta in inlustri posita monumento intueri; inde tibi tuaeque rei publicae quod imitere capias, inde foedum inceptu, foedum exitu, quod uites. (Pref. 10)

[It is this that is particularly healthful and profitable in the study of history: you look on examples for a variety of experience set forth in a clear record. From there you may choose for yourself and your state what to imitate and what, shameful in its conception and shameful in its outcome, to avoid.]

Livy does not explicitly call his own written history a monument, though the implication is there in his later references to some written sources as *monumenta* (e.g., 6.1.2) and to others as *monumenta litterarum* (38.57.8).[23] Instead, he says that to look on a *monumentum* is a benefit of studying affairs *(in cognitione rerum)*. And one does not even look on the *monumentum* itself except as space, a context for the *documenta*. Unlike Horace's famous metaphor "I have constructed a memorial more lasting than bronze," *exegi monumentum aere perennius . . . (Odes* 3.30.1), which emphasizes the size, solidity, and durability of the poet's achievement and draws attention to his building activity *(exigere)*, Livy's words stress the active role that his audience must play to comprehend the past. The reader's study illuminates the record and makes the clear vision possible. The idea of vigorous personal effort is also conveyed in the preface when Livy says: "I call on each man for himself to pay careful attention to these things . . ." *[ad illa mihi pro se quisque acriter intendat animum . . .]* (Pref. 9). Livy's hypothetical student of history aims at seeing, but at seeing as a metaphor for understanding. Studying history

---

23. On Livy's history as a *monumentum*, see Moles, "Livy's Preface," 146. On history as monument in Herodotus and Thucydides, see H. Immerwahr, "*Ergon:* History as a Monument in Herodotus and Thucydides," *AJP* 81 (1960): 261–90.

allows one to look on a *monumentum*, but a clear view is only part of this experience: the encounter with a *monumentum* that produces insight also entails the viewer's awareness of his or her own position in space (that of the *uiator* on the road passing by). While the narrative maneuvers the reader into a position that allows him or her to receive an instructive vision, the ideal student reaches the ultimate goal of understanding the past, at times through vision, at times through determining his or her own position relative to events recorded on the textual "monument," and at times through perceiving the structure and movement of a particular episode.

Movement through space is an essential part of the experience of Livy's *monumentum*. The closer one is to the *monumentum*, the clearer one sees it. However, the viewer who stands too close cannot take in the *monumentum* in its entirety.[24] Finding the right position, close enough to see clearly, far enough away to see comprehensively, is crucial. It is not, though, the end of the process. A clear and comprehensive vision from the appropriate distance produces insight, and insight produces movement. The reader is expected to act after establishing his or her spatial coordinates, to continue on in the direction indicated by the monument by choosing what to imitate and what to avoid (*unde, exitus,* and *uitare* all imply movement).[25] Thus the *monumentum* is a goal that paradoxically comes into view as one nears it; at the same time, it holds the viewer at a certain distance and provides a starting point for future conduct.

This quality of being at once spatial, visual, and mnemonic, of attracting the observer's gaze and then directing his or her memory and subsequent actions, makes the idea of the *monumentum* useful for an analysis of Livy's narrative technique. *Monumenta* provide opportunities for examining what Gérard Genette calls the "focalization" of a narrative, that is, for analyzing it by asking the question, Who sees?[26] Genette identifies types of discourse used to present a story (direct speech,

---

24. Cf. Livy's use of vision and distance at 6.1.2, a passage discussed in Jaeger, *"Custodia Fidelis Memoriae,"* 362–63, and in Miles, *Reconstructing Early Rome,* 57–61.

25. Vasaly (*Representations,* 30) points out that places with historical associations were able to "move" people emotionally and that this was also one of the three chief goals of rhetoric (the others were to please *[delectare]* and to teach *[docere]*). The metaphor is particularly appropriate for *monumenta*, which first convince the passerby to pause and then move him or her on down the road into the future. As a metaphorical *monumentum*, the history gives moral direction to this movement.

26. Gérard Genette's theory of narrative breaks it down into the grammatical categories of tense (the relationship between the narrative and the set of narrated events in terms of order, frequency, and duration), mood (the types of discourse used to present the story and the degrees of narrative representation they entail), and voice (which discusses the act of

reported speech, third-person narrative) and the degrees of narrative representation they entail. He monitors the way information is filtered and narrowed by various perceptors as it passes from narrator to reader. As concrete evidence that reaches from the past to the narrator's present, *monumenta* guide and restrict knowledge of the events they commemorate. And the historian's representations of the monuments restrict it further.

Genette explains that he uses the abstract term *focalization* for this narrowing because it indicates the restriction of knowledge more precisely than terms that involve metaphors of sense perception: one can know without seeing.[27] Still, I think that it is necessary to restore the visual metaphors when we analyze issues of perception and knowledge in ancient historians.[28] *Monumenta* require both vision and memory. As we have seen, ancient historiography emphasized the visual, from ranking eyewitness testimony higher than oral reports, written documents, or rumor, to holding up as an ideal the historian's presence at the events he recounts. Vision also plays an important role in historical narrative. Andrew Feldherr has demonstrated the potency of spectacle in Livy's histories, and James Davidson, who applies some of Genette's ideas to Polybius' *Histories,* writes that "lines of sight form their own structures, linking the protagonists and the readers of the *Histories* together in the act of looking."[29] For this reason Davidson prefers the term *gaze* to Genette's *focalization.*[30] Yet although Livy uses visual metaphors programmatically (e.g., *intueri* in the famous passage from his preface, quoted earlier),

---

narrating and the traces it leaves in the text). His discussion of mood includes the theory of focalization, which he applies to the field of knowledge of both narrator and characters. See Genette, *Figures III* (Paris, 1972), translated by J.E. Lewin as *Narrative Discourse: An Essay in Method* (Ithaca, 1980). See also Genette, "Boundaries of Narrative," trans. A. Levonas, *New Literary History* 8 (1976): 1–13. M. Bal ("The Narrating and the Focalizing: A Theory of the Agents in Narrative," *Style* 17 [1983]: 234–69) identifies some of the problems that arise from Genette's terminology and clarifies his discussion. There is a useful summary in the *Encyclopedia of Contemporary Literary Theory,* ed. Irena R. Makaryk (Toronto, 1993), s.v. "Genette, Gérard."

27. Genette, *Narrative Discourse,* 189.

28. Here, I am following Davidson, who makes this point in "The Gaze in Polybius' Histories," 10–11.

29. Feldherr, "Spectacle and Society," esp. 1–22, 152–91; Davidson, "The Gaze in Polybius' Histories," 11.

30. According to Davidson ("The Gaze in Polybius' Histories," 11), "'focalization,' as a term formulated for the analysis of fictional texts, a complement to 'narration,' is problematic when applied to history, which must participate in what Hayden White has called 'a discourse of the real.'" Davidson also points out that, "'gaze' has the advantage of reflecting the visual metaphors which are used consistently by Polybius, though rejected by Genette as a naive view of narrative."

and although he often indicates a character's field of knowledge by what that character sees, I will not use the term *gaze* very often. Livy's constructive metaphors are different from those of Polybius, just as his project is different, and they require terminology adapted to them.

We have seen that Livy's text occupies physical space and creates metaphorical space, that author and reader traverse these spaces, that a *monumentum* is situated in space and gives meaning to the space in which it stands. We need terminology that extends beyond the visual to include the entire spatial experience of encountering a monument. While the term *gaze* captures the act of seeing, the terms *point of view* and *perspective* connote distance and movement through space better than *gaze* does. *Point of view* throws weight on the position a person takes to adopt their stance, and it implies the movement involved in taking up that position. In a like manner, *perspective* retains the idea of a particular direction and a particular stance that is lost in *gaze*. Therefore, although this study will occasionally use *gaze* to indicate a line of vision, and while it will use the more abstract term *focalization* to discuss the abstract issue of what a given character knows, it will rely heavily on the old metaphorical terms *perspective* and *point of view* to illustrate how space and movement through it, control of it, or simply the ability to see or comprehend it act as physical correlates to cognitive states.

The *Ab Urbe Condita* unites two extended narratives: a story of Rome's history told by an omniscient narrator and an account of writing Rome's history told from a first-person point of view that appears intermittently in asides, discussions of sources, and references to the present (e.g., in the preface).[31] The relationship between these two narratives is most easily understood in terms that are spatial as well as visual, as movement between internal and external points of view relative to the *res gestae populi Romani*. The history's changes in perspective often occur at the monuments, because the monuments endure from the time of the narrated events to the present of the historian's writing. In addition, they sometimes occur at book ends and draw attention to parallels between the space of the physical text and the metaphorical space of the narrative.

These two narratives also reflect two perspectives on the city. Seen from the outside, it appears as a defined shape, space separated from the surrounding land by its religious boundary (the *pomerium*), pro-

---

31. In Genette's terms these are, respectively, a nonfocalized and an internally focalized narrative.

tected physically by its walls, and divided by social, political, and moral polarities—high and low, central and peripheral, public and private. From the inside, to a person on the street, the city appears as a miscellany of details, of landmarks, and of monuments that have specific associations.[32] Thus, on the one hand, a view of the city as conceptually coherent usually entails seeing it from outside or above, from the mapmaker's perspective, just as seeing events as part of a coherent pattern entails adopting the objectivity of an omniscient narrator.[33] A view of it as a miscellany of details, on the other hand, entails seeing it from inside, or from a subjective position. The *Ab Urbe Condita* combines these abstract ideals and documentary particulars in such a way that the monuments, with their specific and often emotional associations, compel the reader to reconsider the abstract polarities that shape the community as well as the landscape, while the schematized landscape rearranges the monuments so that they elicit organized patterns from a hodgepodge of events.

Movements between these points of view are of particular interest, because some of Livy's exemplary characters, by acts of will, change the focalization of the very narrative in which they appear. Characters move from the inside to the outside of their own stories, adopting perspectives from which they determine the historical significance of their own actions. Sometimes the narrative expresses these changes in perspective as movement through space. And sometimes the narrative uses movement through space to maneuver the reader into a new perspective. As a

---

32. E. Gabba ("True History and False History in Classical Antiquity," *JRS* 71 [1981]: 50–62) describes the role of the city as a repository of information. He writes (61): "It seems clear that monuments, statues, toponyms, whose significance was for various reasons unclear, were at first invested with fantastic meaning of different kinds, but always related to legendary episodes or episodes of earliest Roman history; this took place in the context of an antiquarian and guide-book tradition aiming to explain and expound the monuments involved. In a complete reversal of roles, the monuments then became the document which guaranteed the historicity or credibility of the legends or stories which had grown up."

33. See J. Rykwert, *The Idea of a Town: The Anthropology of Urban Form in Rome, Italy, and the Ancient World* (Princeton, 1976), 41–71. On conceptual models of the city, see H. Cancik, "Rome as Sacred Landscape and the End of Republican Religion in Rome," *Visible Religion: Annual for Religious Iconography* 4 (1985): 250–65. In *How to Lie with Maps* (Chicago, 1991), M. Monmonier presents an amusing discussion of the abstraction and deception that all mapmaking entails. A journey connects particular places into an even more significant whole. The journeys in Horace's *Satires* 1.5 and 1.9 come to mind. For a study on a related topic, see S. MacCormack, "*Loca Sancta*: The Organization of Sacred Topography in Late Antiquity, " in *The Blessings of Pilgrimage*, ed. R. Ousterhout (Urbana, 1990), 7–40.

result, in addition to the question of who sees, there arises a less personal question: From what point is their seeing? From a succession of changing points of view, Livy constructs a model reader, who does not play a passive role. The outermost of the narrative's many audiences, this reader participates in constructing the meaning of the text and decodes its various rhetorical gestures even as he or she watches others supply meaning to events and interpret them.[34]

Livy's *monumenta* replace natural time and space with monumental time and space. As *uestigia* marking out direct routes between past and present, they allow the reader to stand outside events, on the threshold between past and present, but they also place the reader on the very edge of events, where representation becomes so vivid that he or she feels the movement of the story and responds to it with an impulsive desire to move in a particular direction. This dual cognitive state is paradoxical. We could call it one of "engaged objectivity." A person watches events from a distance and thus views them with clarity; at the same time, he or she moves in response to the narrative. At the end of her study of place and monuments in Ciceronian oratory, Ann Vasaly concludes that "this constant reliance on the visual and the concrete was but the Roman gateway to the world of ideas."[35] Her words are also relevant to Livy, for whom the "visual and the concrete" are directly and reciprocally connected to that abstract world. Livy conveys abstract ideas in a way that gives the illusion of a sensory experience. This sensory experience, in turn, is commemorated by a *monumentum* in the concrete world. While visual and aural memory can be public and social, tactile memory and memory of movement are essentially private and personal.[36] Thus, the public memories of Rome's past, when transmitted through the restored *monumenta*, become sensory and personal memories, and because the text acts on every single reader, the sensory and personal act of remembering becomes social again, within the community of readers.

The study of the ideas behind monuments and their place in a narrative economy entails an eclectic approach. Not only must we identify the relationship between a monument in the text and the physical world outside, but we must also recognize the significance of its appearance at a

---

34. On the many audiences in the history, see Feldherr, "Spectacle and Society"; on the adaptation of exempla in response to changing audiences, see J.D. Chaplin, "Livy's Use of Exempla and the Lessons of the Past" (Ph.D. diss., Princeton University, 1993).

35. Vasaly, *Representations*, 257.

36. See Fentress and Wickham, *Social Memory*, 1–40.

particular point in the written text and in the story, each of which has its own internal logic. We need to consider the contexts that give monuments meaning, the people they remind, and the type of event they recall. In addition, we must study the relationship between reminder and context, context and person reminded, reminder and person reminded.[37] We must consider the opportunities offered the author and the constraints imposed on him or her by events within the narrative, by topic, and by genre. The rhetorical purpose of the historian, persuasion for the sake of moral improvement, differs, for example, from that of the advocate, which is persuasion for its own sake. So too does his use of landscape and monuments.

The case studies in the chapters that follow describe the location of *monumenta* by their position in the city, in time, in the physical text, and in the story the text tells. Then, since the contexts created for the *monumenta* are both topographically realistic and constructed to support an argument, the various studies ask how particular reminders function in this dual context. From what vantage points in time and space does the reader perceive them? Moreover, Livy presents his *monumenta* as items that have, or at one time had, existence independent of his text; thus they offer material proof of the credibility of his narrative. How, then, does the urban landscape, with its *monumenta,* provide the verisimilar detail that helps the historian to characterize people and events?[38] Finally, how does the image of the city that Livy creates both draw on and influence the reader's perception of the landscape external to the text? And what are the moral, political, and ideological implications of this altered perception?

37. See, e.g., R. von Haehling, *Zeitbezuge des T. Livius in der ersten Dekade seines Geschischtswerkes: Nec vitia nostra nec remedia pati possumus* (Stuttgart, 1989). He includes monuments in his catalog of Livy's temporal references.

38. Vasaly (*Representations,* 25) suggests that Cicero used monuments as inartificial or nonartistic proofs, like documents, laws, or the testimony of slaves under torture, all of which were considered to be "discovered," rather than "invented," by the orator.

Chapter 2

The Battle in the Forum

Sanguinis autem coniunctio et beneuolentia deuincit homines <et> caritate. Magnum est enim eadem habere monumenta maiorum, eisdem uti sacris, sepulchra habere communia.

[The blood tie binds men together through goodwill and affection. For it is a great thing to share the same reminders of ancestors, to employ the same rites, and to have ancestral tombs in common.]
—Cicero *De officiis* 1.55

As one of Rome's great foundation myths, the story of the Sabine women has been told by many authors, with variations in detail.[1] According to Livy's version, after neighboring peoples refused to grant the Romans rights of intermarriage, Romulus and his fellow Romans invited them to Rome for a festival in honor of Neptune.[2] The guests came with their families, including their nubile daughters. When their visitors' attention had been diverted by the horse races, the Romans seized and carried off the young women. The women's families departed in anger; their fathers returned in arms. The Sabines, the last of the wronged peoples to attack, captured the citadel on the Capitoline and held their own in battle against the Romans, until their daughters, now Roman wives and mothers, intervened to prevent their husbands and their fathers from killing one another. The Romans and the Sabines made peace, and the two peoples became one.

It has been suggested that this story associates Roman imperialism with rape and that here, as in accounts of other exemplary women, Livy makes women's bodies into disputed space, the setting for a crisis in

---

1. Authors who relate the story include Livy (1.9–1.13.8), Cicero (*Rep.* 2.12–14), Dionysius of Halicarnassus (2.30–47), Ovid (*Ars Am.* 1.101–34; *Fasti* 3.167–258), and Plutarch (*Rom.* 14–19).
2. The connection between this festival, the Consualia, and the theft of the women is unclear, as is that between the Consualia and Neptune. See Ogilvie, 66–67.

Roman history.[3] Recent work on this legend has tended to focus on the role of the women and on the story's implications for Roman marriage.[4] Yet the women's bodies are not the only kind of space disputed in this section of the *Ab Urbe Condita:* the landscape, including citadel and Forum, is another, and the metaphorical space of the narrative is yet a third. No one of these can be understood without considering how it relates to the others. Accordingly, this chapter places less emphasis on the women so that it can give due attention to the other contested spaces and thus show how the text, by manipulating traditional ideas about historical causation, including the abduction of women, weaves a close and reciprocal network of relationships between landscape, monuments, and historical narrative.

Several features of the episode make it a useful starting point for an inquiry into these relationships. First, it presents a common aetiology for two landmarks that stood some distance apart: the Temple of Jupiter Stator (Stayer of Flight) and the Lacus Curtius (Curtius' Lake). The site of the Temple of Jupiter was somewhere at the base of the Palatine, near the Porta Mugonia, the Old Gate of Livy's narrative, while the Lacus Curtius was part of a swamp at a low spot in the Forum near the location of the Column of Phocas.[5] Second, although each of these monuments has more

---

3. Especially those of Lucretia and Verginia. See S.R. Joshel, "The Body Female and the Body Politic: Livy's Lucretia and Verginia," in *Pornography and Representation in Greece and Rome*, ed. A. Richlin (Oxford, 1992), 112–30.

4. See, e.g., J. Hemker, "Rape and the Founding of Rome," *Helios*, n.s., 12 (1985): 41–47. Miles (*Reconstructing Early Rome*, 179–219) adopts an anthropological approach and analyzes this story as an account of an enemy's co-option into the community via bride theft.

5. The ancient sources agree that the Temple of Jupiter Stator was on the Palatine, at the lowest part of the slope, just outside the Romulean settlement (Livy 1.12.1–8; Dion. Hal. 2.43.1–5, 50.3; Ovid *Fasti* 6.793–94 and *Trist.* 3.1.31–32; Plut. *Cic.* 16.3; Pseudo-Cic. *Or. priusq. in ex. iret* 24). F. Coarelli (*Il Foro Romano*, 2 vols. [Rome, 1983, 1985], 1:26–33) places it along the Via Sacra, on the site of the so-called Temple of Romulus, but convincing arguments for the traditional location are made by A. Ziolkowski (*The Temples of Mid-Republican Rome and Their Historical and Topographical Context* [Rome, 1992], 87–91) and Vasaly (*Representations*, 41 n. 3). On the temple, see S.B. Platner and T. Ashby, *A Topographical Dictionary of Rome* (Oxford, 1929), 303–4; E. Nash, *Pictorial Dictionary of Ancient Rome*, 2 vols. (London, 1968), 1:534; L. Richardson Jr., *A New Topographical Dictionary of Ancient Rome* (Baltimore, 1992), 304. On the Lacus Curtius, see J. Poucet, *Recherches sur la légende sabine des origines de Rome* (Kinshasa, 1967), 241–63; idem, "Le premier livre de Tite-Live et l'histoire," *LEC* 43 (1975), 342–434; and, in the books already cited in this note, Platner and Ashby, 310–11; Nash, 1:542–44; Coarelli, 1:116–19; Richardson, 229. According to Ogilvie (75), it was the *mundus*. For a survey of relatively recent work in the Forum area, see N. Purcell, "Rediscovering the Roman Forum," *JRA* 2 (1989): 156–66.

than one aetiology, the story of the battle with the Sabines is the only one that links the two.[6] And of the many aetiologies in the early chapters of Book 1, these are the first for items called *monumenta*. The word draws attention to their mnemonic function and links them together in the written text, just as the action in the story links them topographically. This raises a question: to what degree is this episode significant for its uniting of the two monuments?

When Livy's contemporaries looked around the Roman Forum, they saw a landscape quite different from the setting for this episode. There was in Livy's time a temple of Jupiter Stator that, of course, did not exist when the battle took place. Livy says later that, although Romulus vowed the *templum,* the temple was not built immediately: the land alone was set aside after Romulus' prayer; the building was not constructed until after the consul M. Atilius Regulus made a similar vow in a battle with the Samnites.[7] A person looking for the Lacus Curtius in Livy's time would not see even the vestiges of a swamp: the Forum had been drained by the end of the sixth century, and the creek that ran through it went underground by the Cloaca Maxima.[8] Although the sight of a flooded Forum was not unknown in Augustan times, the place contained nothing that could be called a *palus* or *lacus,* except by courtesy.[9] The Lacus Curtius was a small polygonal area surrounded by a balustrade; it had been paved over in Sulla's time.[10] In the crowded and developed Forum of the late first century B.C., it would be difficult to imagine an unimpeded dash from hill to hill, except perhaps along the narrow and regularized route of the Via Sacra. Otherwise the Temple of Castor, the Regia, the House of the Vestals, the Julian Basilica, and the Temple of Julius Caesar all

6. We have seen that the Temple of Jupiter Stator has two aetiologies. The Lacus Curtius had three, two of which Livy relates: (1) the conflict with the Sabines (Livy 1.12–13, as well as Varro *LL* 5.148–50, Dion. Hal. 2.42.5–6, and Plut. *Rom.* 18.3–5); (2) the opening of a chasm in 362 B.C., in response to which portent, M. Curtius, armed and mounted, rode his horse into the pit (Livy favors this as the correct aetiology at 7.6.1–6); (3) a lightning strike in the place in 445 B.C., after which it was fenced off and marked with a stone enclosure by the consul C. Curtius (Varro *LL* 5.150). Whatever its origin, this monument was very old and had associations with the underworld. See Ogilvie, 75; J. Bayet, ed., *Tite Live, Histoire romaine,* vol. 1, Budé series (Paris, 1985), 23 n. 1.

7. 10.36.11, 37.15–16.

8. Ovid *Fasti* 6.403–4.

9. J. Le Gall lists the known instances of flooding in *Le Tibre, fleuve de Rome dans l'antiquité* (Paris, 1953), 29–35. Note also that in Plutarch's version of the battle the swamp is the product of a Tiber flood.

10. See Richardson, *A New Topographical Dictionary,* 229; Poucet, *Recherches,* 241.

stood in the way. Instead of picturing the contemporary Forum as the setting for these events, or even starting with an image of the Forum and stripping it bare of buildings, it would be more natural to conjure up a vision of an empty landscape and then add the buildings and landmarks as they appear in the narrative. Livy describes the battle taking place in a setting that no longer exists, one that he himself has of course never seen, as he is writing seven hundred years after a legendary event.[11] Thus whether or not the reader knows the precise topographical details of the Roman Forum is not as important as that he or she knows that it is a low-lying area between two hills and that there is a historical temple to Jupiter Stator and a Lacus Curtius. The reader who knows this much can follow Livy's general argument aptly.

In fact, this episode's moral message lies less in the specific records it preserves than in the vantage point it creates for the reader. The narrative constructs an audience that watches this battle from the sidelines. The reader adopts this audience's perspective so that he or she becomes aware of both the spatial structure of the narrative and the shape of its setting. As the reader does so, he or she gains insight into a critical moment in Roman history, when foreign war becomes civil war, as well as into the important dichotomies in Roman society: Romans versus foreigners; men

11. On the Latin authors' sacrifice of specificity to typology, see N. Horsfall, "Illusion and Reality." Topographical selection and abstraction may have its origin in the rhetorical handbooks (Horsfall, 201). Menander Rhetor (350.26–29) provides a late but illustrative example. When listing ways to praise a city, he points out: "In the most general terms—for it is impossible to cover all the individual patterns—every city lies either entirely on a mountain or a hill, or entirely on the plain <or partly on a mountain and partly> in the plain" (D.A. Russell and N.G. Wilson, eds., *Menander Rhetor* [Oxford, 1981], 41). It is normal, then, to describe a city in terms of hills and plains, and the rhetor praising a city can expect to praise either of these qualities, or both, as Camillus does at 5.54.3: . . . *quotienscumque patria in mentem ueniret, haec omnia occurrebant, colles campique et Tiberis et adsueta oculis regio et hoc caelum sub quo natus educatusque essem.* Such abstraction is also consistent with the suggestion made by writers on the *ars memoriae* that the orator memorize a relatively deserted landscape (*Ad Herennium* 3.31) or imagine loci if suitable real ones are not available: *Cogitatio enim quamuis regionem potest amplecti, et in ea situm loci cuiusdam ad suum arbitrium fabricari et architectari* (*Ad Herennium* 3.32). See Vasaly, *Representations*, 100–102. For another instance of typology influencing the representation of a place, see M. Jaeger, "Reconstructing Rome: The Campus Martius and Horace, *Ode* 1.8," *Arethusa* 28, nos. 2–3 (1995): 177–91.

While a discussion of Roman drama is not within the scope of this work, note that the clean lines of this setting would make a nice backdrop for a play like Ennius' *Sabinae*. T.P. Wiseman (*Remus: A Roman Myth* [Cambridge, 1995], 129–50, esp. 140) has suggested that the Romulus myths took shape in the politically tendentious performances of the *ludi scaenici* in the late fourth and early third centuries. If so, the nature of the space on a stage might have had some influence on the structure of the story.

versus women; and, most important of all, those who see things from a historical perspective versus those who comprehend only the present.[12]

To understand how the narrative constructs landscape, audience, and point of view alike, we must monitor the way it maps space in all dimensions and track movement within it. First, Livy's account of the fighting displays to a heightened degree the symmetry inherent in the ebb and flow of the typical battle narrative.[13] This symmetry receives reinforcement from the setting in which the fighting takes place, the area between the Capitoline and Palatine that eventually becomes the Roman Forum. (I shall call it the Forum for the sake of convenience.) A close relationship between setting and event was part of the tradition Livy inherited, for the fragment of Calpurnius Piso's account preserved in Varro displays a bilateral symmetry of both action and setting.[14]

> Piso in Annalibus scribit Sabino bello, quod fuit Romulo et Tatio, uirum fortissimum Mettium Curtium Sabinum, cum Romulus cum suis ex superiore parte impressionem fecisset, in locum palustrem, qui tum fuit in Foro antequam cloacae sunt factae, secessisse atque ad suos in Capitolium recepisse; ab eo lacum [curtium] inuenisse nomen. (Varro *De lingua latina* 5.149)

> [Piso writes in his *Annales* that in the Sabine war between Romulus and Tatius, Mettius Curtius, a most heroic Sabine, after Romulus and his men had charged from a higher position and had made an onslaught against the Sabines, retired to what was a swampy area in the Forum then, before the sewers were made; after that he withdrew to his own men on the Capitoline. From him the pool acquired its name.]

---

12. On the male/female dichotomy, see, e.g., Hemker, "Rape and the Founding of Rome"; Miles, *Reconstructing Early Rome*, 179–219.

13. On this battle, see esp. Poucet, *Recherches*, 187–213; Ogilvie, 75–79. The story's spatial symmetry is more pronounced in some versions than in others: it is evident but not as obvious in Dion. Hal. 2.41–46, because of the episodic nature and greater topographical complexity of Dionysius' version. It is even less apparent in Plutarch's account (*Rom.* 18.2–19.2), which begins with the Sabines on the citadel, then tells of Curtius and the swamp. Plutarch next relates Hostilius' fall, the Roman retreat toward the Palatine (πρὸς τὸ Παλάτιον), and, finally, Romulus' vow. According to Plutarch, the two sides met shield-to-shield near the site of the Regia and the Temple of Vesta.

14. On the relationship between Piso's version and Livy's, see Poucet, *Recherches*, 197–98.

According to Piso, Romulus charges the Sabines from higher ground *(ex superiore parte),* and Mettius retreats through the swamp and uphill to his men on the Capitoline. The story's symmetry comes from its movement to and fro in a simple setting comprised of the higher ground under Roman control, the low swampy ground of the future Forum, and the Capitoline, a topography easily schematized as hill-Forum-hill.[15]

Livy extends the symmetry already apparent in Piso's simple schema to include the situation, a conflict between two groups of men over one set of women, which we can schematize simply as men-women-men. He extends it further to include even the monuments that commemorate the fight. His account represents the Forum valley as a minimalist landscape defined by a few famous landmarks.[16] When the conflict begins, the Roman army gathers in a place described as a level area bordered by two hills: *quod inter Palatinum Capitolinumque collem campi est* (1.12.1). Then the battle turns within narrower parameters marked off by two *monumenta,* the Temple of Jupiter Stator (1.12.3–4) and the Lacus Curtius (1.12.10). After this, husbands and fathers first resume fighting and then make peace in a place that Livy does not identify specifically, but which he describes precisely in abstract terms as the middle of the hollow between the two hills *(in media conualle duorum montium,* 1.12.10). The attacks and counterattacks, represented vividly as movement through this landscape, enhance the symmetry in the topography, while the topography in turn enhances the symmetry inherent in the battle and in the very conflict between the Romans and the Sabines. The result is an impression of complete reciprocity, as if these events were made for such a landscape and this landscape for such events.

The passage preceding the battle places the first restrictions on the audience's knowledge of events and, at the same time, determines the time and place from which the reader views them. The Sabines captured

15. Since Varro quotes Piso to explain the origin of the Lacus Curtius, he preserves the description of only this phase of the battle. We do not know if or how Piso described the initial Roman attack and the Sabine thrust that pushed the Romans back to the Palatine. Nor, for that matter, do we know how he related the women's intervention. Still, this brief fragment conveys the story's symmetry. See also Dion. Hal. 2.41.2 and 2.42.1.

16. Dionysius of Halicarnassus, in contrast, sketches the topography with less economy (2.37.5–38.1). At the beginning of his account, he locates the Roman and Sabine camps by their positions on the hills they occupy: those of Romulus and Lucumo are on the Esquiline and Quirinal, that of Tatius on the plain between the Quirinal and the Capitoline. Later, he situates the fighting in "the plain between the camps" (τὸ μεταξὺ τῶν στρατοπέδων χωρίον). Livy, however, uses the hills to orient the episode.

the citadel during the night before the battle, as coolly and deliberately as the Romans had stolen their women: *nihil enim per iram aut cupiditatem actum est* (1.11.5).[17] A young woman named Tarpeia betrayed the citadel to the Sabines, who killed her for her treachery, although Livy says it is not certain which side was its target. The account of the battle follows immediately after the narrator discusses the variant versions of her death (1.11.9). It is remarkable, given the frequency of aetiologies in the account of Romulus' reign,[18] that the narrator draws no overt connection between the ancient fate of Tarpeia and the famous Tarpeian Rock. Rather, by discussing the variants, he reorients the account of the capture of the citadel so that it looks back into the past rather than forward into the reader's present. Livy's authorial comment about uncertainty in the tradition represents the past as something obscure and unrecoverable, whether one locates the source of obscurity in the secrecy of the night attack, the death of the one Roman witness, or the variants in the tradition.[19] The Sabine possession of the citadel cannot be accounted for completely. The reader, then, is forced to wonder, along with the Romans gazing up at their occupied *arx* in the light of day, How did this happen?

Since the causes of the occupation are obscure, the occupation itself is a historical first principle. The Forum battle continues and concludes the series of episodes that began with the theft of the women, but occurring as it does the day after the inexplicable capture of the citadel, it opens a new epoch *ab arce capta,* "from the capture of the citadel." The series of reciprocal thefts links this narrative to the greater historiographical tradition by reenacting the series of reciprocal thefts that opens Herodotus' account of the Persian Wars (1.1–5). In Herodotus the abductions of Io, Europa, Medea, and Helen, and the consequent movement between East

---

17. See Miles, *Reconstructing Early Rome,* 186–87.

18. Cf. 10.6–7 on the Temple of Jupiter Feretrius and the *spolia opima (haec templi est origo quod primum omnium Romae sacratum est. . . . bina postea, inter toto annos, tot bella opima parta sunt spolia);* 13.5 on the Lacus Curtius *(Curtium Lacum appellarunt);* and 13.6, which gives the names of thirty curiae and those of three centuries of *equites.* On the fifty temporal references that are linked to topography in the first decade (of which 10.6–7 is one), see Haehling, *Zeitbezuge des T. Livius in der ersten Dekade seines Geschischtswerkes,* 164–65. He attributes their frequency in Book 1 (there are seventeen such references there) and their subsequent falling off to the book's introductory character.

19. The comment reads: *Sunt qui eam ex pacto tradendi quod in sinistris manibus esset derecto arma petisse dicant et fraude uisam agere sua ipsam peremptam mercede. Tenuere tamen arcem Sabini* (1.11.9–12.1). On the use of the variants as rhetorical gestures, see Miles, *Reconstructing Early Rome,* 20–38. According to Miles, the multiple explanations of the Lacus Curtius raise questions about the possibility of knowing with any certainty what happened in the past.

and West, account for hostilities between Greece and the "barbarians" in the murky period before Croesus, whom the historian identifies as a firm starting point for an explanation of the war.[20] The Sabines, of course, do not reciprocate for the theft of their women by stealing the women back. They take the Roman citadel instead, and the reciprocal actions that follow involve the capture and recapture of space. Indeed, the Sabines use the seizure of the woman as an excuse to seize territory, while on the Roman side male desire shifts from the women to the landscape.[21] Even though it recalls the opening passages of Herodotus, this tit-for-tat behavior does not lead to a great war between the two sides, partly because the Sabine women divert the men's anger into an alternate channel, and partly because the confined landscape does not have room to allow any escalation in the violence.

Moreover, the episode's isolation from what has gone before allows the reader to focus on events taking place in a fully schematic and symmetrical landscape free from distractions. And these events begin in a static but unstable condition.

Tenuere tamen arcem Sabini, atque inde postero die, cum Romanus exercitus instructus quod inter Palatinum Capitolinumque collem campi est complesset, non prius descenderunt in aequum quam ira et cupiditate reciperandae arcis stimulante animos in aduersum Romani subiere. Principes utrimque pugnam ciebant ab Sabinis Mettius Curtius, ab Romanis Hostius Hostilius. Hic rem Romanam iniquo loco ad prima signa animo atque audacia sustinebat. Ut Hostius cecidit, confestim Romana inclinatur acies fusaque est ad ueterem portam Palatii.[22] (1.12.1–3)

---

20. Hdt. 1.6. Herodotus' opening remarks display part of what J. Cobet, calls a "rudimentary typology of war," which consists of (1) simple robbery; (2) destruction of a city; (3) defeat, subjection, removal of autonomy, and reduction to tributary status in relation to the conqueror. All of these levels are compressed into the account of the conflict between the Sabines and the Romans, although the second is represented by the capture of the citadel and the killing of Tarpeia. See Cobet, "Herodotus and Thucydides on War," in *Past Perspectives: Studies in Greek and Roman Historical Writing*, ed. I.S. Moxon, J.D. Smart, and A.J. Woodman (Cambridge, 1986), 5–6.

21. Miles (*Reconstructing Early Rome*, 205–11) discusses Livy's use of desire *(cupiditas)* and points out that a susceptibility to passions characterizes the Romans in this episode. On the force of the passions in Livy, see M. Ducos, "Les passions, les hommes et l'histoire dans l'oeuvre de Tite-Live." *REL* 65 (1987): 132–47.

22. I print here the text of the Oxford Classical Text but with a full stop after *ad veterem portam Palati*. (See Ogilvie, *A Commentary on Livy, Books I-V*, p.77 ad 12.3.) Thus the reader's attention is drawn immediately from the Capitoline right to the Palatine.

[However that may be, the Sabines held the citadel. On the next day, when the Roman army had been drawn up and had filled what level ground there was between the Palatine and the Capitoline, they did not descend from it to the level ground until the Romans, their anger and desire to retake the citadel goading their spirits, approached from below. The heroes on each side were stirring up the battle, Mettius Curtius on the Sabine side, and Hostius Hostilius on the Roman. The latter, at the foremost standards, upheld the Roman side in its unfavorable position by his courage and daring. When Hostius fell, the Roman line quickly gave ground and was routed and fled right up to the Old Gate of the Palatine.]

In the first phase of the fighting, the Sabines and Romans press against each other across an imaginary horizontal axis, with the Sabines above it and the Romans below. The opening and closing clauses of the historical period reflect the symmetry of the arrangement: *tenuere tamen arcem Sabini; . . . in aduersum Romani subiere.* The Sabines, the subject of the dramatic initial verb *tenere,* occupy the higher ground. The passage includes no unusual diction, but the cumulative effect of Livy's words is to underscore the role played by gravity. Translating tendentiously, one could say that Hostilius "supported the Roman side from below" *[sustinebat],* "in an uneven position" *[iniquo loco].* When he "fell" *[cecidit],* the Roman line quickly "was moved out of the horizontal" *[inclinatur]* and "was poured out" *[fusaque est].* Even the balanced reference to the two champions *(ab Sabinis Mettius Curtius, ab Romanis Hostius Hostilius)* reflects the static condition produced by the two men applying force, each on his own side. Yet until he fell, Hostilius countered the Sabine pressure by meeting it from below and, therefore, applied more force than Mettius. The verb *sustinere,* which emphasizes his inferior position, recalls, in contrast, the advantage enjoyed by the Sabines, who held *(tenuere)* the citadel from above.

The emphasis on the relative positions of the two armies implies that merely the force of gravity stands behind Sabine success, success that is, consequently, not based on superior valor. The Romans have placed themselves at a disadvantage by ascending the Capitoline; therefore their inferior position helps to account tactfully for their initial retreat. After Hostilius falls, the force of gravity remains in play, and the height of the Capitoline provides the momentum that drives the Romans, and with them Romulus, back to the Old Gate, the Porta Mugonia, on the Palatine. Livy describes the flight across the Forum briefly: "and [the Roman line] fled right up to the Old Gate." The narrative reflects the speed of the Romans' flight by shifting the scene immediately to the other end of the Forum.

> Romulus et ipse turba fugientium actus, arma ad caelum tollens, "Iuppiter, tuis," inquit, "iussus auibus hic in Palatio prima urbi fundamenta ieci. Arcem iam scelere emptam Sabini habent; inde huc armati superata media ualle tendunt; at tu, pater deum hominumque, hinc saltem arce hostes; deme terrorem Romanis fugamque foedam siste. Hic ego tibi templum Statori Ioui, quod monumentum sit posteris tua praesenti ope seruatam urbem esse, uoueo." Haec precatus, ueluti si sensisset auditas preces, "Hinc," inquit, "Romani, Iuppiter Optimus Maximus resistere atque iterare pugnam iubet." Restitere Romani tamquam caelesti uoce iussi; ipse ad primores Romulus prouolat. (1.12.4–7)

[Romulus himself, swept along by the mass of fleeing soldiers, raised his weapons to the sky and said: "Jupiter, it was here, on the Palatine, that, at the bidding of your eagles, I set down the first foundations for the city. Now the Sabines hold the citadel, after buying it by treachery. From there armed men have already passed the middle of the valley and are making their way here. But you, father of gods and men, keep the enemy away, at least from this place. Remove fear from the Romans and put a stop to their shameful flight. In this place I promise to build a temple to you, Jupiter Stayer of Flight, as a reminder to posterity that the city was preserved by your immediate and effective aid." Having made this prayer, he said, as if perceiving that it had been heard, "From this point, Romans, Jupiter the Best and Greatest commands us to resist and to renew the fight." The Romans resist, as if ordered by a heavenly voice; Romulus too flies forth toward the soldiers fighting in the front.]

As Livy represents it, the very landscape suggests that the Romans, unlike the Sabines, do not need to make their counterattack from higher ground. First, the Sabine countercharge drives the Romans back to the Old Gate of the Palatine. The reference to the gate offers tangible proof that Romulus can choose between two actions. He can go through the gate, thus retreating back into the original city and then up the Palatine.[23] But since to do so would be to give ground, Romulus turns directly upward instead. When he raises his weapons to the heavens, prays, vows a temple, and commands his men to make a stand, he makes an appeal that reaches higher than the Palatine or any *arx,* and he does so from a position where valor and divine favor, not gravity, will be decisive. The etymological play of *arcem . . . Sabini habent; inde. . . . hinc . . . arce hostes* helps draw the connection between the place Romulus stands and the citadel, while at the same time, the fact that the Romans take their stand at a point lower than the Sabine-occupied *arx* provides evidence of their superior martial valor. In addition, the phrase relating the Romans' response, *resistere Romani,* with its dramatic initial verb, recalls the Sabine position at the opening of the episode: *tenuere tamen arcem Sabini* (1.12.1). After this point, the Romans recover lost ground in more ways than one, for while they resist and retake, they also repeat—redoing and thus undoing—the past. After Romulus' prayer, Livy repeats the verb *restitere,* placing it in the emphatic initial position.[24] The sense of repetition is also conveyed by the verb *iterare* (to repeat) and is further emphasized by the repetition of *Romani.* All this repetition implies that the narrative is going to tell substantially the same story as it did before, but in the opposite direction. The Romans must recover, in the sense of "cover again," the ground that the Sabines have taken: *superata media ualle.* When they do so, the Roman narrative of success prevails over that of the Sabines.

First, however, the narrative leaps backward in narrative time, so that it reports what Mettius Curtius did before Romulus prayed.[25] This analepsis directs attention back to the other side of the Forum, up to the high ground of the citadel on the Capitoline.

---

23. On the Porta Mugonia, see Coarelli, *Il Foro Romano,* 1:26–38, esp. 27. He identifies it as "the boundary between the Sacra Via and the Palatine. See also Richardson, *A New Topographical Dictionary,* 304. Vasaly (*Representations,* 45) points out that if Romulus retreated any further, he would reenter the fortifications of his original settlement.

24. The prefix *re-* itself denotes movement back or in reverse, withdrawal, reversal of a previous process, restoration, response or opposition, separation, or repeated action. (See *OLD,* s.v. "re-.") On *re-* verbs, see D. Daube, "Withdrawal: Five Verbs," *CA* 7 (1974): 93–112. On the spatial connotations of other compound verbs, those prefixed with *trans-,* see J.E. Phillips, "Form and Language in Livy's Triumph Notices," *CP* 69, no. 4 (1974): 271–72.

25. Vasaly (*Representations,* 44–45) points out that Livy tells the story twice.

Mettius Curtius ab Sabinis princeps ab arce decurrerat et effusos egerat Romanos toto quantum foro spatium est. Nec procul iam a porta Palati erat, clamitans: "Vicimus perfidos hospites, imbelles hostes; iam sciunt longe aliud esse uirgines rapere, aliud pugnare cum uiris!" (1.12.8)

[Mettius Curtius, the first man on the Sabine side, had run down from the citadel and had driven the Romans who were scattered throughout the entire area of the present-day Forum. He was now not far from the Palatine gate, crying out, "We have vanquished the treacherous hosts, the unwarlike enemy; now they know that it is one thing to steal maidens and a far different thing to fight with men!]

The description of Mettius Curtius' attack draws the audience's gaze from the citadel back down into the Forum and across it to the Roman position at base of the Palatine, where like a pendulum the action pauses again and Mettius' speech offers a boastful counterpart to Romulus' prayer. The narrative has related the rush from the Capitoline to the Palatine twice, for the account of Mettius' actions covers the very events related by the words *confestim Romana inclinatur acies fusaque est* (1.12.3); but this rout never appears as a whole. Livy has split the story in half and has told each part separately: only the Roman flight is apparent in the first version, while the second describes not Mettius' pursuit but the state of affairs after it, in a sentence couched in the pluperfect *(decurrerat et . . . egerat).*

Such manipulation of tenses has several functions. First, it represents the Sabine action unemphatically. Expressed in the pluperfect, Mettius' *impetus* ceases to be the main subject of the narrative and becomes the background for the Roman counterattack. This, in turn, produces a curious reversal of roles: after all, the agents of the action should be the main subject of the narrative. Instead, Livy depicts the Roman rout as if it were something that happened without Sabine agency, and he reintroduces the Sabines now so that the Romans have someone to resist. Moreover, by splitting the story, Livy separates the Romans and the Sabines to focus more narrowly on the Romans. Because the narrator has treated the Romans first, the audience hears Romulus' prayer for the future before it hears Mettius' boast about the accomplished (as he thinks) past. While Romulus prays that his city and its history will not cease to exist, that, as it were, the narrative will not stop here, or that it will not stop being a Roman narrative, Mettius, in contrast asserts that the story is over, the lesson learned: "We have vanquished . . . ; now they know. . . ." Romulus vows the temple in the narrative; Livy's contemporary reader knows that it exists in the present and therefore can interpret Mettius' actions and his boast in the correct way. By recounting Romulus' prayer first, the narrator allows the reader a glimpse into the future before returning to Mettius' unfulfilled past, which is now recognizable as such. The end of the Sabine pursuit turns into yet another given, like the capture of the citadel, but with Mettius at the base of the Palatine and Romulus and his men in the advantageous position. The story is about to begin again.

This part of Livy's account matches the fragment of Piso's version quoted earlier.

> In eum haec gloriantem cum globo ferocissimorum iuuenum Romulus impetum facit. Ex equo tum forte Mettius pugnabat: eo pelli facilius fuit. Pulsum Romani persequuntur; et alia Romana acies, audacia regis accensa, fundit Sabinos. Mettius in paludem sese, strepitu sequentium trepidante equo, coniecit; auerteratque ea res etiam Sabinos tanti periculo uiri. Et ille quidem, adnuentibus ac uocantibus suis fauore multorum addito animo, euadit; Romani Sabinique in media conualle duorum montium redintegrant proelium; sed res Romana erat superior. (1.12.9–10)

> [Against him, as he made these boasts, Romulus charged with a throng of the keenest youths. Mettius happened to be fighting from horseback at the time. For that reason it was all the easier for him to be driven off. When he had been, the Romans [with Romulus] pursued him, while the rest of the Roman line, fired by the king's daring, routed the Sabines. Mettius, his horse panicking at the noise of his pursuers, leapt into the swamp, a matter that distracted the attention of the Sabines because of the danger it posed to such a man. Mettius, on his part, with his own side urging him on and calling him, and encouraged by the help of many, passed through to the other side. The Romans and Sabines renewed the battle in the valley between the two hills, but the Roman side had the upper hand.]

Livy's account reverses the landscape of Piso's to show other forces at work. In fact, Piso's account of the Romans driving Mettius from the higher ground of the Palatine to a specific position on the Capitoline does not resemble this passage as much as it resembles Livy's account of the Sabines driving the Romans from the higher ground of the Capitoline to a specific position on the Palatine. Piso's Romulus charges from higher ground *(ex superiore parte),* which is where Livy places the Sabines (1.12.1), only on the Capitoline. The place where Romulus stops, however, at the base of the *clivus Palatinus,* is clearly not the "higher position" of Piso's narrative. Piso's Mettius Curtius retreats up the Capitoline *(in Capitolium),* after making his way through the swamp; Livy, in contrast, does not say where Mettius went after he escaped. Livy locates the point from which Romulus attacked quite specifically at the Old Gate of the Palatine, while Piso simply calls it the "higher position." Finally, while one would expect the Romans to retreat high up the Palatine to regroup, Jupiter, rather than a position higher on the hill, supplies the force to match the momentum of the Sabine downhill rush. The Romans are pressing back, movement that mirrors the Sabine action of pressing down.

When Romulus and the Romans make their counterattack, the action moves from the Palatine back toward the center of the Forum. Once again Livy's account shortens the arc of its swing, for after Curtius escapes from the swamp, the narrative does not follow him up the Capitoline, as Piso's version does. Instead it directs the audience's attention back to the center of the valley, where the fighting resumes. The two sides meet, face-to-face *(Romani Sabinique),* in the middle of a landscape that is symmetrical *(in media convalle duorum montium).*[26] Yet, as we have seen, within this symmetrical physical landscape, the narrative has been working to invert the original imbalance of power and has been shaping a moral landscape in the process. When the battle begins for the second time, the Sabines, who were fighting to retake their women and exact retribution (according to Mettius' boast), have been defeated, while the Romans, who were fighting to retake their citadel and defend their city (according to Romulus' prayer), now prevail.

To understand how and when this inversion happens, let us review the spatial symmetry displayed by the narrative up to this point. That Livy credits the rise of the *res Romana* to Romulus' bargain with Jupiter is clear: the prayer to Jupiter, in a sense, raises the base of the Palatine to an elevation religiously as high as that of the Capitoline.

---

26. Plutarch, whose topography is less economical than Livy's, locates the fighting near

Romulus' attack on Mettius Curtius continues to "tilt" the landscape: in elevating one end of the Forum, the base of the Palatine, it "sinks" the other and with it the main prop upholding the Sabine side, so that Mettius Curtius' escape into the lowest point in the Forum, the swamp, both repeats Hostus Hostilius' fall and forms a mirror image of Romulus' raising of his armor. Unlike Piso, who implies that Mettius crossed the swamp and escaped to the Capitoline, and unlike Dionysius (2.42. 5–6), who says he swam across it and then escaped to his own camp, Livy says only that Mettius Curtius passed through it; then he immediately directs attention back to the middle of the Forum area. At the end of the episode, Mettius Curtius comes out of the depths of the swamp (*ex profunda . . . palude*, 1.13.5). The reader is left with the impression that, instead of crossing this body of water and returning to his own side, Mettius casts himself down into it, disappears from view, and emerges from its depths.[27]

The spatial relationships may be summarized as Palatine up versus Capitoline down and Curtius and Hostilius down versus Romulus' arms up; in Livy's version, Curtius is down for the duration of the battle. Thus the physical superiority of the Sabine position on the Capitoline corresponds to the divine impetus behind the counterattack led by Romulus, the fall of Hostius Hostilius corresponds to the flight of Mettius Curtius, and the momentum of the Roman retreat down the Capitoline Hill corresponds to that of Mettius' horse as it flees from the Palatine down into the swamp.[28] Mettius disappears from the narrative just as Hostius does after his fall. With the Sabine prop fallen, the fighting settles into the middle of the space that was originally described as separating the two hills (*quod inter Palatinum Capitolinumque collem campi est*, 1.12.1) but now is said to join them *(in media conualle duorum montium)*.[29] The two

the Regia and the Temple of Vesta. Livy, in contrast, limits himself to the hills, and to the landmarks made significant by the story.

27. The other aetiologies of the place suggest this vertical orientation. See Varro *LL* 149; Livy 7.6; Dion. Hal. 2.42. The late third-century relief that once adorned the balustrade around the Lacus Curtius is possibly the copy of an archaic work and clearly shows the horse plunging downward. On the relief, see E.S. Strong, *Roman Sculpture from Augustus to Constantine* (New York, 1907; reprint, 1969), 324–27.

28. Piso does not say whether Mettius Curtius was mounted or not, while Dionysius implies that he was on foot (2.42.1–5). Plutarch has the horse. Its presence may be a result of conflating this story with the other aetiologies of the *lacus* (e.g., Livy 7.6).

29. This space is, in fact, where Dionysius of Halicarnassus (2.42.5) places the Lacus Curtius.

hills and the Forum now form a unified and symmetrical landscape, at the center of which Sabine confronts Roman and Roman Sabine.[30]

At this point Livy has brought the two sides face-to-face in a symmetrical landscape. The story of defeat has been told once in one direction (from the Capitoline toward the Palatine) and repeated in another (from the Palatine toward the Capitoline). When the fighting starts anew, repetition in one place *(redintegrant proelium)* replaces the previous oscillation. In renewing the battle, both sides act as one: both are the subjects of *redintegrant*. They now reflect each other as two halves of a symmetrical design.[31] Seeing this symmetry, a viewer could easily conclude that any fighting between these Romans and Sabines in this landscape would be an internal conflict between two halves of a whole.[32] By manipulating Rome's topographical features, Livy has created an image that shows two armies at war becoming two warring factions in one city, one that shows the blurring of the boundary between foreign war and civil war.

The symmetry of this image is apparent to a viewer watching from the sidelines, and Livy has maneuvered the audience to this point by manipulating its gaze. The first sentence of the episode (1.12.1), which alternates main clauses that relate Sabine action and temporal clauses that relate Roman action, introduces an oscillation that is sustained throughout. This alternation of clauses first directs attention to the Sabines atop

---

30. For a useful contrast that highlights the reciprocity between narrative and landscape in this episode, cf. the account of the combat between the Horatii and the Curiatii in 1.25.1–14. See Feldherr's discussion in "Spectacle and Society" (23–36) of the use of the visual and the functions of the various audiences of the episode in making the narrative an account of the separation of two kindred peoples, Roman and Alban. Feldherr (30) points out that "Livy has made the spatial depiction of the fight a metaphor for his motif of discrimination" and that the tombs of the five slain—the two Roman tombs together, the three Alban far apart—reinforce the metaphor (1.25.14). While the placement of the tombs commemorates Horatius' tactics, the narrative does not convey the impression that the landscape changes during the events so that it actually influences them as they happen, the way it does in the story of the Forum battle.

For a discussion of the way a people's myths can shape its landscape, see M. Kahn, "Stone-Faced Ancestors: The Spatial Anchoring of Myth in Wamira, Papua New Guinea." *Ethnology* 29 (1990): 50–66.

31. For a general discussion of doubling in Book 1, see Konstan, "Narrative and Ideology in Livy."

32. Miles (*Reconstructing Early Rome,* 162) points out that Ovid (*Fasti* 3.201–2) portrays this event explicitly as the prototype of civil war. For a discussion of repetition, ideology, and the representation of civil war in the *Aeneid* that is germane to Livy as well, see Quint, *Epic and Empire,* 50–96.

the citadel *(tenuere tamen arcem Sabinae)*, then draws it down to the Romans on the plain *(cum Romanus exercitus instructus quod inter Palatinum Capitolinumque collem campi est complesset)*, back up to the Sabines *(non prius descenderunt in aequum . . .)*, and back down to the Romans again *(prius . . . quam . . . in aduersum Romani subiere)*. The range of oscillation in the audience's line of vision decreases as the two sides draw closer together, but it continues to move to and fro even as its focus is transferred from the opposing armies, to the contested space bordered by the hills, and finally to the women, who are contested space of another kind. When the reader encounters the phrase *sed res Romana erat superior,* the audience's line of vision enters the picture at the center of the landscape *(in media conualle)* and meets the image at a ninety-degree angle.[33]

This is the direction from which the women enter.

Tum Sabinae mulieres, quarum ex iniuria bellum ortum erat, crinibus passis scissaque ueste, uicto malis muliebri pauore, ausae se inter tela uolantia inferre, ex transuerso impetu facto dirimere infestas acies, diremere iras, hinc patres, hinc uiros orantes ne se sanguine nefando soceri generique respergerent, ne parricidio mac-

---

33. This is not unlike the effect of Jacques-Louis David's painting *The Rape of the Sabine Women.* David presents the most dramatic as well as the most obviously symmetrical moment of the story, the moment when the women separate their warring husbands and fathers. The eye lights first on the figure of Hersilia, which splits the composition; behind Hersilia, a red-clad woman throws her arms before her face at the real center of the canvas. Her arms mark a horizontal axis dividing the canvas and her upright torso marks a vertical. The Sabine women—striding, tumbling, and falling—divide Romulus and the Sabine king, the statuesque male combatants who occupy prominent positions in the foreground. The way in which the painting directs the viewer's gaze draws attention to another symmetrical arrangement. Romulus' shield, its convex side turned outward, demarcates the surface that the viewer's gaze cannot penetrate, while Hersilia's right arm, reaching toward the concave surface of Tatius' shield, leads the viewer's gaze into the picture. Hersilia's left palm seems to push Romulus' shield out toward the viewer, while her right pushes the shield of Tatius further into the picture. The effect is to draw the viewer into the scene and to ward him or her off at the same time. Hersilia, then, is the vertical axis around which the composition revolves in three-dimensional space, while the torso of the woman in red is its axis on the two-dimensional plane. Hersilia divides the warring kings, Romulus and Tatius; yet the group of women around her—the woman in red, the old woman baring her breast, and the woman kneeling before the infants in the foreground—comes between Roman husband and Sabine wife. Thus the composition conveys the message that this is a story of strife and intervention, but it is not clear who is set against whom. On the social and political implications of the composition, see E. Lajer-Burcharth, "David's Sabine Women: Body, Gender, and Republican Culture under the Directory," *Art History* 14, no. 3 (1991): 397–430.

ularent partus suos, nepotum illi, hi liberum progenium "si
adfinitatis inter uos, si conubii piget, in nos uertite iras: nos causa
belli, nos uolnerum ac caedium uiris ac parentibus sumus; melius
peribimus quam sine alteris uestrum uiduae aut orbae uiuemus."
(1.13.1–3)

[Then the Sabine women, from whose wrong the war had arisen,
with their hair in disarray and their clothing torn, their feminine
fear conquered by evils, dared to enter the area filled with flying
spears, to rush from the flank into the space between the hostile
armies. They parted the hostile combatants, their fathers on one
side, on the other their husbands, and begged them, fathers-in-law
and sons-in-law not to splash themselves with abominable blood-
shed, not to stain their own offspring with the murder of kin,
grandsons of one side, sons of the other. "If your relationship—if
our marriage—is hateful to you, turn your anger against us! We are
the reason for the war, we the cause of wounds and slaughter for
husbands and fathers. It would be better for us to perish than to live
widowed or orphaned!"]

The only indication of the women's position comes from the topographically vague but geometrically precise indication of direction *(ex transuerso).*[34] Until now Livy has not even mentioned that the women are
watching the battle. The reader has been aware of viewing the action
through the eyes of an audience on the sidelines, but only when the

---

34. Livy uses the phrase *ex transuerso*, always literally and always in military contexts,
to describe attacks from the side. One example occurs at 2.20.3 (the description of the
death of Valerius in pursuit of Tarquinius): *Valerium temere invectum in exsulum aciem ex
transverso quidam adortus transfigit, nec quiqcuam equitis vulnere equo retardato . . .* (note
that the attack does not slow the horse at all). See also 3.62.8, 10.41.5, 22.18.18, 37.42.5
(it is a good way to attack elephants). It is also used figuratively to mean "unexpectedly" or
"by surprise" (*e transuerso*, once in Cicero—at *Luc.* 121.2—and at Petron. *Sat.* 55.3.1 and
Sen. *De uita beata* 15.6 and *Ep. mor.* 117.21.4). Lucretius uses *e transuerso* to describe the
movement of atoms to fill a void (6.1018: they can move in from above, *superne*, or from
the side, *e transuerso*). It is not found in any historians or military writers besides Livy, but
much later it comes to mean "from the collateral line" in Gaius (once) and Justinian (fre-
quently), in contexts dealing with marriage. One would expect the Sabine women to be
watching the fighting from within the fortifications of the Palatine and to make their way
around and past the Romans to intervene from the sides. Yet in Livy's account the women
appear out of the blue when they rush into the area between the lines of fighting men. The
abstract phrase aptly describes a movement that is (a) tactical (an assault on the flanks) and
(b) unexpected.

Sabine women enter the fray does the reader become aware of seeing it from their point of view. This set of viewers, part of an audience that up to this point appears to have been created by the narrative, actually has an independent existence and acts to influence the course of events. Livy has split the audience: the reader sees, but the Sabine women react, entering the text as dramatically as they enter the midst of the conflict. From this position on the sidelines, both the reader and the women can see the situation clearly and can comprehend the awful symmetry of a war between husbands and fathers. By directing the mind's eye as it follows the turning and returning of a symmetrical story in a symmetrical landscape, the narrative creates a point of view sufficiently distant that the viewer can take in the fighting and the landscape as a coherent whole. At the same time, the vividness of the fighting in 1.12 gives the reader the impression of being present at the very event; and it is but a small step from sharing this peripheral but involved point of view with the women to sharing the emotions that launch them on their dangerous course of intervention.[35]

After the fighting resumes in the middle of the Forum valley, the audience's attention, which has moved to and fro between the two hills, now oscillates within the narrowest confines, the area between the battle lines, space that is quickly occupied by the Sabine women themselves.[36] And yet, while the audience looks from side to side, following the trajectories of the weapons flying to and fro, the entrance of the women produces another boundary. The use of anaphora (*diremere . . . acies, diremere iras; hinc patres, hinc uiros; ne . . . respergerent, ne . . . macularent; nepotum illi, hi liberum progeniem*, 1.13.2) produces the impression that half of the women are turning one way, toward the Sabine fathers, and half the other way, toward the Roman husbands.[37] The two sides still mirror one another. As they divide the men by turning to and fro, the women offer themselves as alternate space where Roman and Sabine blood can intermingle and as a way out that does not violate the boundaries

---

35. See Vasaly, *Representations*, 89–104. On the emotional involvement of spectators, see Feldherr's discussion in "Spectacle and Society" (13) of Thucydides' account of the battle in the harbor at Syracuse (Thuc. 7.71.3–4). On the position of the reader relative to other spectators in Livy's battle, see Feldherr, op. cit., 23–35.

36. E. Burck (*Die Erzählungskunst*, 144) points out that the denouement unfolds in three parts: first the entrance of the women, then their plea in indirect speech, and finally their plea in direct speech.

37. See J. Wankenne, "Le chapitre 1.13 de Tite-Live," *LEC* 43 (1975): 350–66. Note also the idea of boundaries in the word *adfinitas (ad + finis)*, which literally means "situated or lying next to."

imposed on the landscape by the restricting hills.[38] They deflect the men's attention by uniting the warring sides against a single common foe *(in nos uertite iras)*.[39]

After the women's intervention, the two sides move in harmony: silence falls; the leaders on both sides come forward; both sides together make one city out of two; both join the rule; both confer all the imperium on Rome. Only then does Curtius return to the narrative.

> Movet res cum multitudinem tum duces; silentium et repentina fit quies; inde ad foedus faciendum duces prodeunt. Nec pacem modo sed ciuitatem unam ex duabus faciunt. Regnum consociant: imperium omne conferunt Romam. Ita geminata urbe ut Sabinis tamen aliquid daretur Quirites a Curibus appellati. Monumentum eius pugnae, ubi primum ex profunda emersus palude equus Curtium in uado statuit, Curtium lacum appellarunt. (1.13.4–5)

> [This event stirs both the masses and the leaders; there is silence and sudden stillness; then the leaders come forward to strike a treaty. They make not only peace but also one state out of two. They unite the government, but locate all the power in Rome. The city thus having doubled, so that some concession might be made to the Sabines the people were named Quirites, from the town of Cures. As a reminder of that battle, they named the spot where his horse brought Curtius out of the depths of the swamp and into the shallows Curtius' Lake.]

As joint subjects of the verbs *prodeunt, faciunt, consociant,* and *conferunt,* the Romans and Sabines continue to mirror each other. The city has been moving toward doubling *(Ita geminata urbe)* all through the course of the battle.[40] The verb *geminare* means to double by addition or by rep-

---

38. Menander Rhetor (351.1–3) points out that one of the disadvantages of a hill site is "confined spaces" [στενοχωρίαι].

39. Miles (*Reconstructing Early Rome,* 179–219) sees this as an explanation of a fundamental hostility within Roman marriage.

40. This joint action is particularly appropriate for events that may have taken place on the site where Livy later places the Temple of Janus Geminus (*ad infimum Argiletum,* 1.19.2). Some sources say that the temple was built to commemorate the doubled people (Serv. *ad. Aen.* 12.198). According to Coarelli, (*Il Foro Romano,* 1:97), the account of the Forum battle is the aetiological myth establishing the cult of Janus in his capacity as *Patulcius* and *Clusius,* since the ideas of opening and closing can be perceived in the activity of the Sabines, occupants of the Capitoline and the Quirinal.

etition. Here Rome does both: the city's population doubles through addition, its landscape and history through repetition.[41] The topography and narrative alike reflect the superimposition of city on city over time by superimposing story on story, that of the Roman advance and Sabine retreat on that of the Roman retreat and Sabine advance. While the fighting began as a conflict with a people outside Romulus' original settlement, the movement between the hills shows the battle turning into a conflict between kindred enemies, as the landscape becomes more and more coherent and symmetrical, and as the people within it come to mirror one another.[42]

The conflict itself is reflected in the doubled space. The initial opposition between Romans and Sabines is reflected by their opposing strongholds on the Palatine and Capitoline. As they come into conflict, it appears in other polarities, those of hill and valley, sky and swamp. Finally, the women's physical intervention collapses the distinction between Roman husbands and Sabine fathers by replacing it with another dichotomy, that between men and women. This too is reflected in the way events and space unfold before the various audiences, as well as before the reader, who sees through the audiences' eyes.

The account of the Forum battle demonstrates the beginning of a reciprocal process by which the landscape influences events while events, in turn, give meaning to the landscape, in the form of *monumenta*. A pair of *monumenta* like the Temple of Jupiter Stator and the Lacus Curtius produce a self-validating system, in which the monumental complex produced by the story is proof of the story that unites them.[43] Thus the account of the battle shows that the relationship between the narrative and the objective landscape is complex and reciprocal: the story ties the monuments together, and the monuments tie the story together. The war with the Sabines generates more than an increased population and an expansion of Roman imperium: it allows Roman history, both the *res gestae* themselves and accounts of *res gestae,* to continue in the very land-

41. Konstan's "Narrative and Ideology in Livy" is invaluable here. Like the first book of the *Ab Urbe Condita*, the story of the Forum battle opens with loss. The Romans are keen to retake their citadel *(reciperandae)*; in this they share the impulse of Romulus, who Livy later says showed his divine nature in his recovery of his ancestral kingdom *(in regno auito reciperando)* from his uncle.

42. There is a trace here of the antiquarian tradition, preserved in Tacitus (*Ann.* 12.24.3), that the Sabines originally were settled on the Capitoline and that Titus Tatius brought it into the city.

43. See Gabba, "True History and False History," 61.

scape that generates them. Although the Romans themselves are not indigenous to the place, their *res gestae* are.

What effect would this dramatic narrative have on the Roman reader's perception of the objective landscape? First, it would link together places whose interrelationship was otherwise unclear. Amid seven centuries' accumulation of physical monuments, it would be difficult to conceive of any relationship between the Temple of Jupiter Stator and the Lacus Curtius without a reminder in ritual or story, especially since their other aetiologies make no connection between them. Moreover, without the story, one would not know what was important about the relative positions of the monuments in the landscape. Was it significant that one monument stood at the place where the Forum sloped upward at the base of the Palatine and that the other was near its lowest spot?

As it brings together the monuments, the narrative guides the reader's attention to other connecting features in the urban landscape. Commentators point out that this story joins the aetiologies of two monuments in the Forum, on the assumption that the Forum is the topographical link between them.[44] But as we have seen, for Livy as for Piso, Dionysius, and Plutarch, the hills play the defining role in this episode. They mark off the original space of the Forum, and they provide the termini for the action.[45] The Roman army filled the plain between the two hills; the Romans were driven from the Capitoline to the Palatine; the Sabines pursued them from one to another *(inde huc);* Mettius ran down from the Capitoline, crossed the entire length of the future Forum, and then, Livy says, approached the Palatine gate, where he made his boast; the fighting resumed not *in medio campo* but *in media conualle duorum montium.*[46] By redefining this place as the hollow between two hills, Livy does two

44. See Vasaly, *Representations,* 43. Vasaly (41–49) gives a good account of the monuments and points out that the story ties together two etiologies. Ogilvie (75) comments, "As the legend of Tarpeia was to account for the name of the Tarpeian rock, so the prominent features of the Forum, the temple of Juppiter Stator and the Lacus Curtius, supplied the material for the present episode."

45. I agree with Coarelli (*Il Foro Romano,* 1:26–27), who focuses on the relationship between this story and a more specific part of the Forum, the Via Sacra. He points out that the story—not just Livy's version, but those of Plutarch and Dionysius as well—touches on the archaic monuments along the road. Coarelli's argument is that the Via Sacra was terminated by the hills; that it began at the base of the Arx and ended at the Porta Mugonia fits Livy's narrative, which is so clearly limited by the hills.

46. Plutarch emphasizes that this is a difficult place for retreat or pursuit, because it is encompassed (περιεχόμενος) by a ridge of hills.

things: he throws emphasis on the vertical components of movement in the episode, and he suggests that the place is a container. Although the two monuments are in different parts of the Forum, the hills exert a constricting pressure that draws them together. The effect is to join the disparate topographical features—the Forum, the two monuments, and the two hills—into one coherent design.[47]

The doubling of the city, with the *res Romana* having the advantage, creates an image in which the *monumentum* to Jupiter's celestial interference is superimposed on the earthy Lacus Curtius. Romulus seems to communicate with the heavens in the place where he vows a temple *(Romulus . . . arma* ad caelum *tollens; Restitere Romani tamquam* caelesti *uoce iussi);* the Lacus Curtius may have been the *mundus,* a place of communication with the world below. Thus the configuration of monuments commemorates the outcome of the conflict. As far as the Romans are concerned, the Temple of Jupiter Stator commemorates the point where the Romans turned from flight to pursuit and where they rewrote, as it were, a story of defeat as one of success. Yet the Temple of Jupiter Stator on the Palatine (rather than the *arx* on the Capitoline) also commemorates the high point of Sabine success in battle. Joined to the Lacus Curtius, a hollow in the ground, the temple commemorates the lost imperium of the Sabine people.[48] Together the two *monumenta* mark a single turning point, from city to twinned city, in the history of *one* people, whose story is told from the point of view of the dominant half. The word *monumentum* functions topographically in the written episode, because it marks out points of return, one for each side: the place where Romulus and Jupiter together turned the battle and the place where Curtius emerged from the swamp. Action turns and returns between the first two items called *monumenta* in the text, as the city doubles. Romulus'

47. The landscape may even become a metaphor for the narrative. Although Livy does not use the words *coniunx* and *iugum* in this episode, it is tempting to see this episode as a *monumentum* that marks out the city in the shape of a *iugum*, which is both a ridge of hills and also a yoke, thus commemorating the *coniuges*. As the population is doubled, the city doubles; as the two peoples are joined by marriage, the hills are joined in a landscape.

48. This was the lowest and most difficult part of the Forum to drain. The draining of the Forum area is a motif that unites the account of the regal period: the Tiber leaves Romulus and Remus at its high-water mark (1.4.4–6); the representative Sabine disappears into the Lacus Curtius (1.12.10), itself dried up by Livy's time; and Tarquinius Priscus builds the sewers that drain the low-lying areas around the Forum—and the *conualles* (1.38.6). Poucet (*Recherches,* 241) observes that the Mettius Curtius episode quite precisely reflects the topographical conditions of early Rome.

prayer reinforces the impression of turning and of doubling in size, population, and history, for it defines the present, in which Jupiter's *praesens ops* plays the decisive role, as the turning point between a past and a future that reverses this past.[49]

Coarelli points out that the annalists may have modeled their narrative of this story on the ritual dance of the Salii, which crossed the city moving from the Forum to the Capitoline in a responsive and mirroring movement *(amptruare/redamptruare)*.[50] The ritual would have commemorated the battle between the Romans and the Sabines. If Coarelli is right, each reading of Livy's text follows the ritual movement through the landscape. The narrative traverses the permanent features of urban space (hills, valley) and ties them together. Yet it also stops at places that are significant for specific historical associations (Temple of Jupiter Stator, Lacus Curtius), and in placing the temple above the Lacus Curtius in the written landscape, it leaves behind a *monumentum* that in its historical specificity complements the ritual repetition, for it signifies not the fighting but the permanent peaceful settlement and the transition from the first city to the doubled city.

Coarelli also points out that the Salii had an "initiatory" character, that they were young men entering military service.[51] The dance of the Salii Palatini (who are to be identified with the Romans), with its movement from the inside to the outside of the city *(amptruare)*, symbolized the departure of the army for the annual campaign season, while that of the Salii Collini (who are to be identified with the Sabines), with its movement from the outside to the inside *(redamptruare)*, alluded to the return of the army and the transition from war to peace.[52] If the original ceremony symbolized the departure for foreign wars and the return to home and peace, then Livy's reconfigured topography, his constriction of two settlements into the tight configuration of hill-Forum-hill, makes the point that this battle is a paradox: one half of the city cannot fight a foreign war with the other half of that same city. There is no way to resolve this paradox, no way out of the *conuallis duorum montium*, except by

---

49. Even the infinitive *resistere* in Romulus' exhortation and the perfect *restitere* relating the men's action are partly morphological mirror images.

50. Coarelli, *Il Foro Romano*, 2:302. On *redamptruare*, he cites Festus, p. 270M: *redamptruare dicitur in Saliorum exulationibus: 'cum praesul amptruauit,' quod est, motus edidit, ei referuntur inuicem idem motus.*

51. See Coarelli, *Il Foro Romano*, 2:302–5.

52. L. Gerschel, "Saliens de Mars et Saliens de Quirinus," *RHR* 138 (1950): 145–51.

moving through a different space, in this case, the bodies of the Sabine women.

This paradox is apparent to the reader and to an audience far enough from the fighting to take in the landscape as a whole. In fact, this episode is remarkable for the extent to which it makes breadth of vision into a measure of historical awareness. The fighting men on both sides experience events subjectively: the Romans, in their anger and desire to recapture the citadel *(ira et cupiditate reciperandae arcis)*, focus their attention on the *arx* alone, look only to the present, and aim only to recoup their recent losses; on the Sabine side, Mettius' boast comprehends only the present moment *(uicimus,* "we have conquered"; *iam sciunt,* "now they know").[53] Both Romulus and the Sabine women view events more objectively, although the women are at the edge of society and on the sidelines of the fighting, while the king is at the center of both (he is surrounded by a throng *[cum globo . . .]* when he attacks Mettius). Romulus engineers events, including the theft of the women and the Roman rally, while the women, who at first are powerless, in the end manipulate the fighting men as much as he does. Yet the foreign women and the city's founder share the ability to stand both inside and outside of events, although the women are placed in a marginal position by their origin and gender, while Romulus is a privileged viewer because of his semidivine nature. The women's pleas show that their comprehension of events includes the past (their fathers), the present (themselves and their husbands), and the future (their children). Romulus speaks of the present in a similar way: when vowing a temple of Jupiter, he recalls the founding of the city *(iussus auibus hic in Palatio prima urbi fundamenta ieci);* then he promises a reminder, a *monumentum,* for the future. Both the women and Romulus historicize the critical place and time in which they stand. Yet Romulus places the immediate moment in its wider context to make his way out of a tight spot; the women, having seen the paradox of fathers and husbands fighting, make their way to its center.

The narrator and reader also work together to create meaning. The

---

53. Mettius misreads even the present. His declaration "now they know it is one thing to steal maidens and quite another to fight with men" is premature, for this is something the Romans do *not* know. Stealing maidens *is* the same thing as fighting with men for them, at least in effect, since both work toward expansion and the domination of neighboring peoples. According to J. Hemker ("Rape and the Founding of Rome," 43), "[t]he seizure of the Sabine women is, in effect, the equivalent of conquering the entire Sabine tribe. The Roman soldiers' control over the forces of reproduction ensures the strength of the Roman state."

narrator, like Romulus, takes the initiative, while the reader, like the Sabine women, responds to the situation. We have seen that the peripheral point of view from which they watch the ebb and flow of battle gives the women and the reader insight that they could not gain from any other position. Sharing the perspective of the Sabine women incites the reader to plunge into a critical situation just as they do. This complicates the moral lesson offered by the narrative: it is not simply their passionate willingness to dash into the no-man's-land between the Roman and Sabine battle lines that makes the Sabine women an instructive exemplum; it is their deliberate willingness to do so as a result of the insight they have gained from their objective point of view.

Romulus, who is at the center of the fighting and the center of the state, and the women, who stand on the sidelines, both see the past and the future as parts of a larger whole. By endowing these social and political polar opposites with a broad historical vision, Livy expresses the complete inclusiveness of the set of people who can act to save the state in a crisis. Livy has written, as it were, an initiatory rite into his schematized topography, and this rite opens outward to include the reader. Romans and Sabines move to and fro, but others participate: Romulus turns the battle with a prayer to an outsider and an impulsive counterattack, then the women, who perceive the mirror image of these enemies fighting in this particular landscape, respond to it by entering the battle and, with their own action and speech, deflect the men's hostility from one another (*impetum facit,* 12.9; *impetu facto,* 13.2); the narrative shows movement through space, the reader follows the movements indicated by the narrative. At the critical point in this episode, the historian's achievement in vivid representation exceeds the standard rhetorical goal of placing narrated events before the mind's eye of his audience *(sub oculos subiectio)* and, in fact, goes so far as to place the audience before the narrated events, first pushing it away from and then drawing it into the action. This spatial manipulation produces a paradoxical objectivity: Livy maneuvers the audience into a distant position from which it comprehends the image of war becoming civil war, yet when the women make their emotional entrance into the midst of the conflict, they do so from that same marginal position. There is a moral message here: while Livy's audience can fall anywhere on the sociopolitical continuum, it must be able to stand outside of events and then move to participate in them, like the Sabine women, or to participate in events even while finding his way out of them, like Romulus. Together this narrative and this landscape produce the crucial vantage point on the threshold between objectivity and engagement. By focalizing the events through an unspecified audience and identifying that audience with the Sabine women, Livy's account of the Forum battle creates a reader who adopts a point of view advantageous to the state and remembers it when he or she looks on the monuments in the landscape or recalls or imagines them in absentia.

Chapter 3

The Rise and Fall of
Marcus Manlius Capitolinus

In the story of the Sabine women, Romulus' prayer to Jupiter Stator ties Rome's origins to its future and binds together the captured citadel, the Forum valley, and the original settlement on the Palatine (1.12.4–5). Romulus' words are the first from a Livian character to portray the landscape of legendary Rome. No explicit causal connection is drawn here between his comprehensive vision of the historical landscape and the subsequent rally of the Roman troops; but other characters at other critical moments in the *Ab Urbe Condita* clearly do influence events by means of allusions to the city and its monuments. Camillus' famous speech persuading his fellow citizens not to abandon Rome for Veii after the Gallic sack comes immediately to mind.[1] One effective weapon in his arsenal is the panorama of Rome's historical and religious topography (5.51.1–54.7).[2] Livy compares him explicitly to the city's founder: Camillus celebrates his triumph over the Gauls shortly before this speech, with his men calling him "Romulus, and father of the country, and a second founder of the city" [*Romulus ac parens patriae conditorque alter urbis*] (5.49.7). The author considers Camillus' prevention of the move to be as important as his annihilation of the Gauls: "there is no doubt that, hav-

An earlier version of the section of this chapter entitled "The Fall" appeared as "*Custodia Fidelis Memoriae:* Livy's Story of M. Manlius Capitolinus," *Latomus* 52, no. 2 (1993): 350–63. I am grateful to the editors of *Latomus* for permitting me to reuse some of that material here.

Works of general use for this chapter include I. Kajanto, *God and Fate in Livy*, Annales Universitatis Turkensis, vol. 64 (Turku, 1957); Luce, *Livy*; A.H. McDonald, "The Style of Livy," *JRS* 47 (1957): 155–72; Ogilvie; D.W. Packard, *A Concordance to Livy*, 4 vols. (Cambridge, Mass., 1968); and Walsh, *Livy, His Historical Aims and Methods*.

1. His words produce action: *mouisse eos Camillus cum alia oratione, tum ea quae ad religiones pertinebat maxime dicitur* (5.55.1).

2. Andrew Feldherr has discussed Camillus' effective use of historical and religious topography in "*Caeci Auaritia:* Avarice, History, and Vision in Livy V" (paper presented at the annual meeting of the American Philological Association, Atlanta, Ga., 1994).

ing preserved the city in war, he saved it again in peace, when he prevented the move to Veii" [*servatam deinde bello patriam iterum in pace haud dubie servavit cum prohibuit migrari Veios*] (5.49.8). Camillus resembles Romulus in his ability to meet a crisis with both military force and a vision of the city, although for Camillus the crisis comes in two separate stages.

Views of the city also play an important role in the career of Marcus Manlius, another hero of the Gallic invasion, who saves the citadel from a night attack (5.47). Camillus and Manlius complement each other: Manlius defends the citadel from the inside, and Camillus comes to its rescue from the outside. After this their lives diverge: Camillus goes on to lead Roman armies in wars of expansion; Marcus Manlius, however, stays in Rome, stirs up sedition, and is thrown to his death from the Tarpeian Rock (6.11–20). If Camillus is a second Romulus, Marcus Manlius is his rival and antithesis, not exactly a *conditor alter urbis,* but, on the order of Remus, a would-be *conditor alterius urbis.*[3] This chapter discusses Manlius' heroism and sedition, first in isolation and then in the context of Camillus' actions. The words, deeds, and lives of these two men arise from and exemplify their views of the city. Indeed, in the account of their lives, the historical landscape is linked to issues critical in the late Republic and early Augustan Age: how to define the role of the extraordinary man as he moves from military to civil life, how to commemorate his achievements, and how to limit his influence at home after the crisis that brought him to power has passed.[4]

The account of Manlius' sedition in Book 6 has rightly been called a tragedy, and scholars have pointed out its self-sufficiency as a drama.[5] Yet readers who progressed steadily from Book 5 on to the second pentad would see Manlius' heroism and subsequent sedition as two parts of one story. Indeed this is how Livy presents it in the concluding *sententia:* "and the same place, in the case of one man, was the reminder of both his

---

3. For a discussion of Remus as twin and alternate founder, see Wiseman, *Remus,* with reference to earlier work.

4. See A. Wallace-Hadrill, "*Civilis Princeps:* Between Citizen and King," *JRS* 72 (1982): 32–48. Octavian faced this challenge after Actium. See W. Eder, "Augustus and the Power of Tradition: The Augustan Principate as Binding Link between Republic and Empire," in *Between Republic and Empire: Interpretations of Augustus and His Principate,* ed. K.A. Raaflaub and M. Toher (Berkeley and Los Angeles, 1990), 101.

5. E. Burck (*Vom Menschenbild in der romischen Literatur: Ausgewahlte Schriften,* ed. Eckard Lefevre, 2 vols. [Heidelberg, 1966, 1981], 1:94) points out the self-sufficiency of the drama. For a catalog of scholars' comments on Livy's dramatic tendencies, see D.A. Pauw, "The Dramatic Elements in Livy's History," *Acta Classica* 34 (1991): 33–49.

the city along cultural lines, for the aged ex-magistrates who choose to await death impassively in the atria of their houses represent an enormous sacrifice of accrued civic memory.[13]

The Romans who have taken refuge on the citadel look outward from it at the destruction of their city. Livy suggests that their hold on their past, private as well as public, loosens as they watch the city fall.

Quocumque clamor hostium, mulierum puerorumque ploratus, sonitus flammae et fragor ruentium tectorum auertisset, pauentes ad omnia animos oraque et oculos flectebant, uelut ad spectaculum a fortuna positi occidentis patriae nec ullius rerum suarum relicti praeterquam corporum uindices, tanto ante alios miserandi magis qui unquam obsessi sunt quod interclusi a patria obsidebantur, omnia sua cernentes in hostium potestate. (5.42.4)

[And wherever the shout of the enemy, the wailing of women and children, the roar of fire and the crash of falling buildings had directed their attention, they fearfully turned their minds and eyes, as if placed by fortune before the spectacle of their falling country. And they were not left champions of anything they owned, except their bodies, more pitiable than any other who had ever been besieged, in that they were being besieged having been shut off from their native land, and seeing everything they owned in the hands of the enemy.]

Witnesses of slaughter and destruction, the Romans on the citadel are paradoxically excluded from their own city by being confined within its core (*quod a patria obsidebantur interclusi*, 5.42.3–5).[14] Yet for these Romans, watching the city's destruction brings about a salutary forgetting in the same way that watching the Forum battle made the Sabine women forget about their own fear. Present evil weans them from the past, from thoughts of their own affairs and their own property.

---

13. Burck (*Die Erzählungskunst*, 126–29) discusses the moral reversal. Feldherr pointed out the Gauls' "misreading" of the ex-magistrates' behavior in "*Caeci Auaritia.*"

14. This is, of course, the primary purpose of a citadel, which as a defendable site was not included in the *pomerium*; on this and on the usages *arx et urbs* and *arx et Captolium*, see A. Magdelain, "Le Pomerium Archaïque et le Mundus," *REL* 54 (1976), 94. Richardson (*A New Topographical Dictionary*, 69) observes that the phrase *arx et Capitolium* is probably a tautology and that the *arx* and the *Capitolium* are inseparable.

Nihil tamen tot onerati atque obruti malis flexerunt animos quin etsi omnia flammis ac ruinis aequata uidissent, quamuis inopem paruumque quem tenebant collem libertati relictum uirtute defenderent; et iam cum eadem cottidie acciderent, uelut adsueti malis abalienauerant ab sensu rerum suarum animos, arma tantum ferrumque in dextris uelut solas reliquias spei suae intuentes. (5.42.8)

[Still, although burdened and overwhelmed with evils, they did not waver—even when they had seen everything in flames and in ruin—in their resolve to defend with courage the hill left to freedom, which they held, however small and resourceless. And by and by, since the same things kept happening everyday, as if inured by their sufferings, they detached their minds from the perception of their own affairs, looking only to their arms and the iron in their right hands, as if they were their only remaining hope.]

In this passage spatial orientation reflects historical perspective. Looking outward from the citadel, these Romans, like the Sabine women, occupy a position on the periphery of events. As they watch the destruction of everything they own, they see the obliteration of their past. This unites them and initiates them into a society that has nothing to fight for save *libertas* and the "hill left to freedom, . . . however small and resourceless" (5.42.7).[15] The representation of the Capitoline as a place inadequate to the demands made on it calls attention to those demands and recalls its fundamental nature as a high and fortified place.[16] By diminishing the Capitoline and emphasizing the Romans' alienation from their surroundings, Livy gives the impression that, in addition to suffering a painful cure for avarice, the Romans have been transformed into soldiers holding a

---

15. Feldherr ("Spectacle and Society," esp. 24–48) emphasizes the ability of spectacle to unify an audience. He points out (18 n. 47) that calling this scene a spectacle *(spectaculum)* creates irony: the scene is all too real for the Romans. Yet I would add that it also emphasizes their separation from their city's destruction and their helplessness, since they are shut away and cannot intervene.

16. Cf., in contrast, the burning of the Capitoline in Tac. *Hist.* 3.71, where the historian Tacitus says that the long period of peace had allowed the construction of high buildings around the Capitoline. Thus it was possible to attack it from a level or higher position. Inadequacy is the essential quality of other emergency refuges, such as the place Cn. Scipio occupied in Spain, when he made his futile last stand against the Carthaginians: he led his men to "a certain mound, one that was not secure enough" *[tumulum quendam non quidem satis tutum]* (25.36.2).

defensive position in enemy territory. This metamorphosis becomes clear when the Gauls, attacking the citadel in the light of day, finally meet an impermeable boundary: no longer panicking in the face of attack, the Romans wait for them to advance uphill and then rush down to meet them. Their cool use of the place to their own advantage recalls the Sabine charge down the same slopes (1.12).[17] The two descents from the Capitoline, one at each end of the pentad, together produce an impression of topographical symmetry: the Sabine seizure and defense of the citadel led to the first doubling of the city; the Roman defense comes when the city has been reduced to its core. Thus the end of the pentad mirrors the beginning.

After this unsuccessful attack, control over the city's space begins to reverse. The Gauls never again make such an overt attempt. Now their number begins to dwindle, as foraging parties leave Rome for Ardea (5.43.3). Moreover, the repulse of the day attack sets off a chain reaction, as the foragers inspire first the attack of Camillus from Ardea, then that of Caedicius from Veii, and after that the establishment of communications between Ardea and Veii and between Veii and Rome (5.46.4–11). This network of activity begins to form a Rome in exile, albeit a fragmented city, with its potential dictator in Ardea and most of its army in Veii.[18] Obeying constitutional requirements to the letter, the exiled Romans refer decisions to the Senate on the Capitoline (5.46.7), and this recognition of political authority gives the inchoate city shape. While Caedicius' army is a strong body that needs Camillus as a head (*sed corpori ualido caput deerat,* 5.46.6), the Senate is still the head of public deliberation (*caput publici consilii,* 5.39.12).[19] The implication is that preserving the core, both Capitoline and *caput,* is crucial to the rebirth of the city.

Marcus Manlius performs his heroic act in the context of this siege. And the stark situation on the Capitoline, one in which the necessities of

---

17. *Auersus quos Romani nihil temere nec trepide* (5.43.2). Livy emphasized the coolness of the Sabines when capturing and using the citadel in Book 1, to draw a contrast between them and the Romans, who acted out of anger and desire (at 1.11.5 he writes of the Sabines, *nihil enim per iram aut cupiditatem actum est;* at 1.12.1 he writes of the Romans, *ira et cupiditate reciperandae arcis stimulante animos*). See my discussion in chap. 2.

18. Luce ("Design and Structure in Livy," 280–81) observes that Livy is making the most of "division by place" as a way of prolonging suspense.

19. Luce ("Design and Structure in Livy," 280 n. 24) points out how Livy subordinates the fighting around Ardea and Veii so that the climactic reversal takes place at Rome.

life both limit possibilities and serve as tokens of exchange, provides
Manlius with the worldview that inspires his later sedition.

As the Roman forces gather outside the city, the Gauls nearly capture
this core.

Dum haec Veiis agebantur, interim arx Romae Capitoliumque in
ingenti periculo fuit. Namque Galli, seu uestigio notato humano
qua nuntius a Veiis peruenerat seu sua sponte animaduerso ad Carmentis saxo in adscensum aequo, nocte sublustri cum primo iner-
mem qui temptaret uiam praemisissent, tradentes inde arma ubi
quid iniqui esset, alterni innixi subleuantesque in uicem et trahentes
alii alios, prout postularet locus, tanto silentio in summum euasere
ut non custodes solum fallerent, sed ne canes quidem, sollicitum
animal ad nocturnos strepitus, excitarent. Anseres non fefellere
quibus sacris Iunonis in summa inopia cibis tamen abstinebatur.
Quae res saluti fuit; namque clangore eorum alarumque crepitu
excitus M. Manlius qui trennio ante consul fuerat, uir bello
egregius, armis arreptis simul ad arma ceteros ciens uadit et dum
ceteri trepidant, Gallum qui iam in summo constiterat umbone
ictum deturbat. Cuius casus prolapsi cum proximos sterneret, trepidantes alios armisque omissis saxa quibus adhaerebant manibus
amplexos trucidat. Iamque et alii congregati telis missilibusque
saxis proturbare hostes, ruinaque tota prolapsa acies in praeceps
deferri. (5.47.1–6)

[While these things were happening at Veii, the citadel and Capitoline at Rome were, for a time, in great danger. For the Gauls
[attacked], whether they had noticed human footprints where the
messenger from Veii had got through, or whether their attention had
been drawn of its own accord toward the shrine of Carmenta, where
the rock is level for an ascent; in any case, during a moonlit night,
having sent an unarmed scout in advance to test the ascent, passing
along their weapons wherever the climbing was rough, leaning on
and pushing each other up in turn, each man drawing the other after
him, as the place demanded, they reached the top so quietly that not
only did they escape the notice of the guards but they did not even
disturb the dogs, who are usually alert to any commotion at night.
They did not, however, fool the geese, which, being sacred to Juno,

even at a time of greatest hunger, were left untouched. And this saved the citadel, for roused by their cry and the sound of their beating wings, M. Manlius, who had been consul three years earlier, a man exceptional in warfare, seizing up his weapons while summoning the rest to arms, entered into the fray. While the others hesitated in fear, he struck a Gaul who had already reached the summit and with a blow from the boss of his shield knocked him down from the rock. As the Gaul's body fell and carried with it those who were closest, Manlius slaughtered the rest. They were clinging in terror, dropping their weapons and gripping the rock with their hands. Now the other Romans too had come together, and using spears, javelins, and stones, they drove forth the enemy until the entire column of Gauls collapsed and fell headlong.]

Once again, the shape of Livy's written space emerges in the details of the narrative. Livy organizes his account of the attack around the simple spatial pattern of rise and fall; the structure of the narrative reflects the plot, the ascent and descent of the hill. The elaborate construction of the sentence that describes the climb mimics the elaborate human scaffolding made by the Gauls pushing and pulling each other to the summit, according to the demands of the place *(prout postularet locus),* and it sets up conditions for their domino-like fall. The division of the plot between rise and fall, which, as Walsh points out, is accompanied by a shift from the Gallic to the Roman point of view, throws emphasis on the turning points of the story: the actions of the geese and then of Manlius.[20] These are themselves located at the center of the narrative.

Marcus Manlius uses his shield against the first Gaul to reach the top, a detail that appears to be a Livian variation, as does the specific reference to the boss of the shield *(umbo).* Both Dionysius and Plutarch say that Manlius severed the sword arm of the first Gaul to reach the top, then beat back the second with his shield.[21] Livy emphasizes the critical nature of this moment by calling attention to its centrality and extremity.

---

20. For a comprehensive analysis of this passage, see Walsh, *Livy, His Historical Aims and Methods,* 250–51. On details, see Ogilvie, 734–35.

21. Dion. Hal. 13.8; Plut. *Cam.* 27.4. This suggests that Manlius' use of a sword was in Claudius Quadrigarius, the source common to Livy and to Dionysius, who in turn may have been Plutarch's source. See H. Peter, *Die Quellen Plutarch in den Biographieen der Romer* (Amsterdam, 1965), 17–27.

It unites the extreme of hunger (summa *inopia*), the top of the citadel *(in summo)*, and the boss of the shield. Defense of the center comes at a critical moment by means of a center. Manlius' bivalent action of striking with a shield, using it as a defensive and offensive weapon, makes the boss of the shield both a center from which the space under Roman control must expand (this is as far inward as Rome will withdraw) and a turning point (this is as close as the Gauls will come to capturing the city completely). While the *umbo* is the spatial turning point of the attack, the actual reversal of the story occurs between *abstinebatur* and *quae res saluti fuit,* at the moment when the geese sound their alarm. Until now, many things have been running out for the Romans: space, population, food, and, it seems, time. But the *pietas* that made the hungry Romans abstain from the geese now buys them just enough time to ensure that a few Romans can retain their hold on a limited amount of space. Piety, then, precedes and (by implication) leads to military success, as it does in the entire account of the Roman recovery from this invasion.[22] The carefully constructed human edifice crashes in a chain reaction set off by the force of the concussion *(ruinaque tota prolapsa acie in praeceps deferri).* Manlius' blow with the *umbo* produces a dramatic turn on a small scale: before he strikes, his fellow Romans fear *(dum ceteri trepidant);* afterward, the Gauls are afraid *(trepidantes).* Manlius has made a tight spot into a turning point, a distinction he shares with Romulus, who, as we have seen, turned the battle in the Forum.

In fact, the narrative raises the possibility here that Marcus Manlius is a second founder of the city, for the passage that describes the activity on the morning after the attack suggests that Roman history has a potential new starting point, just as it did the day after the Sabines captured the citadel. The description shows the Romans on the citadel developing the nucleus of a group history.

---

22. D.S. Levene (*Religion in Livy* [Leiden, 1993], 199) writes, "Only Livy points to the act of piety involved, and then, indeed, goes on to connect it directly with the fortunate result." This continues the leitmotiv of gods and men acting in harmony that Luce ("Design and Structure in Livy," 272) identifies at each crucial stage of the story (38.1, 39.9–10, 40.10, 49.1). For general discussions of religion in Livy, see W. Liebeschuetz, "The Religious Position of Livy's History," *JRS* 57 (1967): 45–55; J. Linderski, "Roman Religion in Livy," *Xenia* 31 (1993): 53–70. Linderski (54) writes: "The *Annals* treat of *res divinae* and *res humanae,* in that order. They treat of Rome's relationship with its gods, its internal history, and its wars. Peace with the gods and peace among the citizens, *pax deum* and *concordia,* form the two pillars on which the imperium of Rome is built." Manlius' rise is a result of the former, his fall a result of tampering with the latter.

Luce orta uocatis classico ad concilium militibus ad tribunos, cum et recte et perperam facto pretium deberetur, Manlius primum ob uirtutem laudatus donatusque non ab tribunis solum militum sed consensu etiam militari; cui uniuersi selibras farris et quartarios uini ad aedes eius quae in arce erant contulerunt,—rem dictu paruam, ceterum inopia fecerat eam argumentum ingens caritatis, cum se quisque uictu suo fraudans detractum corpori atque usibus necessariis ad honorem unius uiri conferret. Tum uigiles eius loci qua fefellerat adscendens hostis citati; et cum in omnes more militari se animaduersurum Q. Sulpicius tribunus militum pronuntiasset, consentiente clamore militum in unum uigilem conicientium culpam deterritus, a ceteris abstinuit, reum haud dubium eius noxae adprobantibus cunctis de saxo deiecit. Inde intentiores utrimque custodiae esse, et apud Gallos, quia uolgatum erat inter Veios Romamque nuntios commeare, et apud Romanos ab nocturni periculi memoria. (5.47.7–8)

[At sunrise a bugle call summoned the soldiers before the tribunes for an assembly. A reward was owed for the deed done rightly and punishment for the deed wrongly done. First, Manlius was praised for his courage and rewarded with a gift, not only by the military tribunes but even by the soldiers who agreed, all of them, to bring half a pound of barley and a quart of wine to his house, which was on the citadel—a small thing to speak of, but the lack of food had made it a great token of their affection, since each man, depriving himself of his own provisions, brought together, to honor one man, what he had taken away from his own bodily needs. Then the guards who had been stationed at the place where the enemy had climbed the citadel unnoticed were summoned. Although Q. Sulpicius, the military tribune, had announced that he was going to punish them according to the military custom, he was prevented from doing so by the unanimous outcry of the soldiers, who cast the blame on one guard. So he refrained from punishing the rest, but the man who was without a doubt guilty of wrongdoing was thrown from the rock, with everyone's approval. After this the watches on both sides were more careful, the Gauls because it was common knowledge that messengers were coming and going between Veii and Rome, and the Romans because they remembered the danger the night had brought.]

As the military tribunes pass judgment on the events of the previous night, they provide exempla: the praise and reward given Manlius in contrast to the humiliating summons of the careless guards and the execution of the guilty one. This kernel of the larger Rome now has a nucleus of a history, a full cycle from *res gestae* to commemoration, one that aims to inspire more and greater *res gestae* by the force of its exempla. Thus the narrative has presented the night attack on the citadel and the events of the following day as a self-contained unit moving from the great danger *(in ingenti periculo)* to the memory of that danger *(ab nocturni periculi memoria)*.[23] The parallels between the citadel and the account of the assault are striking: the episode represents in miniature the large-scale pattern of invasion, repulse, and commemoration that occupies the last half of Book 5, just as the citadel and its garrison represent the space and population of the entire city in drastically reduced form (5.39.12).

Manlius has defended the citadel in a crisis; the narrative displays the nucleus of a new history starting from his heroic act. Yet this history, like the reborn city, has only a limited future unless the citadel makes contact with the outside. Failure to connect with the reinforcements gathered at Veii will mean the end for this Rome, just as failure to obtain rights of intermarriage threatened the city in its early years. The narrative makes it clear that neither the citadel nor this episode can stand alone. A pointed reference to interaction between Rome and Veii introduces the episode *(dum haec Veis agebantur, interim arx Romae Capitoliumque . . .)*. In addition, Livy suggests that the tracks of the messenger from Veii may have guided the Gauls in their ascent. The topographical details point to greater issues: while the Rome that is coalescing in exile looks to the center as its head, the center has just as much need of the city that is taking shape outside Rome, beyond the Gauls.

Indeed the physical limitations of the citadel produce the preconditions for Manlius' sedition. The morally corrupting influence of wealth and luxury and, in converse, the bracing effect of poverty *(inopia)* are major themes in Book 5. As Gary Miles points out, Rome's obsession with wealth and luxury after the destruction of Veii contributes to the decline in *pietas* that causes the city's downfall.[24] In the impoverished

---

23. On the episodic nature of Livy's narrative in general, see K. Witte, "Über die Form der Darstellung in Livius' Geschechtswerk," *RhM* 65 (1910): 270–305, 359–419. Burck (*Die Erzählungskunst*, 128) divides the account of the siege into three parts: 43.1–46, 47, 48–49.

24. Miles, *Reconstructing Early Rome*, 79–88.

and limited situation on the citadel, however, there is no wealth to speak of; there are only the necessities and not enough of them. Rome's wealth has shrunk to a small space, an insufficient amount of food, some nervous geese, and a few people defending their bodies because they have nothing else.

Rome's metamorphosis from a place of luxury into one of dearth suggests that the reader should place more interpretive weight on references to food. Although Dionysius of Halicarnassus and Plutarch mention the shortage of rations on the citadel (in Plutarch, even the geese are alert from underfeeding), Livy mentions food more often than they do, and his details are suggestive. The Gauls crossed the Alps on account of the attractiveness of Italian agriculture and the novelty of wine (5.33.2); an excess population of Gauls (too large to rule) results from an overabundant food supply (5.34.2).[25] The Romans decide to gather the food and the young fighting men on the citadel (5.39.9) but will not turn back noncombatants, even if it swells the number of mouths to feed (5.40.4). Since there is neither room nor food on the citadel for everyone, the plebeians make for the Janiculum (5.40.5). Having thoughtlessly destroyed the food supplies in the city, the Gauls divide after their daytime assault on the citadel and send half their army on foraging raids (5.43.4). The Gallic foragers, bloated with wine and sleeping, are dispatched by the Ardeans, led by Camillus, who has predicted an easy slaughter of sleeping drunkards (5.44.6). When the Gauls attack by night, the famous geese, still uneaten despite the food shortage, wake Manlius, who, having saved the place, is rewarded with food. After this, Livy tells us that evil hunger oppresses both besiegers and besieged (5.48.1). Despite their ever shrinking supplies, the Romans bombard the Gauls with bread to dispel rumors that they are facing starvation (5.48.4).[26] They negotiate only when hunger has left them too weak to hold their weapons (*et cum stationes procederent prope obruentibus infirmum corpus armis,* 5.48.6–7), a detail that appears in neither Dionysius nor Plutarch.

In rewarding Manlius and throwing bread from the citadel, the Romans deprive themselves of sustenance to use food symbolically

25. Kraus ("No Second Troy," 275 n. 35) writes: "The motif of leaving a place because it has too much produce is very odd." Dionysius of Halicarnassus (13.10) does not mention food as a necessity but emphasizes the luxurious qualities of Italian figs, wine, and olive oil in contrast to Gallic barley water and lard. Plutarch (*Cam.* 15) says that the Gauls' own country was not able to sustain them.

26. For another such use of food during a seige, see Caes. *Civ.* 3.48.

instead. In a limited situation like a siege, such symbolic actions are ambiguous because of their practical implications. Livy calls the reward "a great token of affection" *(argumentum ingens caritatis),* and modern readers see other praiseworthy meaning in it: just as the refusal to eat the geese signifies the return of *pietas,* so too the gift of grain and wine indicates victory over personal avarice.[27] The Romans' willingness to deprive themselves of a limited necessity contrasts sharply, for example, with their earlier hostile response to Camillus' request for contributions of a tenth of the booty from Veii, to help him to fulfill his vow to Apollo (5.23.8–12).[28]

Confined to the day after the attack and the nucleus of a history, Manlius' reward is a good thing; its only apparent flaw is its meagerness (Livy calls it a *res parua dictu).* Yet Manlius' reward appears different when reconsidered in broader contexts. After saying that everyone brought food to Manlius' house, the narrator compares the smallness of the gift and the greatness of the honor from a more distant perspective by adding a second clause, an editorial remark that does not appear in the other extant versions of this story. Livy says that the gift was a great thing, "since each man, depriving himself of his own provisions, brought together, for the honor of one man, what he had taken away from his own bodily needs" (5.47.8). While this comment simply repeats the point of the previous clause (all the Romans brought food to Manlius) and expands the theme of the magnitude of the gift, it makes the reader consider the practical implications of the reward. For although the reward is bestowed with good intent, and although it receives praise in the immediate context, it presages Manlius' future disaffection and anticipates the account of his downfall in Book 6.

In referring to the food as a great token of affection, Livy uses a form of the word *caritas,* which, as both Feldherr and Miles have pointed out, is an important word in Livy: Camillus uses it when he expresses his affection for the land, and this affection for the land *(caritas ipsius soli)* makes possible Rome's early existence as a free republic.[29] The narrator,

---

27. On the degenerative force of Roman greed and luxury, see Miles, *Reconstructing Early Rome,* 79–94. Luce ("Design and Structure in Livy," 271) sees Manlius' reward as one of a series of exaggerations marking Roman moral recovery: (1) the self-sacrifice of the elders, (2) Fabius Dorsuo's daring, (3) the careful observance of procedure in nominating Camillus dictator.

28. See Lintott, "Imperial Expansion and Moral Decline," 630.

29. See Feldherr, "Spectacle and Society," 91–108; Miles, *Reconstructing Early Rome,* 90–91, 204–5.

who has the benefit of hindsight, may be implying here that to direct such affection toward Manlius is to misplace an emotion that belongs properly to the place. At the very least, while praising the reward, he foreshadows the identification of man and place that is so central to the account of sedition in Book 6.

A comparison with another such *conlatio* is illuminating. In the early years of the Republic, Horatius Cocles receives a similar reward for defending the bridge against an Etruscan attack: "private zeal too was conspicuous among the public gestures of recognition: for although there was a shortage of food, each person gave him what he could according to his means, skimping on his own rations to do so" *[privata quoque inter publicos honores studia eminebant; nam in magna inopia pro domesticis copiis unusquisque ei aliquid, fraudans se ipse uictu suo, contulit]* (2.10.13). In this case, Livy does not specify the quantity of food that everyone gives. Each person acts on his own in contributing something *(aliquid)*, with the amount determined by what his household can offer *(pro domesticis copiis)*, and the contribution is a private mark of favoritism, in marked contrast to the public honors. Manlius' reward, however, is both unanimous *(uniuersi)* and uniform. Livy indicates the precise amount of the contribution *(selibras farris et quartarios uini)*, a precision that is indicative of rationing.[30] And although Livy says that every man skimped on his own rations to give food to Horatius *(fraudens se ipse uictu suo)*, he does not say that each robbed his body of essentials. (The food given Manlius is "taken away from [each man's] own bodily needs" *[detractum corpori atque usibus necessariis]*) Nothing like Livy's editorial remark appears in Dionysius or Plutarch.

A siege is a matter of confinement and the manipulation of will, on the part of both besieger and besieged, and rationing is intended to make limited necessities last longer than they otherwise would. In a siege, one doles out these necessities over time and, conversely, measures the time one can endure by the quantity of necessities available. In this stationary situation, Livy's usual analogue for time—space—gives way to another material factor. Since food is the limited necessity, food becomes a currency that buys time until the besiegers lose their will to continue the siege or until help arrives. Livy makes it clear that it was only a matter of time before hunger and plague would drive the Gauls away (5.48.1). The

---

30. Indeed, Dionysius of Halicarnassus (13.8) and Plutarch (*Cam.* 27.5) say that the men each gave Manlius a day's ration. Ogilvie (735) calls Livy's precise figures suspicious, arguing that "[they] can hardly have been preserved by the tradition."

men waiting on the citadel for Camillus to come with help needed to buy time (5.48.6). In saying that the Romans endured until they were too weak to lift their weapons, Livy implies that a little more food, just another day's rations, would have allowed them to hold the citadel until the arrival of Camillus with the army from Veii, instead of negotiating with the Gauls over ransom, a matter Livy calls a *res foedissima*.[31] But if every man gave a day's rations to Manlius, that was one less day the citadel could hold out. Thus, in Manlius' case, Livy raises the question of the consequences of this reward. On the one hand, extraordinary men, like people who save citadels, should be rewarded; on the other, the Romans reduced their collective strength by rewarding Manlius.

Manlius' reward and the bread tossing allow Livy to account for the negotiations in the Forum in terms of Roman mores. Just as the geese allow Livy to imply that the rescue of the citadel was a result of Roman piety, so too the emphasis on food in the aftermath of the night assault makes it possible to represent Brennus' *Vae uictis,* the *uox intoleranda* (spoken when Romans and Gauls are haggling over gold and there is a danger of Rome's greed resurfacing), not as a consequence either of Roman greed or of military ineptitude at the Allia but as the price of Roman defiance in the face of starvation and Roman generosity toward a man exceptional in war.[32] Marcus Manlius defends the citadel; the story of his reward defends the collective Roman ego.

But even if Marcus Manlius' reward is praiseworthy in the short term, a more distant view reveals a pattern of behavior that has dangerous effects in the long run. Livy includes another detail omitted by Dionysius and Plutarch: in honoring Manlius, all the Romans bring food to one place, his house on the citadel.[33] (Note the repetition *contulerunt; conferret* in 5.47.7–8.) The city contracts once again by repeating on a small scale the initial withdrawal to the citadel. This time the Romans move not away from a foreign enemy but toward one man and one man's house. Bringing food to Manlius' house is a sign of respect, which,

31. Livy removes blame from Camillus by shifting the scene's temporal perspective so that he arrives just in time to prevent the disaster of actually paying the ransom (5.49.1). Luce ("Design and Structure in Livy," 281) points out the rise of suspense to its climax at Camillus' intervention.

32. In this account, the monuments that Livy says exist in his time—the shrine of Aius Locutus (5.32.6), the Doliola (5.40.8), the Gallica Busta (5.48.3)—commemorate the presence of the Gauls. The crooked streets of the rebuilt and reoriented city (5.55.3–5) are permanent reminders of the loss of the past. See Kraus, "No Second Troy," 285–87.

33. Dion. Hal. 13.11; Plut. *Cam.* 27.5.

although it is not technically so, has the flavor of a *salutatio*.[34] To his fellow Romans, Manlius is now a virtual *patronus*. Yet this act centralizes a man who is actually isolated from his fellow citizens, for from the perspective of Livy's audience, which is filling a schematized mental map of Rome with the buildings and landmarks referred to by the text, Manlius' house stands apart from the ruins of the city. Manlius is among the fortunate group that lived on the Capitoline and that, consequently, did not see its own homes destroyed by the Gauls.[35] This privileged position, however, implies that Manlius was not initiated into the society of Romans intent only on defending their freedom. Even to defend the citadel was to defend his own house. Now Livy makes no comments about Manlius' motives in defending the *arx*, and he suggests Manlius' isolation at the center only implicitly, first by placing stress on the outward orientation of the Romans as they watch the destruction of the city, and then by editorializing about their unanimous convergence on Manlius' house. But the story of Manlius' sedition was famous, and Livy's audience would be attentive to details that anticipated the sequel to Manlius' heroic act: in the future, his house and the nocturnal meetings there would pose another severe threat to Roman freedom. In addition, the Romans' purpose for depriving themselves of food, to honor one man *(ad honorem unius uiri)*, introduces the slogan *uir unus*, one of Manlius' favorites in Book 6.11–20; and the antithesis of *uir unus* and *uniuersi* anticipates his favorite rhetorical antithesis, "one versus all."[36] The narrative suggests another antithesis through its topographical references, that all but one of the Romans in this episode learn a valuable lesson about the relationship of the individual to the community. When we turn to the second half of Marcus Manlius' story, we see that the food given as a sign of affection whets his appetite for that other necessity that is always limited in a competitive society: *gloria*.

Because the account of Marcus Manlius' reward is concomitant with the continued reduction of Roman space, it conveys yet another lesson. As

---

34. On the morning visit, the *salutatio*, as a sign of deference and respect, see T.P. Wiseman, *Roman Studies* (Liverpool, 1987), 263–66. Ogilvie (735) compares this to the custom by which clients brought gifts to patrons on New Year's Day. On the social and political significance of the Roman house, with emphasis on the interior experience, see A. Wallace-Hadrill, "The Social Structure of the Roman House," *PBSR* 56 (1988): 43–97; idem, *Houses and Society in Pompeii and Herculaneum* (Princeton, 1994), esp. 3–61.

35. Camillus organizes a college of priests for the Ludi Capitolini from the members of this fortunate group (5.50.40). See Ogilvie, 740.

36. See, e.g., 6.11.3–5, 15.11, 17.5, 18.6, 18.8, 18.9.

part of the extended account of the capture of Veii and the Gallic invasion, a narrative in which wealth, greed, and luxury play important roles, this episode repeatedly poses the question, how much is enough? Only the substance at issue changes, from territory, to food, to citizens, to gold. Although the account begins by describing the conditions produced in Rome by excessive wealth and at the edge of the known world by an excess of food, it reduces by stages Rome's territory and population, which wealth and food are supposed to support. As space implodes and the city dwindles to survive, Livy distinguishes between what is necessary to its survival and what is not. Deprived of wealth and territory, its local religious ritual reduced to observance of one family's cult and abstinence from the sacred geese, the city can still retain its identity. But the movement choreographed on and around the citadel continues to raise questions: How much territory can Rome lose? How many citizens can one remove and still have a *ciuitas*?[37] What epitomizes Rome? Livy makes it clear that the city can afford to lose the old ex-magistrates and that it can allow private houses to go up in flames as long as it keeps the Capitoline, the Senate, and the fighting men intact (5.39.12). But it cannot be reduced beyond this; even the Capitoline itself cannot endure as a "hill left to freedom" without help from outside. Still less can the city be reduced to one man and one house. Although he deflects the sneak attack heroically, Marcus Manlius is the antithesis of a "second Romulus," for unlike Romulus in the Forum battle, and unlike Camillus at the end of Book 5, Manlius never conveys a vision of the city that leads his fellow Romans to build on what he has done. It is not his role to do so.[38] His heroism is properly the stuff of anecdote. He remains inside the narrative of events, praised and rewarded, but, for now, silent. Instead of reestablishing the city's military and cultural foundations, he is the hypothetical last Roman at the center of the disappearing city.

The Fall

The account of the attack on the citadel toys with the idea of taking the reduction of Rome to its logical conclusion: one man and one place epit-

---

37. Note that it also relates the reduction of the Gallic multitude, of which no one survived: *castra capiuntur et ne nuntius quidem cladis relictus* (5.49.7).

38. This is not to suggest that Livy or any ancient author might have put a stirring speech in Manlius' mouth and made him lead a breakout as L. Marcius does in Book 25 (see my discussion in chap. 4). There was no such tradition. Manlius' heroism was the alternative to the greater evil, the version in which the Gauls did capture the citadel. Moreover, such action on Manlius' part would usurp Camillus' role in ending the siege.

omizing the city. The account of Manlius' bid for power, however, focuses on the relationship between the whole of an expanding city and a part, whether that part is a person or a place. The issues foreshadowed in the account of the Gallic sack, Manlius' centrality and isolation, become topics of open debate as the city rebuilds.[39] This tragedy of a hero turned demagogue takes place at the center of Rome's historical landscape. A Roman reader could see the citadel and Capitoline that Manlius had saved; the Campus Martius, where his trial was initially held; the Petiline Grove, to which it was transferred; the Tarpeian Rock, from which he was thrown; and the Temple of Juno Moneta, built on the former site of his house.[40] Livy encodes his analysis of Marcus Manlius' behavior in this topography by using polar opposites—high and low, center and periphery, upward and downward, inward and outward—to represent polarities in political and social values. At the end, the story of Marcus Manlius is commemorated by a *monumentum* that reminds the viewer of both Manlius' particular political downfall and the risks inherent in any extreme political ambition. The account of Manlius' sedition closes with the rhetorically satisfying *sententia* that commemorates the hill he saved and from which he was cast, as a reminder of the dramatic

---

39. Burck (*Vom Menschenbild*, 118–43) points out the contrast in this episode between an Augustus-like Camillus and a Manlius who resembles Catiline and other *populares* of the generation before Livy. On their roles as exempla, see E. Burck, "Aktuelle Probleme der Livius-Interpretationen," *Gymnasium* 4 (1964), 21–45; P. Panitschek, "Sp. Cassius, Sp. Maelius, M. Manlius als *exempla maiorum*," *Philologus* 133 (1989): 231–45. The appendixes in J. Bayet, ed., *Tite-Live, Histoire romain*, 2d ed., vol. 6, Budé series (Paris, 1989), offer a thorough analysis of the episode. On the dramatic structure of this story, see Lipovsky, *A Historiographical Study of Livy*, 33–38. For discussion of Book 6 in general and for commentary on specific points, see C.S. Kraus, *Ab urbe condita Book VI* (Cambridge, 1994). On the topography, see N. Horsfall, "From History to Legend: M. Manlius and the Geese," *CJ* 76 (1980–1981): 298–311; Wiseman, *Clio's Cosmetics*, 43; idem, "Topography and Rhetoric: The Trial of Manlius," *Historia* 28 (1979): 32–50, reprinted and cited here as *Roman Studies*, 225–43; A. Ziolkowski, "Between Geese and the Auguraculum: The Origins of the Cult of Juno on the Arx," *CP* 88, no. 3 (1993): 206–19. On Manlius' rhetorical use of place, with discussion of this passage, see Jaeger, "*Custodia Fidelis Memoriae*"; Vasaly, *Representations*, 15–16. On Livy's use of earlier tradition, especially political topoi from the Sullan era, see A. Valvo, *La Sedizione di Manlio Capitolino in Tito Livio*, Memorie dell'instituto Lombardo, Accademia di Scienze e Lettere, vol. 38, no. 1 (Milan, 1983).

40. On the legend of Juno's geese, see Horsfall, "From History to Legend." On the site, see Wiseman, *Roman Studies*, 232–33. On the temple and the cult, see Ziolkowski, *The Temples of Mid-Republican Rome*, 71–73; idem, "Between Geese and the Auguraculum"; Richardson, *A New Topographical Dictionary*, 215; *LTUR* 226–34; Platner and Ashby, *A Topographical Dictionary of Rome*, 289–90.

turn in his life (6.20.12).[41] Livy plots a metaphor, the rise and fall of fortune, onto the urban landscape and commemorates it through a significant place.[42]

In Book 6 the Capitoline is no longer "the hill left to freedom, . . . however small and resourceless" (5.42.7) but the center of a Rome whose territory and population are once again expanding. Those Romans who did emigrate to Veii return under threat of punishment and begin to rebuild, and the new city grows quickly from the united efforts of its citizens and magistrates (6.4.5–6). Now it attracts substance: Camillus, triumphing over the Volscians, the Aequians, and the Etruscans, brings to the Capitoline gods tokens of their increased dominion in the form of three gold platters *(paterae)* inscribed with his name. Livy says that these platters remained in the Temple of Jupiter until the Capitoline burned in 83 B.C. (6.4.1–3). In addition, a public construction project reinforced the slopes of the Capitoline Hill, work, says Livy, that was still worth seeing even among the architectural splendors of his day *(opus uel in hac munificentia urbis conspiciendum,* 6.4.12). The long-lasting *paterae* and enduring substructure of squared stone together reinforce the sense of permanence, stability, and centrality associated with the place. Thus Book 6 introduces the Capitoline in a manner that establishes it as a fixed point of reference for a discussion of continuity and change in civic memory.

Framed by episodes that show Camillus acting in the interests of Rome and the Senate and that show people willingly submitting to his authority, the story of Manlius' sedition has been rightly called a negative exem-

---

41. Wiseman (*Roman Studies,* 225–43) identified the Tarpeian Rock as the southeastern cliff of the citadel, the part overlooking the Forum, by showing that, as the scene of Manlius' exploit, it is a late addition to the story. Livy changed the location of Manlius' heroism only in the story of the sedition, for in 5.47.2–4, the Gauls climb the *saxum Carmentis,* which is on the other cliff of the citadel, the one nearest the Tiber. Wiseman argues that Livy's problem with empirically accurate topography comes from a desire to use the rhetorically satisfying "same place" *sententia* that he inherited from his late annalistic sources. We can see this example as part of Livy's larger project of creating an abstract landscape, one in which absolute positions like center and edge bear a great deal of moral and didactic weight and are of more concern to the writer than empirical topography.

42. The idea of the dramatic reversal remains a prominent theme early in Book 6, just as it was at the close of Book 5, when Veii, Camillus, Rome, and the Gauls all suffered extreme fluctuations in fortune. Luce ("Design and Structure in Livy," 268–69) sees two major dramatic reversals in Book 5: one at the beginning of the siege (5.39.8) and another when Camillus interrupts the negotiations over ransom (5.49.1). See also Burck, *Die Erzählungskunst,* 216–17, 224–26.

plum in an ongoing lesson about the proper handling of power.[43] When we consider it in the broader context of Books 5 and 6, as a counterpart both to Manlius' own defense of the citadel and to Camillus' wide-ranging and continuous service to the state, the sedition offers a second political lesson: how and how not to perceive and represent the city and its monuments. As the story of Manlius demonstrates, perspectives on the city influence behavior and can themselves be communicated to others by means of persuasive speech. An audience can adopt them for its own use and pass them on in turn.[44] While the political battle fought between Manlius and his opponents demonstrates the threat to freedom posed by one man's attraction of popular support, it also shows how historically significant places influence the course of events. That Livy tells the story of Manlius' sedition so as to make it a particularly appropriate opening to the second pentad becomes clear when we consider the role of the Capitoline.[45]

Finally, while Manlius' story teaches the specific lesson that a person should not agitate for power and prestige by making seditious popular appeals, it also conveys a general one: a person must contemplate any given event in a broad context to achieve a clear view of the past. Manlius' impulsive defense of the citadel appears a greater deed when the citadel is all that remains free in a captured city; it appears a lesser one when that same place is the center of an expanding city.[46] In addition, it is important to know and to remember the entire history of a place, because a single place can point back to multiple and contradictory memories: the Capitoline is Manlius' *monumentum*; it commemorates

43. See Kraus, *Ab urbe condita Book VI*, 118. Camillus leads expeditions against the Volsci, Antium, and Etruria in 7.1–10.6; he receives another extraordinary command against the Volsci and saves the day when his colleague, L. Furius, leads the army into battle prematurely (22.5–25.6).

44. See esp. Vasaly, *Representations*. The reader of Cicero's speeches is witness to the speech from only the speaker's point of view, while in Livy's narrative, the speaker is privy to both the speaker's point of view and that of the audience. Thus we can follow rhetorical uses of a place as they are communicated between different characters.

45. Bayet (*Tite-Live, Histoire romaine*, 6:111) observes that the Capitoline plays a prominent role in the narrative, as a place of refuge during the Gallic invasion, as a central and unifying site of the priesthood organized by Camillus, and as the alleged hiding place for the gold recovered from the Gauls, but he does not comment further on issues of topography.

46. Livy continues to make the growth in narrative scope parallel the expansion of Rome's influence. Books 6–15 deal with the conquest of Italy; in Book 7.29.1–2, Livy signals another outward step in this process, with what Burck (*Vom Menschenbild*, 325 n. 5) calls an "interior prologue." See also Kraus, "No Second Troy," 269–70.

both his heroism and his execution. Since the Capitoline itself is spatially multivalent—a turning point, a peak, and a center—it commemorates not just a specific event but a cluster of interrelated dramatic reversals: the repulse of the enemy; the rise and fall, first of the Gauls and then of Manlius; the city's rebirth from a core. The narrative makes the case for viewing past events as part of a comprehensive picture, because an isolated and unintegrated memory of one event is just as limited and just as limiting as a view of the city that takes in only one place from only one point of view. Livy illustrates different degrees of historical comprehension by means of different perspectives on the Capitoline.

Livy divides Manlius' story into three parts that alternate with discussions of external affairs.[47] It begins four years after the Gallic invasion, when, in response to the threat posed by the Antiates and the Etruscans, Camillus' colleagues in the military tribunate voluntarily cede their authority to him (6.6.6–7). During the following year, Manlius begins to court the favor of the plebeians; in the next, he is tried on charges of attempting to establish a tyranny, convicted, and cast to his death from the Tarpeian Rock.

Camillus' eminence prompts Manlius' initial complaint.

Qui nimius animi cum alios principes sperneret, uni inuideret eximio simul honoribus atque uirtutibus, M. Furio, aegre ferebat solum eum in magistratibus, solum apud exercitus esse; tantum iam eminere ut iisdem auspiciis creatos non pro collegis sed pro ministris habeat; cum interim, si quis uere aestimare uelit, a M. Furio reciperari patria ex obsidione hostium non potuerit, nisi a se prius Capitolium atque arx seruata esset; et ille inter aurum accipiendum et in spem pacis solutis animis Gallos adgressus sit, ipse armatos capientesque arcem depulerit; illius gloriae pars uirilis apud omnes milites sit qui simul uicerint: suae uictoriae neminem omnium mortalium socium esse. (6.11.2–5)

---

47. On the dramatic structure, see Lipovsky, *A Historiographical Study of Livy*, 33–38. The tragedy of Manlius fits into the tradition of Hellenistic tragic-pathetic histories. On this, see Pauw, "Dramatic Elements in Livy's History." On tragic history, see B.L. Ullman, "History and Tragedy," *TAPA* 73 (1942): 25–53; F.W. Walbank, "History and Tragedy," *Historia* 9 (1960): 216–34, reprinted, and cited here as *Selected Papers: Studies in Greek and Roman History and Historiography* (Cambridge, 1985), 224–41.

[Manlius, overweening in spirit, while scorning the other leading men but envying one, M. Furius Camillus, who was outstanding in both honors and virtues, bore it ill that Camillus should occupy magistracies alone, that he alone should command the army, that he was now so preeminent that he considered men elected under the same auspices not as his colleagues but as attendants, while, in fact, anyone who wanted to make a true assessment could see that the country could not have been retaken from the siege by M. Furius had the Capitoline and citadel not first been saved by him [Manlius]. Moreover, Camillus attacked the Gauls while they were distracted by the matter of the ransom and relaxed in the expectation of peace; he, Manlius, drove them off when they were in arms and in the process of capturing the citadel. A good part of Camillus' glory belonged to all the soldiers who conquered with him; but no mortal shared Manlius' victory.]

Livy introduces Manlius as an unlikely source of sedition by pointing out his fame and patrician rank, but he conveys the competitive side of his character implicitly, by giving him a keen interest in hierarchy and a tendency to set himself apart from others and to make comparisons.[48] Manlius cannot tolerate Camillus' prestige: to do so would mean accepting a place among the *uniuersi*.

Marcus Manlius also presents a narrow and restricted version of Rome's recent history: his thoughts include no events from the years before the Gallic invasion and none from the years between the defeat of the Gauls and Camillus' extraordinary appointment. Moreover, the past focalized through him uses a model of the city in which the Capitoline predominates. This introduces an analogy between breadth of historical memory and breadth of vision that Livy sustains throughout the episode. Manlius' complaint also implicitly correlates hill and power: he who saved the "head" of Rome should be the "head" of Rome. The correlation is not new. Livy first identified the Capitoline as the center of Roman political power in Book 1, when, during the reign of Tarquinius Superbus, the last of the Etruscan kings, workmen digging foundations for the Temple of Jupiter Optimus Maximus discov-

48. Kraus (*Ab urbe condita Book VI*, 149) notes Manlius' interest in the vertical and observes that Manlius uses the historiographical technique of *syncrisis,* a point-by-point comparison of the accomplishments of great men.

ered a human head, the portent of Rome's future status as the "head" of a world empire (1.55.5–6).[49]

The second act of the drama represents these spatial associations even more vividly, in direct speech. The Senate appoints A. Cornelius Cossus dictator, ostensibly, says the narrator, in response to the prospect of war with the Volscians, but really to deal with the suspect behavior of Marcus Manlius, who has begun to rescue bankrupt citizens from debt slavery. Manlius' experience on the citadel has influenced his worldview to the extent that he defines his actions by their relationship to his rescue of the place. They are simply extensions of his earlier heroism. Seizing one wretch in the middle of the Forum, Manlius declares, "Then it was in vain that I saved the Capitol and citadel with this right hand, if I see a citizen, and my fellow soldier, led off to chains and servitude as though he were captured by the Gauls" (6.14.4). Freed from his debt, the grateful citizen hails Manlius as his liberator *(liberator suus)*. Manlius promises to help as many debtors as he can afford and divests himself of his Veian real estate to finance the project, a gesture that inspires the people to pronounce him the champion of their freedom *(uindex libertatis,* 6.14.10).

Manlius views these private favors as continued expenditure of the symbolic capital he acquired saving the citadel, capital he considers just as liquid as the money raised from his Veian holdings.[50] Yet by selling his Veian property *(fundum in Veienti),* which the narrator calls his *caput patrimonii,* Manlius has confined his sphere of interest to the city alone. The narrative reinforces this sense of constriction by shifting the reader's attention from the sale of the property to Manlius' haranguing the plebs at his own house: "In addition, at his house he made speeches in the manner of harangues that were full of accusations against the patricians" *[ad*

---

49. On the Capitoline myth, see P. Borgeaud, "Du mythe à l'idéologie: La tête du Capitole," *MH* 44 (1987): 86–100. Manlius' obsession with the "head"of Rome calls to mind Cicero's words when, at *Pro Murena* 51, he reports the speech of another demagogue, Catiline. Indeed "head" puns lie thick on the ground in this narrative. Camillus is *caput rei Romanae* (6.3.1), there is the *capitalis poena* (6.4.4–6), and Manlius' Veian holdings are the *caput* of his *patrimonium* (6.14.10). In one of his seditious speeches, Manlius declares that "Dictatorships and consulships must be leveled to the ground so that the plebs can raise its head" *[solo aequandae sunt dictaturae consulatusque, ut caput attollere Romana plebes possit]* (6.18.14). On *caput rei Romanae,* see J. Pinsent, "Livy 6.3.1 *(caput rei Romanae)*: Some Ennian Echoes in Livy," *LCM* 2 (1977): 13–18.

50. I draw the term *symbolic capital,* used to define accumulated prestige, from P. Bourdieu, *Language and Symbolic Power,* trans. G. Raymond and M. Adamson (Cambridge, Mass., 1991), 14.

hoc domi contionantis in modum sermones pleni criminum in patres]
(6.14.11).

Manlius' continued attempts to alleviate debt and his inflammatory claim that some patricians have embezzled the Gallic gold force the dictator to return from his military duties abroad to lead a rhetorical battle in the Forum against Manlius and his supporters. Manlius' view of the past continues to focus narrowly on the Capitoline and thus to determine his interpretation of the present. Summoned to the tribunal, he defends himself by invoking the rescue of the citadel.

at enim quid ita solus ego ciuium curam ago? nihilo magis quod respondeam habeo quam si quaeras quid ita solus Capitolium arcemque seruauerim. Et tum uniuersis quam potui opem tuli et nunc singulis feram (6.15.11)

[You ask why I alone am thus concerned for the citizens? I can no more answer that than if you were to ask why I single-handedly saved the Capitoline and citadel. Then I brought what aid I could to all men, just as now I shall bring it to individuals]

Although Manlius represents his present actions on behalf of individuals as extensions of his previous action on behalf of all, they are actually antithetical to it. Manlius views *libertas* as a personal possession, just as he considers saving Rome to be his own personal accomplishment. His use of private property to aid individual debtors and his repeated appeals to an audience that shows signs of becoming a personal following threaten to undermine the entire state's political freedom.[51] Though hailed by the people as *uindex libertatis*, Manlius champions individual freedom only.

Arrested despite vociferous references to his own former heroism, Manlius increases the intensity of his appeal to the Capitoline; focusing still more narrowly on the rescue, he presents a closer and more detailed image of the place. As he is led off to imprisonment in the *carcer* (prison) below it, he addresses the gods and goddesses resident on the hill, reminding them that he saved them from the Gauls and now merits their support.

---

51. On the incompatibility of *libertas* and individual predominance, see C. Wirszubski, *Libertas as a Political Idea at Rome* (Cambridge, 1950), 4–6.

'Iuppiter' inquit, 'optime maxime Iunoque regina ac Minerva
ceterique di deaeque, qui Capitolium arcemque incolitis, sicine
uestrum militem ac praesidem sinitis uexari ab inimicis? haec dex-
tra, qua Gallos fudi a delubris uestris, iam in uinclis et catenis erit?'
(6.16.2)

["Jupiter Best and Greatest," he said, "Queen Juno, Minerva, and
the other gods and goddesses who dwell on the Capitoline and
citadel. Do you allow your champion and defense to be harassed by
his enemies in this way? Is this right hand, with which I routed the
Gauls from your shrines, now to be chained and shackled?"]

Manlius' appeal wins the sympathy of those who see and hear it, and
only their long habit of obedience to the dictator prevents the tribunes
and the people themselves from interfering in the arrest. Manlius' hierarchical conception of the city takes an ironic turn with his imprisonment
in the *carcer* below the Capitoline.[52]
    Livy illustrates the potency of Manlius' rhetorical use of the Capitoline
by showing that it is transferable as well as inflammatory: adopting it,
Manlius' supporters place before their audience an even more vivid and
detailed image of the Gallic assault, one complete with Gauls, the Tarpeian
Rock, and Manlius himself, armed and covered with sweat and blood.

Non obuersatam esse memoriam noctis illius quae paene ultima
atque aeterna nomini Romano fuerit? Non speciem agminis Gallo-
rum per Tarpeiam rupem scandentis? non ipsius M. Manli, qualem
eum armatum, plenum sudoris ac sanguinis ipso paene Ioue erepto
ex hostium manibus uidissent? (6.17.4)

[Was not the memory of that night before them, that night that was
almost the last, forever, for Rome? Did they not see the image of the
row of Gauls climbing up by the Tarpeian Rock? Did they not see
Manlius, armed as he was then, covered with sweat and blood, with
Jupiter himself rescued almost from the very hands of the enemy?]

His supporters link the memory of Manlius' heroism to the place even
more specifically by focusing on one part of the Capitoline, the Tarpeian

---

52. On this irony, see Kraus, *Ab urbe condita Book VI*, 187.

Rock.[53] Their scenario invokes the Capitoline gods, and they elaborate Manlius' appeal when they argue that someone so closely linked to Jupiter, a divinity of the sky, should not be incarcerated in a subterranean prison below the Capitoline.[54] Thus they draw further attention to the vertical features of the place and with it to the idea of the rise and fall.

Moreover, in adopting his use of the Capitoline, Manlius' supporters reinterpret his cognomen. *Capitolinus* now signifies not just the savior of the Capitoline but a person almost divine and ranked with Jupiter himself (*prope caelestem, cognomine certe Capitolino Ioui parem,* 6.17.5). Manlius' supporters have divorced his cognomen from the circumstances in which he obtained it and have disassociated him from Juno's geese to place emphasis on the loftier connection to Jupiter. Their words imply that Manlius did not earn the name *Capitolinus* for saving the Capitoline; rather the name recognizes a divinity inherent in the man. Thus they attribute to Manlius the qualities of the place he saved.[55]

The efforts of his supporters free Manlius, and during the following year, one of peace abroad, the sedition reaches a critical point. Manlius refers once again to his acts on behalf of individual citizens (6.18.8). His speech to the leading plebeians includes yet another reminder that he rescued the Capitoline: just as he defended the people against the barbarian enemy (*a barbaris hostibus*), so too, says Manlius, he will defend them against arrogant Romans (*a superbis ciuibus,* 6.18.9). And he asks that the gods may grant the people the inclination to do the same for him.

The Senate has its own concerns. Recounting its thoughts, Livy adds a detail that explains its anxiety, the fact that Manlius' house, where he has convened the plebeian leaders, is right on top of the citadel: "But on its part, the Senate discussed the withdrawal of the plebeians into a private house, located even on the citadel, and the menace to liberty" [*at in parte altera senatus de secessione in domum priuatam plebis, forte etiam in*

---

53. Kraus (*Ab urbe condita Book VI,* 194) points out that the plebeians invoke the story of the attack, not the attack itself. Wiseman (*Roman Studies,* 233–38) points out that this is not where the attack occurred (see Livy 5.47.2) but that its transfer to the Tarpeian Rock adds to the irony of Manlius' death.

54. Levene (*Religion in Livy,* 206) points out that Livy's version emphasizes the religious elements in the story of Manlius more than the other versions do. On the close topographical association of citadel and prison, see David, "Du *Comitium* à la roche Tarpéienne," 131–39.

55. As Bayet (*Tite-Live, Histoire romaine,* vol. 6) and others (e.g., Ziolkowski in "Between Geese and the Auguraculum," 210) point out, this kind of rhetorical connection lies behind the story that Manlius received the cognomen as a reward.

arce positam, et imminenti mole libertati agitat] (6.19.1). From the Senate's point of view, and from that of a Roman audience familiar with the type characters of rhetoric, Manlius' obsession with the Capitoline is that of a tyrant who lives on the citadel, a fearful thought for Livy's Romans since the days of Valerius Publicola (2.7.5–12).[56] By focalizing this scene through the Senate, the narrative has changed the reader's perspective on the Capitoline, which, since Manlius' defense (6.15.11), has been presented only from his point of view or that of his supporters. Moreover, the reader is reminded that, at the crucial moment of Manlius' heroism, the boundaries of Manlius' own interests coincided with those of the state. Once the setting for Manlius' heroism—the "hill left to freedom, . . . however small and resourceless" (5.42.8)—the Capitoline has become associated with a menace looming over the city.

The Senate's revised view of the place as citadel, private house, and looming threat ultimately undoes Manlius, for the tribunes present at the meeting see it too, and it reminds them of other boundaries that coincide. They perceive that their own power is coterminous with everyone's freedom (. . . *eundem suae potestatis, quem libertatis omnium, finem cernebant,* 6.19.4). Knowing that in the vertically oriented city envisioned by Manlius such boundaries would be narrow indeed, they subordinate themselves to the authority of the Senate. The tribunes suggest reinterpreting Manlius' behavior to the people in such a way that they realize Manlius is not their friend but a threat to their freedom instead. Then, they say, the very sight of Manlius will bring about his conviction: the people will look on a defendant who is a patrician, will perceive the charge of attempted tyranny, *regni crimen,* and will cherish nothing more than their own liberty (6.19.7). For the Senate and tribunes the new perspective on the Capitoline offers a new perspective on Manlius. They plan to transmit this view of Manlius to the plebeians in a way that will influence them politically, just as Manlius communicated his view of his relationship to the Capitoline to his supporters, who in turn passed it on to their audience.

But when Manlius comes to trial again, the Senate's perspective on

---

56. See Bayet, *Tite-Live, Histoire romaine,* 6:109 n. 6, 111. On the topos of a young man excessively attached to the acropolis, see D.A. Russel, *Greek Declamation* (Cambridge, 1983), 32–33. Dio's version of the story says that Manlius and his supporters actually seized the citadel (7.26.2). On this as an example of rhetorical color, see Wiseman, *Roman Studies,* 239.

Manlius comes into conflict with Manlius' use of the Capitoline. (Livy admits that he does not know all of the specific allegations involved in the charge of *regnum*, but he says that they must have been weighty, since as far as the plebeians were concerned, the obstacle to Manlius' condemnation lay not in the legal case but in the location *(locus)* of the trial, 6.20.5). The tribunes understand perfectly well that an audience is influenced by what it sees; yet their prediction that the people will look on a defendant who is, after all, a patrician, that they will condemn the crime and value freedom above all else, does not anticipate Manlius' continued rhetorical use of the Capitoline. Having saved the Capitoline, Manlius uses it to save himself.

Describing the trial, Livy says that he lists Manlius' accomplishments to show how Manlius negates them by his foul lust for rule *(foeda cupiditas regni,* 6.20.5). There follow the testimonials to Manlius' achievements (6.20.5–9): four hundred men redeemed from debt; spoils stripped from thirty enemies; decorations received for saving fellow citizens in battle or leading an attack over a city wall; the name, in lieu of the man himself, of a *magister equitum* whom Manlius had saved; and, as a climax, an oration as magnificent as his deeds, at the conclusion of which Manlius bares a breast scarred in battle and, looking up at the Capitoline itself, begs his audience to gaze on it as they pass judgment on him. He asks the people to look not at him, the accused patrician, but at the gods whose temples are on the Capitoline.

Capitolium spectans Iouem deosque alios deuocasse ad auxilium fortunarum suarum precatusque esse ut, quam mentem sibi Capitolinam arcem protegenti ad salutem populi Romani dedissent, eam populo Romano in suo discrimine darent, et orasse singulos uniuersosque ut Capitolium atque arcem intuentes, ut ad deos immortales uersi de se iudicarent. (6.20.9–11)

[Gazing at the Capitoline, he called on Jupiter and the other gods for help in his peril, and he prayed that they give the people, in his crisis, the same attitude they had toward him when he was defending the Capitoline and citadel for the safety of the Roman people, and he begged them, one and all, to gaze on the Capitoline and citadel, and to turn to the immortal gods when passing judgment on him.]

The sight of the hill, the temples, and Manlius gesturing toward them recalls his heroism and banishes thoughts of his crime. The tribunes realize that they must free the people from this sight and thus from the memory of Manlius' heroism (6.20.10). Since the memory associated with the Capitoline arouses sympathy toward a man who apparently aims at *regnum*, it threatens Rome's freedom. Blocking it has become crucial to the outcome of the case and, by implication, to preserving republican *libertas*.

More important, however, the tribunes can free the people from the memory of Manlius' heroism because, while Manlius has linked his heroism to one place, they have an entire city in which to maneuver. The gods answer Manlius' prayer, in a sense, for just as he blocked access to the Capitoline *(protegere)* to save the Roman people *(ad salutem populi Romani)*, the tribunes of the people are inspired to block it again for the same purpose. The trial moves from the Campus Martius to the Petiline Grove, from which, says Livy, the Capitoline cannot be seen *(ita prodicta die in Petelinum lucum extra portam Flumentanam, unde conspectus in Capitolium non esset, concilium populi indictum est,* 6.20.11).[57] There the people, who remember only what appears before their eyes, lose the memory of Manlius' heroism, just as they lose sight of the Capitoline. The accusation that is true *(uerum crimen)* prevails in men's minds long enough for Manlius to be convicted and executed. He is thrown down the Tarpeian Rock, a spur of the Capitoline, an ironic touch that allowed Livy and others (cf. Plutarch *Cam.*38.6) a rhetorically satisfying conclusion.

> Tribuni de saxo Tarpeio deicerunt locusque idem in uno homine et eximiae gloriae monumentum et poenae ultimae fuit. Adiectae mortuo notae sunt, publica una, quod, cum domus eius fuisset ubi nunc aedes atque officina Monetae est, latum ad populum est, ne quis patricius in arce aut Capitolino habitaret, gentilicia altera, quod gentis Manliae decreto cautum est, ne quis deinde M. Manlius uocaretur. Hunc exitum habuit uir, nisi in libera ciuitate natus esset, memorabilis. (6.20.13–14)

> [The tribunes cast him down from the Tarpeian Rock. Thus the same place became the reminder of one man's greatest glory and his

---

57. On the possible location of this place, see Wiseman, *Roman Studies*, 225–27.

supreme punishment. Two stigmas were attached to him after his death. One was attached by the people. Since his house had been where the temple and mint of Juno Moneta are now, a motion was proposed to the people that no patrician live on the citadel or Capitoline. The other was brought against him by his clan, that no one be named Marcus Manlius. This was the end of a man who would have been worthy of record, had he not been born in a free city.]

The antagonism between memory and freedom comes to the fore at the end of Manlius' story. Not only does the memory of Manlius' heroism threaten Rome's freedom, but after his death, considerations of freedom insure the destruction of his memory. His destroyed house, the Temple of Juno Moneta, and the disappearance of the praenomen *Marcus* from the Manlian gens are consequences and reminders of Manlius' precipitous departure *(exitus)* from life, citadel, family, and community alike.[58] He is erased from the city's visible superstructure.

Still, Marcus Manlius saved the citadel in a moment of crisis, and Livy has reminded his reader of this heroic deed repeatedly, in his own voice or through the words of Manlius and his backers. Livy says that Manlius is not *memorabilis*, that is, not worthy of record. Why then does he keep reminding the reader of Manlius' heroism, when even the Manlian gens and the people take action to destroy his memory, erasing both his name and his house? What are we to make of this?

The answers are partial and interrelated. Like all acts of *damnatio memoriae*, this one calls attention to the fact of obliteration. Just as Livy's sentence structure reflected the Gauls' attempt to climb the citadel, their repulse, and their fall, so too the conditional clause in the final assessment of Manlius undercuts his heroism and sends his reputation tumbling (. . . *uir, nisi in libera ciuitate natus esset, memorabilis*). In doing so it repeats the pattern that gives shape to the larger narrative of Manlius' life. One reason Livy reminds the reader of Manlius' accomplishments before telling of his condemnation and death is to reinforce his suggestion that Manlius, by using honors as reminders first in a bid for kingship and then to save himself after his attempt fails, destroys the very *monumenta* that would have remained to remind posterity of his accomplishments had he died after a long and useful life, like Camillus, or while

---

58. Kraus (*Ab urbe condita Book VI*, 218) observes that Livy ushers him out of history as well, by pointing out that in the final reckoning he is not *memorabilis*—not worthy of inclusion in history.

fighting on Rome's behalf. In and of themselves Manlius' deeds were heroic; only the foul lust for power *(foeda cupiditas regni)* made them hateful.

Another of Livy's purposes is to give Manlius the character of a would-be tyrant. Tyrants traditionally occupy citadels, and Manlius is obsessed with a citadel in word and deed.[59] Marcus Manlius' character, which Livy did not develop in Book 5 beyond calling him an ex-consul and a man outstanding in battle (5.47.4), emerges vividly in his restricted and vertically oriented conception of the city. By making it plausible that Manlius is plotting tyranny, Livy justifies the actions of the Senate and the tribunes. The narrative also implies that Manlius' ties to one place, the Capitoline, produce the very conception of the city that motivates his seditious behavior. His actions, speeches, and gestures all arise from an excessively intimate relationship with the hill: his house is there; he claims sole responsibility for the well-being of the place; and nearly every time he speaks, he mentions that he saved it.

Manlius' limitations are all the more apparent and all the more suggestive because he has a foil in Camillus. If we measure the characters of the two men simply by their comprehension of the city and movement in and around it, they differ markedly. Even their physical separation in Book 6, a product of Livy's episodic technique, contributes to the impression of their antithetical natures. Manlius and Camillus never meet in Livy's version of the sedition, although they do in others.[60] In fact, Manlius never leaves the city in Book 6, while Camillus is almost always pictured outside it and seems to be everywhere at once. Even in Book 5, Manlius has vanished from the text by the time Camillus reenters Rome and expels the Gauls.[61]

---

59. The obsession with the citadel is all the more necessary for Manlius' characterization, because he does not appear to show other typical traits of a tyrant (e.g., *crudelitas, lubido, superbia,* and *avaritia*). See J.R. Dunkle, "The Rhetorical Tyrant in Roman Historiography," *CW* 65 (1971): 12–20; Jaeger, *"Custodia Fidelis Memoriae,"* 358–59.

60. Dio (frag. 25.10 = Zonaras 7.24) makes Camillus dictator for the fourth time in 384 B.C. A. Momigliano ("Camillus and Concord," *CQ* 36 [1942]: 111–20) argues that Camillus' connection with the matter is not in the earliest tradition but is post-Gracchan in origin. He also argues that Livy plays down Camillus' role in preserving concord between the orders to play up his prevention of the move to Veii, an accomplishment that suits his role as second Romulus and proto-Augustus. See also Wiseman, *Roman Studies,* 238.

61. This technique of separating episodes prolongs suspense, and while it does not always separate characters, it can contribute to their characterization when it does. See Luce, "Design and Structure in Livy," 280–81.

Like Manlius, Camillus uses places and monuments to persuade; unlike Manlius, he aims to preserve the city rather than himself. Using the Capitoline as a reference point, we can see how his famous speech opposing the move to Veii (5.51–54) differs markedly from Manlius' talk in its conception of Rome. Camillus' repeated references to the Capitoline consistently integrate it into a comprehensive picture of the city.[62] The hill appears as a discrete and important part of Rome, but as only part of it (*capta tota urbe Capitolium tamen atque arcem dique et homines Romani tenuerint; . . . reciperata urbe arx quoque et Capitolium deseretur, 5.51.3*).[63] When Camillus points to the Capitoline as the home of the gods, he immediately connects it to a larger context by referring first to the places in the city in which the Romans hid sacred items during the invasion and then to the towns that served as hiding places outside the city (5.50.9). His recollection of C. Fabius courageously performing religious ritual during the siege draws connections between the citadel, from which Fabius descended *(degressus ex arce)* and the Quirinal, where he performed the rite (*in colle Quirinali, 5.52.3*). His catalog of ancient cults starts at the Capitoline, then moves to the Temple of Vesta and to the Quirinal (5.52.6–7); that of new ones moves from Veii back to the Capitoline by way of the Aventine and the Nova Via (5.52.10–11).

Camillus mentions the citadel as part of the city once again (5.52.12) before presenting an overview of public assemblies that is also spatially comprehensive, since it moves from civil assemblies inside the *pomerium* to the military assemblies outside on the Campus Martius (5.52.15–17). His recapitulation of the Gallic invasion moves from the military defeat outside the city, to the capture of the city, and then to the siege of the Capitoline: *hoc ad Alliam fuga, hoc capta urbs, hoc circumsessum Capitolium . . .* (5.53.5). Moreover, Camillus refers to the citadel and Capitoline as the parts of the city that are still intact, using them as compelling evidence in his argument for rebuilding the rest (5.53.9). Finally, in his eulogy of the Roman landscape, Camillus represents it as a whole.

---

62. In drawing together Rome's past, its landmarks, and its religious ceremonies, Camillus takes on the role of cultural historian. This was pointed out nicely by Feldherr in "*Caeci Avaritia.*" Feldherr also discusses Camillus' use of the landscape to evoke Rome's past, in "Spectacle and Society," 17–20. The point I am making here is somewhat narrower, namely, that for Camillus it is a mental habit to contextualize the city, especially its center, the Capitoline.

63. See also 5.44.5, where Camillus speaks to the Ardeans about the situation at Rome: *Patentem cepere urbem: ex arce Capitolioque iis exigua resistitur manu.*

... quotienscumque patria in mentem ueniret, haec omnia occurrebant, colles campique et Tiberis et adsueta oculis regio et hoc
caelum sub quo natus educatus essem. (5.54.3)

[. . . Whenever I thought of my homeland, all these came to mind:
the hills and plains and Tiber, this familiar countryside, and the sky
under which I was born and raised.]

And:

Non sine causa di hominesque hunc urbi condendae locum elege-
runt, saluberrimos colles, flumen opportunum. . . . (5.54.4)

[Not without reason did gods and men choose this as the place for
founding a city, the health-giving hills, the useful river. . . .]

Even his last and climactic sentence, which, like Manlius' last, looks to
the Capitoline and its gods, also includes Vesta and the rest, whose
shrines are in other places and whose rituals connect different parts of the
city.

Hic Capitolium est, ubi quondam capite humano inuento responsum est eo loco caput rerum summamque imperii fore; hic cum
augurato liberaretur Capitolium Iuuentas Terminusque maximo
gaudio patrum uestrorum moueri se non passi; hic Vestae ignes, hic
ancilia caelo demissa, hic omnes propitii manentibus uobis di.
(5.54.7)

[Here is the Capitoline, where once a human head was found and it
was foretold that in this place there would be the seat of an empire;
here, when the Capitoline was being cleared, Juventus and Termi-
nus refused to move, to the great joy of your forefathers; here are
the fires of Vesta; here are the shields [of Mars] sent down from
heaven; here are all the gods who, if you stay, will be favorable to
you.]

Camillus' words are as comprehensive as they are affectionate and as
his feelings are pious. In his reverence for the land that raised him, Camillus resembles Romulus; but the similarity of their outlook extends

beyond this shared affection for a place.[64] Both see the city comprehensively, and both rally their fellow citizens in a critical moment by giving voice to this comprehensive vision, Romulus during the battle with the Sabines (1.12.6) and Camillus in this speech. Manlius, however, is as unable to think synthetically about Rome as Camillus is to think narrowly. Manlius' antithetical pattern of thought and his fixation on prestige appear to stem from his inability to place a detail in its context or to broaden the scope of his vision so that it takes in more than a vertical line. Thus the narrative suggests that, in the end, the extraordinary man is commemorated by as much of the city as he is willing to comprehend: the entire rebuilt city of the second pentad commemorates Camillus as a consequence of his breadth of vision; but Manlius' narrow and tightly focused view of the city makes remembering him through the landscape a matter of reproach rather than praise.

Camillus' other rhetorical uses of the city offer additional points of contrast. Even before the Gallic invasion, when the tribunes first propose the move to Veii, Camillus uses urban topography to convince the Senate that it should persuade the people to stay (5.30). He urges the Senators to enter the Forum on voting day as men who remember that they must fight for their altars and hearths, for the temples of the gods, and for the soil on which they were born (5.30.1). Once again his view of the city is comprehensive and his topographical rhetoric contagious. The Senators refer to Rome's religious significance just as Camillus did, and they point out the Capitoline and other sites as they do so: *Capitolium, aedem Vestae, cetera circa templa deorum ostentantes* (5.30.5–6). Their pleas, in turn, affect the voting tribes, who decide against the move.

But Camillus uses a negative argument as well, one that the Senators do not adopt, perhaps because they would rather not repeat it. After exhorting his audience to remember that it is fighting for its native land, Camillus, like Manlius, supports his argument by reference to his own achievements and the places that commemorate them. He does not talk about Rome, where he and his audience actually are, but about the alternate Rome, Veii. He prefaces his reminder by pointing out that he hesitates to recollect *(meminisse)* personal connections in such a crisis, then he says that, as far as he is privately concerned *(quod ad se priuatim attineat)*, he would be honored by the move. He then conjures up in the minds of his competitive peers a troubling vision: Veii as a reminder of his

---

64. On Camillus' affection for the land, see Miles, *Reconstructing Early Rome*, 90–91.

glory (*monumento gloriae suae,* a phrase that anticipates *eximiae gloriae monumentum* in Manlius' story at 6.20.13); a city captured by him *(urbem ab se captam)* and paraded in his own triumph *(urbem latam in triumpho suo),* a place where everyone would set foot in the traces of his praise (*instigare omnes uestigiis laudum suarum,* 5.30.2). Camillus' rhetorical manipulation of Veii as a place that constantly commemorates him (note the reflexives *suae, ab se, suo, suarum*) has the deterrent effect he intends. It inspires the Senators to adopt his rhetorical use not of Veii but of Rome, for they cling to their city in the face of the alternative that Camillus has made appear far more threatening to their own prestige. The story of Manlius' sedition, a clear demonstration of the threat to political liberty posed by a *monumentum gloriae,* dramatizes on a limited scale and in a limited space what life would be like in an "other Rome" defined as a city that commemorated the glory of one man. Manlius is *memorabilis,* not in a free city, but in that hypothetical other Rome.

By organizing his account of Manlius' sedition around the only place that remained intact during the Gallic invasion, Livy contrasts the permanent and steadfast nature of the Capitoline with the abrupt changes in the status of the rest of the city and in Manlius' fortunes.[65] In the last half of Book 5 and the first half of Book 6, the Capitoline retains its integrity while taking on different roles, all of them determined by fluctuations in the status of the space around it. The center of the city before the Gallic invasion, it becomes the only space at Rome under Roman control during the sack, an armed camp in the middle of enemy territory. After the invasion, Roman military success gradually transforms it into the center of a city that is also the political center of Italy. As Roman influence expands in the second pentad, the Capitoline becomes the center of a series of larger concentric circles; it symbolizes not just the head of Rome but the head of Rome as the head of Italy. Rome rises again, stronger and greater, not as a village founded by a king, but as an entire city refounded by Camillus, a figure of unparalleled civic and military virtue; it is threatened by Manlius, whose character flaw is the egocentrism of his actions and thoughts. The physical city provides topographical correlates to each man's attitudes and accomplishments. All Rome is a monument to Camillus, its second

---

65. According to Livy, the citadel was never taken, but this claim is belied by the other literary evidence. On the tradition that it was captured, see esp. O. Skutsch, ed., *The Annals of Quintus Ennius* (Oxford, 1985), 407–8; Horsfall, "From History to Legend." T.J. Cornell ("The Annals of Quintus Ennius," *JRS* 76 [1986]: 247–48) does not agree.

Romulus, who sees the city from afar, comprehends it in its entirety, and, after Book 5, is most active outside of it. But Manlius, who defended the last boundaries of a dwindling Rome in Book 5, becomes obsessed with a deed located in one place, the place associated intimately with him and with the sovereignty of the state. His act of heroism, however, is not transferable and does not lead to expansion. His narrow perspective causes him to disappear from the history and from the landscape as well.

Livy's brilliant portrait of this noble anachronism conveys Manlius' tragic flaw, his inability to make the transition from Rome under siege to Rome reborn, implicitly, through the tension between Manlius' various vertically oriented representations of the urban landscape, on the one hand, and the more inclusive and expansive topography comprehended by his fellow Romans, on the other. The portrait of Manlius encourages a shift in perspective on the part of Livy's audience and persuades it to see the city and its past in a different way. The reader of Book 5 who presses on through Book 6 moves from the brief account of Manlius' heroism related by an omniscient narrator to a story incorporating so many perspectives on the past that its outcome depends on a point of view.[66] The repeated accounts of Manlius' heroism in Book 6 make it difficult to remember his rescue of the Capitoline except as an event filtered through the story of his sedition. To focus on either heroism or sedition exclusively is—for Livy's audience as for Manlius—to deny the continuity of history and the importance of placing events and anecdotes in a broader context. To see both entails first seeing the Capitoline with Manlius' eyes as the epitome of the city, then seeing it from Camillus' perspective as just a part, albeit an important one, of a place that is expanding. The insight produced by this ambiguous *monumentum* is the importance of learning to shift between these points of view.

---

66. Kraus (*Ab urbe condita Book VI*, 147) writes, "The narrative itself is preoccupied with the same issues as the story it tells: power, deception, and above all, authority—whose version of history is finally to be believed?"

Chapter 4

Memory and Monuments
in the Second Punic War

Book 27 of the *Ab Urbe Condita* closes with the Roman victory over Hasdrubal's forces at the Metaurus River, a major turning point in the Second Punic War. After describing the disbelief and rejoicing at Rome as the city receives first the initial reports, then confirmation of the victory, and finally the victorious consul himself, Livy sketches the grisly recognition scene that takes place when the consul returns to the field.

> C. Claudius consul cum in castra redisset, caput Hasdrubalis quod seruatum cum cura attulerat proici ante hostium stationes, captiuosque Afros uinctos ut erant ostendi, duos etiam ex iis solutos ire ad Hannibalem et expromere quae acta esset iussit. Hannibal tanto simul publico familiarique ictus luctu, adgnoscere se fortunam Carthaginis fertur dixisse. (27.51.11–12)

> [When the consul C. Claudius [Nero] had returned to camp, he ordered that Hasdrubal's head, which he had carefully saved and brought with him, be thrown out before the enemy's guard posts; that the African captives be displayed bound, as they were; that two of them, moreover, be released and go to Hannibal to disclose what had happened. It is said that Hannibal, stricken with such great grief—grief that was at the same time both public and personal—said that he recognized the destiny of Carthage.]

Hasdrubal's head is a focal point for lines of sight: Hannibal sees the head; Livy's audience, envisioning the scene, is drawn to this gruesome detail. But the head also evokes a memory that guides the interpretation

---

A version of the section of this chapter entitled "Marcius the Historian" was delivered as a paper at the annual meeting of the American Philological Association, Atlanta, Ga., 1994.

of events.[1] In throwing out Hasdrubal's head, displaying the captives in chains, and freeing two prisoners to tell what happened, the Roman consul sends Hannibal a series of tokens that forces him to acknowledge his city's inevitable defeat, since defeat is part of Hannibal's public and personal past. Rome conquered Carthage in the First Punic War, when Hannibal's father fought; now Hannibal's brother has fallen, dying in a manner worthy of his father and brother.[2] The *fortuna* of Carthage is the same as it was before: to be defeated by Rome again, and again.[3] The next sentence, the last of Book 27, describes Hannibal gathering his forces into Bruttium, the very corner of Italy *(extremum Italiae angulum).*[4] The order of narrated events (Hannibal recognizes the fortune of Carthage, and Hannibal goes away) implies that Hannibal moves his army because he acknowledges the inevitability of defeat. In this scene, then, memory results in recognition ("that is my brother's head"), recognition produces grief and insight ("this means Carthage will be defeated"), and these in turn produce the speech act ("I recognize the fortune of Carthage") and possibly the physical gesture as well (the removal to Bruttium).

Hannibal was only alleged to have said that he recognized Carthage's fortune *(Hannibal . . . fertur dixisse)*. By acknowledging the uncertainty of the tradition, Livy draws attention to his own point of view, that of a Roman historian who could not have personally heard remarks made two hundred years earlier in an enemy camp. This suggestion of authorial distance vouches for the accuracy, if not the historicity, of Hannibal's words, since Livy's audience, who shares his distant Roman van-

---

1. Recognition produces various emotions: e.g., the sorrow felt by Horatius' sister (1.26.2); the Gauls' anger when they recognize a Roman legate despoiling their general (5.36.7–8); a rebellious "army's" remorse when it recognizes Roman standards (7.40.1–2). Recognition involves the kind of memory with which ancient writers credited animals as well as humans, instead of memory aided by artificial techniques. Cf. Quint. *Inst.* 11.2.6: *eo magis quod illa quoque animalia, quae carere intellectu uidentur, meminerunt et agnoscunt et quamlibet longo itinere deducta ad assuetas sibi sedes reuertuntur.* On the two kinds of memory, see Blum, *Antike Mnemotechnik*, 152.

2. *Ibi, ut patre Hamilcare et Hannibale fratre dignum erat, pugnans cecidit* (27.49.4).

3. Cf. 26.51.11–14, where the Carthaginian generals react to Scipio's capture of New Carthage. They refuse to acknowledge the severity of the loss, even though they realize that it is a crippling blow. Davidson ("The Gaze in Polybius' Histories") discusses the importance of such acknowledgments in Polybius.

4. *Castrisque inde motis ut omnia auxilia quae diffusa latius tueri non poterat in extremum Italiae angulum Bruttios contraheret, et Metapontinos ciuitatem uniuersam excitos sedibus suis et Lucanorum qui suae dicionis erant in Bruttium agrum traduxit* (27.51.13).

tage point, knows that Carthage actually was defeated and eventually destroyed.[5]

Livy says that the battle at the Metaurus appeared to be an equivalent exchange for the disaster at Cannae.[6] The structure of the third decade reflects this reciprocity. Erich Burck has observed that Claudius' triumphant return to Rome at the end of Book 27 is an apt counterpart to the return of the defeated Terentius Varro at the end of Book 22.[7] Livy's audience would envision Hannibal's response to the sight of his brother's head with the equally memorable Roman response to Varro in mind.

Nec tamen eae clades defectionesque sociorum mouerunt ut pacis usquam mentio apud Romanos fieret neque ante consulis Romam aduentum nec postquam is rediit renouauitque memoriam acceptae cladis; quo in tempore ipso adeo magno animo ciuitas fuit ut consuli ex tanta clade, cuius ipse causa maxima fuisset, redeunti et obuiam itum frequenter ab omnibus ordinibus sit et gratiae actae quod de re publica non desperasset; qui si Carthaginienium ductor fuisset, nihil recusandum supplicii foret. (22.61.13–15)

[All the same, the disasters and defections of the allies failed to cause any mention of peace to be made on the part of the Romans, either before the consul's arrival in Rome, or after he returned and renewed the memory of the blow they had suffered. And at precisely that time, the city was so generous in spirit that when the consul returned from such a great defeat, although he had himself been at fault more than anyone, a crowd of all ranks came out to meet him on the way and gave thanks because he had not despaired of the state, whereas had he been a Carthaginian leader, no punishment would have been denied.]

For the Romans the days after Cannae were the darkest of the war. That this passage follows immediately after the list of allied towns defecting

---

5. On Livy's expressions of doubt and their rhetorical function, see Miles, *Reconstructing Early Rome*, 20–31.

6. *Nunquam eo bello una acie tantum hostium interfectum est, redditaque aequa Cannensi clades uel ducis uel exercitus interitu uidebatur* (27.49.5).

7. E. Burck, *Einführung in die Dritte Dekade des Livius* (Heidelberg, 1950), 132–35. On the third decade in general, see also W. Hoffmann, *Livius und der zweite punische Krieg* (Leipzig, 1942); E. Burck, "The Third Decade," in *Livy*, ed. T.A. Dorey (London, 1971), 21–46; P. G. Walsh, "Livy and the Aims of 'Historia': An Analysis of the Third Decade," *ANRW* II.30.2 (1982): 1058–74.

from Rome after Cannae underscores the gravity of the situation. Yet the anecdote conveys an impression of unanimity, unanimity of opinion, expression, and suppression: on the one hand, there is no discussion of making peace, or *mentio pacis;* on the other, the entire community greets and thanks Varro.[8] The narrative presents the Romans' actions from a point of view that is external and omniscient.[9] There is no doubt about the historicity of the events or the consul's responsibility for the defeat. The perfect concord among the Romans and the narrator's omniscience draw attention to the only discordant note sounded in the passage, the difference between the Romans' view of events and the one offered by the narrator. The narrator mentions disaster *(clades)* three times *(eae clades, acceptae cladis, tanta clade)* and thus reminds the reader just how devastating the defeat at Cannae was, while the Romans, in contrast, refuse to acknowledge the devastation at all.

The closing scenes of Books 22 and 27 make it clear that Rome and Carthage have traded the roles of victor and vanquished. They also suggest that memory plays a part in the exchange.[10] The Romans did at first respond to the news of Cannae with terror, uproar, and grief *(pauor, tumultus,* 22.54.8; *luctus,* 22.56.4). Therefore, one would expect the

---

8. In Carthage, Hanno, leader of the party opposing the war, picks up this fact. He asks whether the Romans have made any gestures of capitulation and whether they have made mention of peace (again, *mentio pacis*). When he hears that there has been no spoken capitulation, he says, "Then we have a war that is as whole as it ever was." He adds that Carthage should offer peace now, while it has the upper hand, for "there are many of us surviving who remember how inconstant victory was in the previous war" *[quam uaria uictoria priore [Punico] bello fuerit plerique qui meminerimus supersumus]* (23.13.3).

9. Polybius does not report Varro's return (3.116.13). See Hoffman, *Livius und der zweite punische Krieg,* 42–45. Note also that in the parallel passage in Plutarch *(Fab.* 18.4–5), there is no reference to memory and no discussion of suppressing talk about peace.

10. Burck ("The Third Decade" and *Einführung,* 1–26) has shown how Livy uses the structure of the decade to organize events. Book 21 opens with a preface introducing this war as the most memorable *(memorabile)* of all (21.1.1). The narrative moves from Hannibal's march on Italy to the Roman disasters at Lake Trasimene and Cannae (Books 21–22), then through examples of Roman steadfastness and courage in the face of Carthaginian success (Books 23–25) to Roman victory in the end (Books 26–30). The ends of Books 21 and 29 coincide with the ends of years, thus setting off the beginning and end of the war. In addition, a strong caesura at the center of the decade divides the war into two halves: Books 21–25, in which Hannibal and the Carthaginians predominate; and Books 26–30, in which Rome gains the upper hand. Space plays a role in the arrangement of the narrative: the decade begins with events in Carthage, and, as Luce *(Livy,* 27) points out, both halves of the decade record Hannibal marching on Rome near the start. While there is a general movement from Carthage to Rome in Books 21–22, there is a general movement from Rome to Carthage in Books 29–30. Finally, the city receives a great deal of attention at the midpoint of the decade: the description of the Shield of Marcius on the Capitoline (25.39.16–18) is followed by the discussion of the arrival in Rome of the spoils from Syracuse (25.40.1–3);

memory of Cannae, which was renewed by the consul's return, to repro-
duce first these emotions and then a desire to punish the man responsible
for the disaster. This does not happen. Instead, the Romans deflect the
memory of defeat by their act of will: in a show of solidarity, they express
thanks, transforming Varro, who we would expect to be a reminder of
incompetence, into a symbol of determination. The Romans' *animus
magnus* enables them to direct their memory away from a potentially
debilitating event toward one that is a source of strength.[11] By commemorating what the consul did and felt after the defeat, the Romans render
his role in the defeat less memorable; by ending the book with his return
instead of with the defeat itself, Livy renders the memory that was most
useful for the Romans into a lasting impression for his audience as well.
Moreover, with the words *is rediit renouauitque memoriam*, Livy points
out that the city has moved past the disaster, that it has, to a degree forgotten it, since only a memory that has lapsed can be renewed, just as
only a consul who has left the city can return. To remember Cannae,
then, is to remember surviving a temporary, if staggering, setback. For
the reader comparing the closing scenes of Books 22 and 27, the striking
contrast is between the self-control the Romans display when faced with
the reminder of their disaster and grief, on the one hand, and Hannibal's
less inhibited response to a reminder of Carthaginian defeat, on the
other.[12]

Between the disaster at Cannae and the victory at the Metaurus, the
Romans repeatedly suppress harmful expressions of emotion and divisive
talk; in addition, they reconstruct the past in ways that divert attention
from debilitating memories. This chapter examines Livy's use of memory,

---

the second pentad of the war opens at the beginning of a new year, with the Senate meeting
on the Capitoline (26.1.1); a few chapters later, Hannibal is at the gates (26.10.3). The
major turning point in the war, then, is reinforced by the breaks between books and years
and is accompanied by a focus on Rome.

11. On *animus magnus* or *magnitudo animi* as qualities that make one rise above fortune, see T. Moore, *Artistry and Ideology: Livy's Vocabulary of Virtue* (Frankfurt, 1989),
141–47. See also Livy's assessment of Cannae: *Nulla profecta alia gens tanta mole cladis
non obruta esset. Compares cladem ad Aegates insulas Carthaginiensium proelio nauali
acceptam, qua fracti Sicilia ac Sardinia cessere, inde uectigales ac stipendiarios fieri se passi
sunt, aut pugnam aduersam in Africa, cui postea hic ipse Hannibal succubuit; nulla ex parte
comparandae sunt nisi quod minore animo latae sunt* (22.54.10–11).

12. On the passions in general, see Ducos, "Les passions." Ducos argues that Livy's representation of human nature shows that two parts are effective in history, one irrational
(sometimes called *impetus*) and another rational *(consilium)*. These opposing forces are at
work from the beginning of Rome's history, according to Ducos, and their presence links
Livy to the New Academy.

space, and monuments in his account of the Second Punic War. It does so through three studies of progressively narrowing scope. The first surveys a selection of instances in which the Romans use *monumenta* and memory to control their response to disaster and direct the course of the war after Cannae. The second presents a detailed reading of a mnemonically rich incident at the center of the decade: the account of Lucius Marcius' heroism after the deaths of the Scipios in Spain (25.37.1–39.18). The third compares two descriptions of monuments, that of the Shield of Marcius and that of the spoils brought to Rome from Syracuse (25.40.1–3). Together they suggest that, if the manipulation of the future, which the Romans call *fraus Punica* (Punic deception), is Carthage's greatest psychological weapon, then adept management of the past, including its *monumenta*, is Rome's.[13]

The Use of Memory after Cannae

The defeat at Cannae, like the Sabine capture of the citadel and the Gallic sack, opens a new historical era in the *Ab Urbe Condita*. This new era has its own designation: the Romans speak of events *post Cannensem cladem* [after the slaughter at Cannae].[14] Since the fighting took place some distance from Rome, it is the initial rumor of the disaster that terrifies the city (22.54.7). Livy's account of the Roman response to the news falls into three phases: first, the repression of grief, despair, and panic in the interests of security (22.55.1–57.1); second, the extreme measures taken to appease the gods (22.57.2–6); third, the recruitment and outfitting of a new army (22.57.9–12). The first and last of these will concern us here, since they discuss the manipulation of human behavior and are, therefore, particularly important for understanding the associations Livy makes between space, emotion, strategy, and memory.

According to the narrator, words could not convey adequately the Romans' fear and consternation at the news of the defeat: "and so I shall give way under my burden and not attempt to tell what I will make less than the truth by expounding" *[itaque succumbam oneri neque adgrediar*

---

13. On Punic treachery, see, e.g., 21.34.1–4, 22.23.4–5, 22.48.1–2. Chaplin ("Livy's Use of Exempla," 156) connects Rome's ability to use the past advantageously to its abundance of exempla.

14. For *post Cannensem cladem*, see, e.g., 23.4.6, 23.30.11, 23.30.19, 23.35.1, 24.18.3, 24.45.2, 25.22.3, 26.41.13, 27.1.4, 27.2.2. Cf. *post fugam Cannensem*, 25.6.7; *post Cannensem pugnam*, 26.7.3; and even *ante Cannensem cladem*, 23.5.9.

narrare quae edissertando minor uero faciam] (22.54.8).[15] Yet the emotional effects of Cannae, which the narrator conveys deftly by disavow-
ing his ability to represent them, could certainly be invoked, and
throughout the rest of the third decade, Romans call on the memory of
Cannae again and again. Cannae, in fact, becomes a much used rhetorical exemplum.[16] Livy's account of the response to the defeat shows how
the Romans manage these emotions carefully from the start, thus taking
a crucial first step that determines what emotions arise in the future when
Cannae is recalled. The narrative conveys an impression of order being
imposed on several forms of expression: the narrative itself is carefully
controlled, for example, and limits on time and place are imposed on the
women's laments.[17]

Livy's description of the situation in Rome after the initial news of disaster emphasizes the noise and confusion of the initial Roman reaction
(22.56.1–6).[18] The passage is replete with references to grief: *luctus*
(three times) and *lugentibus* (22.56.4–5). There is "fear" *[pauor]*, "commotion" *[tumultus]*, "the outcry of lamenting women" *[clamor lamen-
tantium mulierum]*, and "the mourning of families" *[comploratus famil-
iarum]*. The narrative associates emotional upheaval and cognitive
confusion with disordered civic space. The Senate is summoned to the
Curia Hostilia, but its attempts to plan the defense of the city are frus-
trated by an uproar in which space, sound, and understanding are

---

15. G.M. Paul ("*Urbs Capta*: Sketch of an Ancient Literary Motif," *Phoenix* 36 [1982]:
144–55) suggests that Livy gains a special effect by avoiding the usual description.

16. When Rome despairs at news of disaster in Gaul, Ti. Sempronius invokes Cannae
to put heart into the Senate (23.25.1–3). At Nola, Marcellus cheers his soldiers by reminding them of the Punic army's decadence and telling them that Capua was the Carthaginians'
Cannae (23.45.4). When Hannibal marches on Rome, Q. Fabius Maximus uses Cannae to
support a policy of unflinching resistance (26.8.3–4). When the young P. Cornelius Scipio
addresses the armies of his dead father and uncle in Spain, he calls Cannae a *monumentum*
and reinterprets it not as a fearful reminder but as a challenge (26.41.10–13). He encourages his men by pointing out that they have already set a precedent in the post-Cannae era:
"you soldiers, were the first of all to oppose Hasdrubal as he was making his way toward
the Alps and Italy after the defeat at Cannae, and if he had joined his brother, there would
no longer be a people of the Roman name" (26.41.13). For a more thorough discussion of
the use of Cannae as an exemplum, see Chaplin, "Livy's Use of Exempla," 82–93. Chaplin
points out that each person who uses this exemplum tailors it to his particular rhetorical
goal.

17. Walsh (*Livy, His Historical Aims and Methods,* 171) observes that Livy devotes
twice as many chapters to the Roman reaction after Cannae as to the battle itself, "so that
Livy may impress us with the native courage and determination adapting themselves to the
critical situation." See also Burck, *Einführung,* 92.

18. See Walsh, "Livy and the Aims of 'Historia,'" 1071–74.

equally confused: "but when in dangers both immense and unfamiliar not even deliberation was of any use, and the clamor of mourning women resounded, and it was not yet clear who was alive and who was dead, and men were indiscriminately mourned throughout almost every house, then Quintus Fabius Maximus decreed . . ." (22.55.3). Livy goes on to tell how Q. Fabius Maximus restores clarity and calm by imposing order on civic space.[19] Fabius commands that horsemen set out on the Via Latina and Via Appia to meet incoming survivors and spy on Hannibal (22.55.4–5). The horsemen help Rome regain control of the past as they travel the routes by which the first confused information arrived and return with more precise details about the fate of the consuls and army. Their action is also preemptive: they acquire important information more quickly by going out to meet fugitives and, at the same time, prevent unorganized and disruptive news from entering Rome. The set of indirect questions that relates their assignment, to find out what happened and where Hannibal went, what he is doing and what he is going do (*referant . . . quo se Hannibal post proelium contulerit, quid paret, quid agat acturusque sit*, 22.55.5), as it changes tense from the past to the present and then to the future, reflects the nature of their mission as its purpose changes from retrieval to acquisition.

Q. Fabius Maximus also imposes order on the city in a way that links the control of expression to the control of space. He tells the senators to keep the women out of the public sphere and inside their own houses. His commands, conveyed in a series of short clauses, divide the work of imposing order into several discrete tasks that clear space by restricting and removing: "they must keep the wives away the public space" [*matronas publico arceant*], "they must constrain each one to be confined within her own threshold" [*continerique intra suum quamque limen cogant*], "they must restrain the mourning of households" [*comploratus familiarum coerceant*], and "they must produce quiet throughout the city" [*silentium per urbem faciant*] (22.55.6–7). Adding to the sense of order are the verbs used in these commands: "to keep away," *arcere*; "to constrain to be confined," *contineri cogere*; and "to restrain," *coercere*. The restoration of order moves outward from the interior of the mourn-

---

19. His disposition of citizens follows textbook precepts; see Aeneas Tacticus, esp. 1.1–3.6, 5.1, 6.1–6.7. Hoffman (*Livius und der zweite punische Krieg*, 45) points out that Livy assigns Fabius Maximus a less prominent role in the aftermath of Cannae than he plays in Plutarch and Plutarch's pre-Livian sources. Livy is interested in focusing attention on the *magnus animus* of the people as a whole.

ing households to the entire area enclosed by the city walls, for the entire urban population, not just the women, must be restrained. The senators are to see to it that all messages are delivered to the praetors *(nuntios rerum omnium ad praetores deducendos curent)*. Last, the senators are to post guards at the gates who will allow no one to leave and who will compel men (again Livy uses the verb *cogere*) to hope for no safety except on condition that the city and its walls are secure (22.55.8). Only after the uproar is settled is the Senate to be summoned back to the Curia to plan the defense of the city.[20] Burck has observed that Fabius' example of calm authority radiates outward from him, through the Senate, to the rest of the city.[21] A diagram of his influence would show a series of concentric circles, with Fabius at the center, the Senate in the first ring, the guards at the gates in the next, and the other citizens further out (with the male citizens one ring closer to the center than their wives and other household members). The closer one is to the center of authority, the more freedom of movement one has: the Senators move to and fro under Fabius' direction; the guards restrict the movement of the citizens to the space within the city; the male citizens, in turn, keep the women at home.

Moreover, order in the narrative itself contributes to the impression of order restored in the city. When the consul writes telling of his efforts to regroup the survivors, his letter presents exactly the information Fabius sent the spies to discover, in the very order in which Fabius requested it: first the fate of the slain consul and army (*L. Aemilium consulem exercitumque caesum*, 22.56.2; cf. *referant . . . quae fortuna consulum atque exercituum sit*, 22.55.4), then the location of survivors (*sese Canusi esse reliquias . . . colligentem*, 22.56.2; cf. *referant . . . ubi eae copiae sint*, 22.55.5), and, finally, Hannibal's position and activities (*Poenum sedere ad Cannas, in captiuorum pretiis praedaque alia . . . nundinantem*, 22.56.3; cf. *referant . . . quo se Hannibal post proelium contulerit, quid paret . . .* , 22.55.5). The narrative, then, diverts the reader's attention from the initial horror and panic at the news of Cannae to the restoration of calm, first with the narrator's own refusal to describe Rome's fear and consternation, then with the careful observance of order throughout the separate layers of discourse, from expressions of grief to official dispatches. For Livy's audience, then, the memorable impression left by the

---

20. *Ubi conticuerit [recte] tumultus, tum in curiam patres reuocandos consulendumque de urbis custodia esse* (22.55.8); see also *Ceterum cum sedato urbis tuultu reuocati in curiam patres essent . . .* (22.56.6).

21. Burck, *Einführung*, 100–101.

Roman response to Cannae is not of the confusion itself but of the restoration of order.

The city grows calm; it learns the details of the disaster and buries its dead in an orderly manner, with limits imposed on periods of mourning; it performs human sacrifice to appease the gods and sends Q. Fabius Pictor to consult the oracle at Delphi.[22] Then Rome rearms: "They order that arms and missiles and other implements be obtained, and they remove ancient spoils from shrines and porticos. Moreover, the shortage of free men and exigencies of the situation even brought about another kind of new levy: they bought and equipped at public expense eight thousand young slaves, having asked them first individually if they were willing to serve in the army" [*Arma, tela, alia parari iubent et uetera spolia hostium detrahunt templis porticibusque. Et aliam formam noui dilectus inopia liberorum capitum ac necessitas dedit: octo milia iuuenum ualidorum ex seruitiis, priusquam sciscitantes singulos uellentne militare, empta publice armauerunt*] (22.57. 10–11).[23] These measures underscore the city's desperation. The narrative, however, sets the age of the spoils (*uetera spolia*) against the unprecedented levy of slaves, as if the antiquity of one compensates for the innovation in the other: the *spolia* co-opt this makeshift army into the community by equipping it with the dignity and the triumphs of the past. Indeed, later, when Livy says that the dictator recruited debtors and men condemned on capital charges, he becomes more emphatic and more precise about the distinguished pedigree of their weapons: the dictator, says Livy, equipped them with spoils from C. Flaminius' Gallic triumph (23.14.2–4).[24] The provenance of the weapons illustrates the extremity of the situation and at the same time compensates for the background of the men who carry them. Instead of armed criminals, the new recruits become living reminders of past victories.

---

22. The sacrifice consists of the burial of an unchaste Vestal Virgin at the Porta Collina and of pairs of foreigners in the Forum Boarium (22.57.2–6). On the executions, see P. Fabre, "'*Minime Romano sacro*': Note sur un passage de Tite-Live et les sacrifices humains dans la religion romaine," *REA* 42 (1940): 419–24.

23. Cf. Appian *HR* 7.27, which reports the purchase of eight thousand slaves and says that the magistrate ordered everyone to produce weapons and missiles (cf. Livy's *arma, tela, alia parari iubent*, 25.57.10); Appian does not mention spoils taken from temples and porticoes. Livy adds the detail about the spoils after he says that the city sent for soldiers from the Latin allies and before he says the city bought slaves for soldiers, thus isolating the most extreme measure, the recruitment of slaves from the recruitment of free men.

24. Aeneas Tacticus (2.2) says that the Spartans used tripods from their sanctuaries to make barricades against the Thebans.

The use of the spoils correlates nicely with the city's decision to recruit new soldiers by buying slaves instead of ransoming the men taken prisoner at Cannae. The negotiations between the Senate and the delegates representing the prisoners draw an implicit contrast between the prisoners, who capitulated by surrendering themselves and their camp, and the Romans in the city, who energetically make shift with whatever they can find, even if that means taking spoils from temples and arming slaves. While the delegates justify the prisoners' capitulation with the argument that they had no alternative, Manlius Torquatus, a senator of "ancient and, as it seemed to many, excessively harsh severity" [*priscae ac nimis durae ut plerisque uidebatur seueritatis*] (22.60.5), argues against ransoming the prisoners, largely on the grounds that they neither attempted to break out of the camp (indeed, he says, they tried to prevent others from doing so) nor defended it to the last (22.60.16–25).

The delegates, who speak first, draw on earlier examples of Roman capitulation, including the ransom paid to the Gauls after the citadel surrendered to Brennus. They represent their ordeal as a reenactment of the Gallic seige: like their forbears on the citadel, the survivors of Cannae were surrounded by the enemy and suffered from the lack of supplies. The Romans on the citadel were the epitome of the city. The delegates portray themselves and their fellow prisoners as the epitome of the army: "we did not think it a crime that some Roman soldier should survive Cannae, when fifty thousand from our ranks had been killed" (22.59.5). When they refer to the disgrace of being replaced with slaves, they show that they still think they are central to the community and can, therefore, decide who is and who is not a Roman (22.59.12). Yet their interpretation of their experience trivializes the past: they endured for one day and night, instead of many, and surrendered when they ran out of water, not food (22.59.5–6).

Manlius Torquatus' response secures Rome's cultural boundaries, as it were, against such a breach. He points out the impropriety of figures at the margins of society behaving as if they were at the center. When he restates the delegates' arguments, Camillus-like he directs attention not toward the center, the survivors of Cannae, but toward their surroundings: "fifty thousand fellow citizens and allies lie around you [*circa uos*], cut down on that very day. If so many examples of courage do not stir you, nothing ever will. If such great slaughter did not make you hold your life cheap, no slaughter will" (22.60.14). According to Manlius Torquatus, then, one must strive to surpass the exempla one invokes;

one must not use them to justify bad behavior. He even corrects the delegates' version of the Gallic exemplum. In a sentence that recalls Livy's account of starvation on the citadel in Book 5, Manlius suggests how the prisoners might have acted appropriately if they wanted to imitate their ancestors: they would have endured as long as possible, at least for days; they would have refused to give in until they could no longer hold up their weapons for hunger.[25] Turning the delegates' chosen exemplum against them, Manlius implies that their version of their experience is the first step in a debilitating use of history. His argument raises the possibility that future Romans will expect to be ransomed after holding out for a shorter time—perhaps even without fighting at all—and that they will invoke the ransoming of prisoners after Cannae to justify their expectations. Manlius' argument prevails, and the Senate's refusal to ransom the prisoners conveys clearly the message that the city cannot afford to recognize citizens who threaten the usefulness of the past.

The Romans suppress harmful talk in the field as well as at home, again through the manipulation of memory. The recruits mustered after Cannae and armed with old *spolia* become an army of Roman soldiers at the hands of their general, Sempronius Gracchus (23.35.5–9). Gracchus trains his men until they are accustomed to follow their standards and to recognize their ranks in the battle line (*ut tirones . . . adsuescerent signa sequi et in acie agnoscere ordines suos*, 23.35.6). With great care Gracchus instructs *(praeceperat)* his legates and tribunes to repress expressions of contempt for any man's past that might sow conflict among the ordines (*ne qua exprobatio cuiquam ueteris fortunae discordiam inter ordines sereret*, 23.35.7). The veteran and the new recruit, the free man and the slave—all are to be equal. The legates, tribunes, and soldiers follow these teachings *(praecepta)* with equal care (23.35.9). This deliberate repression of talk about background produces concord: "and soon all the

---

25. Cf. Torquatus' words: *Dies noctesque aliquot obsessi uallum armis, se ipsi tuti uallo sunt; tandem ultima ausi passique, cum omnia subsidia uitae deessent adfectisque fame uiribus arma iam sustinere nequirent, necessitatibus magis humanis quam armis uicti sunt* (22.60.23). And cf. the description of the Gallic siege: *Itaque, dum dictator dilectum per se Ardea habet . . . interim Capitolinus exercitus, stationibus uigiliis fessus, superatis tamen humanis omnibus malis cum famem unam natura uinci non sineret, diem de die prospectans ecquod auxilium ab dictatore appareret, postremo spe quoque iam non solum cibo deficiente et cum stationes procederent prope obruentibus infirmum corpus armis, uel dedi uel redimi se quacumque pactione possent iussit, iactantibus non obscure Gallis haud magna mercede se adduci posse ut obsidionem relinquant* (5.48.5–7).

men's minds had come together with such harmony that it was almost entirely forgotten from which station in life each man had become a soldier" [*breuique tanta concordia coaluerant omnium animi ut prope in obliuionem ueniret qua ex condicione quisque esset miles factus*] (23.35.9).[26] In learning to recognize their military positions, the men forget their social positions. Discord between the ranks *(discordia inter ordines)* gives way to harmony *(concordia)* among the ranks. Livy's repetition of the word *ordo* in two different senses (in *agnoscere ordines suos* and *discordiam inter ordines*) draws attention to the transition. In Gracchus' army, only distinctions relevant to military success carry any weight.

The suppression of difference that produces this harmony receives its own monument. After the Roman victory at Beneventum, Gracchus rewards all the slave volunteers with freedom. He bestows this reward on both those who fought bravely and those who lagged behind in the camps. But to preserve some distinction between courage and cowardice (*ne discrimen omne uirtutis ignauiaeque pereat*, 24.16.12), he orders that those who held back from the fighting eat standing up throughout their tour of duty. Accordingly, at the banquet given for the soldiers by the grateful citizens of Beneventum, one that Gracchus stipulates must take place outdoors in front of the Beneventines' houses, all the newly freed volunteers wear liberty caps or white fillets to signify their freedom, but some recline and some stand (*alii accubantes, alii stantes*, 24.16.18). Back in Rome, Gracchus orders an image *(simulacrum)* of the banquet to be painted in the Aedes Libertatis on the Aventine (24.16.18–19).[27] Since in Livy's account the description of the feast immediately precedes the statement that Gracchus decided to commission "a picture of that festive day," the order of the narrative implies that the painting portrays the feast just as it was described: those who fought bravely are sitting, while those who held back stand. The *monumentum* thus focalizes the past it commemorates: the reader who sees the painting perceives the distinction between ex-slave and freeborn soldier only through the filter of the officially recognized distinction between courage and cowardice.

---

26. See also the comments of C. Sempronius Blaesus at 26.2.10–11.

27. On the Aedes Libertatis, see Richardson, *A New Topographical Dictionary*, 234. On this artwork as a continuation of past commemorative practices, see Gruen, *Culture and National Identity*, 94.

After Cannae, then, in discrete phases and on different fronts, and largely through the influence of extraordinary men, the Romans manage their emotions and their memory so they will not aggravate the damage already done and to ready themselves for continuing the war. Fabius Maximus checks Rome's initial display of emotion by imposing order on civic space and private grief. The Romans rearm themselves with weapons that are reminders of past success, and convinced by Manlius Torquatus, they forget the soldiers who cannot learn from the past. By greeting the defeated consul with a unanimous show of gratitude, they deflect the memory of Cannae from the defeat itself to the aftermath of the battle. Finally, by making his men forget one thing and remember another, Ti. Sempronius Gracchus creates an army that recognizes only the difference between courage and cowardice. In sum, the manipulation of memory and of the emotions it evokes plays a crucial role in Rome's ultimate victory over Carthage.

Marcius the Historian

When a well-trained soldier is also an inspired speaker, that one man's memory can provide valuable service to the state. A case in point is the story of Lucius Marcius, who salvages Roman affairs in Spain after the deaths of the Scipios.[28] Killed in separate battles less than a month apart, the Scipio brothers leave two Roman armies without generals until first Claudius Nero and then the young Scipio arrive the following spring. Into the breach steps Marcius, a hitherto unknown Roman knight, who forges the remnants of two armies into one effective force. Under his leadership, the Romans repel a Carthaginian attack; then, inspired by a speech that Marcius delivers, they attack and destroy two Carthaginian camps. As a crucial link between two generations, a stand-in, first for the two dead Scipios and then for Scipio Africanus, Lucius Marcius embodies an important idea: the fortune of any one noble house is not the fortune of the state.[29] Marcius does not have to be a Scipio to lead his men effectively; he—and by extension any Roman—need only act like one.

---

28. The deaths of the Scipios are discussed at 25.32–36. Marcius' story (25.37–39) falls at a turning point in the greater narrative. It closes the pentad's discussion of affairs in Spain. It also looks ahead to events in Books 26–30, especially to the young P. Cornelius Scipio's election as commander of the army in Spain and his activities there.

29. P. Cornelius Scipio himself argues this at 28.28.10–14.

To convey this lesson, Livy emphasizes the role that memory and training play in a crisis, and he draws attention to the commemoration that preserves memory and transforms it from an uncontrolled force into a tool a person can use for managing others. The emphasis on memory makes the very idea of one man saving the state into a paradox, for the person who invokes memory does not act entirely alone.[30] Written history is one part of this memory system, and two lessons, the specific lesson that one need only act like a Scipio and the more general one that a reconstruction of the past can turn defeat into victory, are dramatized together when Marcius, who remembers his lessons so well, who preserves in himself the training of one generation of Scipios and anticipates the charisma, daring, and rhetorical skill of the next, and who links the generations by means of memory and images, takes on the voice of a historian. Marcius provides a practical exemplum of *doctrina* and *ars* put to use in a crisis. Moreover, by linking memory with the control of space in and around the Roman and Carthaginian camps, Marcius' story demonstrates the importance of memory to boundaries, both physical and psychological, and of boundaries to group identity. Finally, the monument Marcius leaves behind makes this story an accessible part of Roman civic memory and a source of historical insight for Livy's contemporary audience.

The carefully constructed episode opens with a brief description of its hero.[31]

Cum deleti exercitus amissaeque Hispaniae uiderentur, uir unus res perditas restituit. Erat in exercitu L. Marcius Septimi filius, eques

---

30. Hoffmann (*Livius und der zweite punische Krieg*, 111) calls Marcius a pale and unrealistic character. This results, I think, from Livy's representation of him as a sort of everyman. On the "one man" motif, see F. Santoro L'hoir, "Heroic Epithets and Recurrent Themes in *Ab Urbe Condita*," *TAPA* 120 (1990): 221–42, esp. 232–35 on Marcius. Santoro L'hoir (230) calls this "the highest compliment the historian can bestow on one of his characters." She sees in Marcius parallels to the young Octavian, and she ties this story to the pacification of Spain in 19 B.C. She also stresses that the *uir unus* acts alone, often against opposition. While this is true of the immediate situation, to those seeing it in a broader context it is clear that others work with him (e.g., Horatius Cocles held the bridge alone at first, but we should not forget that other Romans were destroying it from below).

31. The composition of the entire Marcius passage is (A) introduction of the episode (37.1), (B) Marcius' background and election (37.2–6), (C) the Carthaginian attack (37.8–15), (D) Marcius' speech (38.1–22), (c) the Roman counterattack (38.23–39.11), (b) Marcius' monument (39.12–17), (a) conclusion of the episode (39.18).

Romanus, impiger iuuenis animique et ingenii aliquanto quam pro fortuna in qua erat natus maioris. Ad summam indolem accesserat Cn. Scipionis disciplina, sub qua per tot annos omnes militiae artes edoctus fuerat. (25.37.1–3)

[When the armies appeared destroyed and the Spains lost, one man restored the desperate affairs. There was in the army one L. Marcius, a Roman knight, the son of Septimus, a keen youth, and one of spirit and talent somewhat greater than the fortune in which he had been born. To his nature had accrued the discipline of Cn. Scipio, under which he had been taught all the arts of soldiery through so many years.]

The first sentence describes Marcius as acting alone: he is "one man" *[uir unus]*.[32] Yet the next, which defines him by what he inherited or learned from others, undermines this isolation. One man rescues Roman affairs in Spain because two men made him what he was: those men were his father, who gave him the position in which he was born and his natural talent (he is *Septimi filius*), and Cn. Scipio, whose training *(Cn. Scipionis disciplina)* developed that talent. Livy lays stress on the duration of this schooling: although Marcius is a *iuvenis,* he has fought and learned under Scipio for so many years *(per tot annos).* This *uir unus,* then, represents an accrual of training, of *disciplina* and *ars,* to native energy and ambition. Marcius therefore embodies a paradox: the *uir unus* enters the narrative as his father's son and Scipio's pupil. Like Marcius, the new Roman army is a hybrid, its fathers the dead Scipios and its living teacher Marcius; like Marcius, it is better than the *fortuna* into which it was born. (This is, after all, the army that will take New Carthage.) The story of its success follows the pattern of Marcius' life, for it represents the addition of training and education to what is already there, in this case an animal impulse prompted by a very basic kind of memory.

---

32. The first sentence may echo Ennius' famous line "one man, by delaying, saved the state for us" *[unus homo nobis cunctando restituit rem]* (*Ann.* 370). If so, the narrative inverts the famous line, for the paradoxical achievement of Marcius' *audacia* is delay: *quietae deinde aliquamdiu in Hispania res fuere, utrisque post tantas in uicem acceptas inlatasque clades cunctantibus periculum summae rerum facere* (25.39.18). On this line and its permutations in other writers, see Skutsch, *The Annals of Quintus Ennius,* 529–32; G.R. Stanton, "*Cunctando Restituit Rem:* The Tradition about Fabius," *Antichthon* 5 (1971): 49–56. On this line in Livy, see Pinsent, "Livy 6.3.1."

Marcius unites the remnants of the Roman armies into what Livy calls "an army not to be despised" *[haud contemnendum exercitum]* (25.37.4). It begins fortifying a camp and unanimously elects him leader. Livy is quite emphatic about the Roman defenses: the men construct the camp (across a natural barrier, the Ebro), before electing a leader (25.37.5); they stand guard while voting (25.37.6), and after Marcius has been awarded the command *(summa imperii)*, they continue to prepare their defenses: "all the time after that—and it was not much—the army spent in fortifying the camp and gathering supplies" *[omne inde tempus—exiguum id fuit—muniendis castris conuehendisque commeatibus consumpsit]* (25.37.7). In this short period of time, a new *disciplina*, the *disciplina Marcii*, begins to take effect, for as they obey Marcius' orders, the Romans assume his characteristics: Livy describes Marcius as "keen" *[impiger]*; the Roman soldiers obey him "keenly" *[impigre]*; Marcius is "of greater spirit" *[maioris animi]* than his fortune; the Romans fortify their camp "with a spirit that is by no means downcast" *[haudquamquam abiecto animo]* (25.37.7). As they build their rampart, the Romans begin to take on a group identity by following the example set by their leader. Yet these mental and physical steps do not, at first, seem enough to defend them from the Carthaginians, for the Romans' reaction to the news that Hasdrubal has crossed the natural barrier of the Ebro is to panic.

> Ceterum postquam Hasdrubalem Gisgonis uenientem ad reliquias belli delendas transisse Hiberum et adpropinquare adlatum est signumque pugnae propositum ab nouo duce milites uiderunt, recordati quos paulo ante imperatores habuissent quibusque et ducibus et copiis freti prodire in pugnam soliti esset, flere omnes repente et offensare capita et alii manus ad caelum tendere deos incusantes, alii strati humi suum quisque nominatim ducem implorare. Neque sedari lamentatio poterat excitantibus centurionibus manipulares et ipso mulcente et increpante Marcio, quod in muliebres et inutiles se proiecissent fletus potius quam ad tutandos semet ipsos et rem publicam secum acuerent animos et ne inultos imperatores suos iacere sinerent; cum subito clamor tubarumque sonus—iam enim prope uallum hostes erant—exauditur. Inde uerso repente in iram luctu discurrunt ad arma ac uelut accensi rabie discurrunt ad portas et in hostem neglegenter atque incomposite uenientem incurrunt. (25.37.8–11)

[But after the news was brought that Hasdrubal, son of Gisgo, coming to obliterate the leavings of war, had crossed the Ebro and was drawing near, and when the soldiers saw the standard for battle set out by the new leader, remembering what kind of generals they had had so recently and what kind of leaders and forces they had relied on when they went forth to fight, they all suddenly wept and beat their heads; some raised their hands to heaven and accused the gods; others flung themselves onto the ground and called on their own generals by name. And the weeping could not be stilled, even with the centurions urging the leaders of maniples and with Marcius himself at the same time encouraging them and rebuking them for casting themselves into womanly and useless tears instead of sharpening their spirits to save themselves and the state with them and in order not to leave their own leaders unavenged; then suddenly the uproar and the sound of horns was heard, for the enemy was now very close to the fortifications. Thereupon, with grief turned suddenly to anger, they ran to arms, and as if kindled with madness, they ran to the gates and rushed into the enemy, who was approaching carelessly and in disarray.]

While the enemy is still some distance away, the Romans dwell on their past, with recollections that isolate them from one another. As the Punic army draws near, each man calls on his own lost general. The Romans' gestures reflect the disunity of their thoughts: some raise their hands to the sky; others fling themselves to the ground. These actions are futile, since the gods do not respond (in fact, they play no part in this episode), and the dead Scipios do not at this point do anything to inspire. Yet the Romans, who panic because of their incapacitating memories of the past, actually have another memory that gives them just enough time and space to defend themselves. This is located in their response to a stimulus, the sound of the common enemy at their rampart. For the Romans have two sets of conflicting memories, the divisive memories of the two lost generals, which prevails until they hear the Carthaginians, and the unifying memory of their one enemy. While news of the enemy approaching from a distance terrifies the Romans, the sound of the Carthaginians themselves makes the memories that cause grief yield to the memory that causes anger.[33] The narrative links the transition to space. When the

---

33. It triggers a response similar to that evoked from Aeneas by the baldric of Pallas in Vergil's *Aeneid* (12.945–49).

enemy comes close enough to be heard, it is close to the rampart *(iam enim prope uallum hostes erant)*. Here recognition triggers emotion in the Romans within the rampart and produces an immediate reaction: the men run every which way to prepare. But there is unity within this disunity: the Romans all dash about (note the repetition of *discurrunt . . . discurrunt*) and dash out from the camp together *(incurrunt)*. They respond to the memory evoked by the sound of the enemy as quickly as they did to the news of the enemy's approach and to the sight of their own battle standards (cf. *flere omnes* repente and *inde uerso* repente *in iram luctu*).

At this point in the story, however, there is little to suggest that the Romans' response to a familiar sound is anything but a reflex. Of the two memories that compete in the passage just quoted, the memory that saved the army and the memory that almost incapacitated it, only the latter is presented as a memory; the other is a mere animal impulse. Saying only that grief turned suddenly to anger *(uerso repente in iram luctu)*, the narrative uses the change in emotions and the movement around the camp to reflect the substitution of one memory for another.

Livy's description of the signs that trigger these reactions—the news of the army's approach, then the *signum pugnae,* and finally the sound of the Carthaginian army itself—further associates the Roman army's confusion and panic with its memory and identity. Indeed, from a more distant vantage point, the reader can see that the Romans' memory and identity determine how they receive and interpret information. At the beginning of the episode, what the men hear, that Hasdrubal has crossed the Ebro and is approaching to destroy the leavings of the war, and what they see, the sign for battle set out by their new general, balance each other as an extremely threatening challenge and a pathetically inadequate response. They are also ambiguous signs. The *signum pugnae* that is set out to indicate a battle in the offing points to the past instead and evokes debilitating memories. The news that Hasdrubal is approaching "to destroy the leavings of the war" *[ad reliquias belli delendas]* is not exactly straightforward either. It is not clear who is responsible for the information brought by scouts, since the narrative does not distinguish here between the words they used to convey the news and those of Hasdrubal whose intent they convey. *Reliquiae belli,* then, is no more the Carthaginians' definition of the Roman soldiers than it is the label that the Romans have placed on themselves. (Indeed the narrator has already referred to them as "an army not to be despised" *[haud contemnendum exercitum].*) For when one compares the announcement of Hasdrubal's approach to the actual attack, the menace appears to have been exaggerated. The terrifying sense of purpose conveyed by the phrase *Hasdrubalem . . . uenientem ad reliquias belli delendas* contrasts sharply with the reality the Romans find when they attack an enemy that is both careless and disorganized *(in hostem neglegenter atque incomposite uenientem incurrunt).* The Romans are the "leavings of war" because, until they hear Hasdrubal's army, they remember a past that defines them in this way. The narrative, then, associates the rampart of the camp with a series of transitions: the remains of two armies become one; news of the enemy's approach gives way to the unambiguous announcement of his presence; the invisible and internal—thought, memory, and identity—all give way to action.

This united action provides the foundation for future success. The Carthaginians melt away, driven back from the rampart to their own camp *(ab hostium uallo acti . . . in castra abeunt,* 25.37.15) and wondering what produced such a forceful response. They do not yet perceive that the Romans now comprise one new and intact army: "they were equally careless in guarding their camp, for even if the enemy was near, nevertheless the thought occurred to them that these were the remains of two armies destroyed a few days earlier" *[par neglegentia in castris custodiendis fuit; nam etsi propinquus hostis erat, tamen reliquias eum esse duorum exercituum ante paucos dies deletorum succurrebat]* (25.37.16). The Carthaginians compensate for the proximity of the enemy not by fortifying their camps but by giving the Romans a comforting identity: "the remains of two destroyed armies." Livy's reader realizes that this label is not accurate. Yet both Romans and Carthaginians have now fortified their own camps according to this identical and inaccurate assessment of the Roman forces. The Carthaginians fail to understand that a successful defense has changed the Romans' way of thinking about themselves, and this failure prevents them from realizing that they need to consider their situation from the perspective of an approaching enemy and, accordingly, give some thought to their fortifications, as the Romans did.

This is when Marcius presents his daring plan. Marcius first comments on what has just happened, then exhorts his men to follow his new plan. Successful defense has made the memory of the dead Scipios a useful tool in his hands, and it is by his speech as much as by the attempt at generalship that preceded it that Marcius restores Rome's *res perditae*, for although the Roman soldiers awarded Marcius the *summa imperii*, not until he delivers this speech do they respond to him as their *dux*. Let us consider the Roman counterattack first and then return to Marcius' speech. The narratives of Carthaginian attack and Roman counterattack are approximately the same length, and in their use of space, signs, and sounds, they mirror each other (the attack is narrated at 25.37.8–15, the speech at 25.38.2–22, and the counterattack at 25.39.1–11).

The Roman counterattack takes place at night. Once again the Romans use their time well: they sleep much of the night and place a cohort in ambush between the two Carthaginian camps to prevent communications between them. The leisure and deliberation with which they prepare stands in marked contrast to their frantic digging before the fight, and this contrast becomes even more striking when they attack. Because there are no guards at the Punic gates or on the ramparts (*cum statio nulla pro portis neque in uallo custodiae essent*, 25.39.2), the Roman soldiers find no one to oppose them when they enter the Punic camp. Only when they are inside do they make noise: *inde signa canunt et tollitur clamor* (25.39.3). The disposition of the Roman forces in the clauses describing the attack underscores how thoroughly the Romans penetrate the heart of the Punic camp before they make their presence known. Livy divides the Roman army into three groups, starting from those at the most vulnerable part of the camp, the Carthaginians' own beds, and moving outward: "Some slaughter the half-asleep enemy; some cast fire on the huts covered with dry thatch; some take up position at the gates to prevent flight" [*pars semisomnos hostes caedunt, pars ignes casis stramento arido tectis iniciunt, pars portas occupant ut fugam intercludunt*] (25.39.3). There is no time for recognition or memory to spark a defensive reaction here, since the *signum* and *clamor* announcing the attack arrive at the same moment as the attack itself. The slaughter, noise, and fire contribute to the confusion of the Carthaginians allowing them neither to hear nor to anticipate: "they can neither hear nor anticipate anything" [*nec audire nec prouidere quicquam*] (25.39.4). Livy's use of the metaphoric *prouidere* instead of the literal *uidere* illustrates his sensitivity to matters of perception: the Carthaginians cannot see anyway because it is still dark. In addition, it draws attention to the function of visual signs later in the episode.[34] The ability to plan and historical insight become linked through vision, the dominant sense for the historian.

The Carthaginians panic just as the Romans did, in a disunited and incoherent manner: "Some rushed for the gates; others, since the paths were blocked, leapt over the rampart and, as soon as each one escaped, made for the other camp" *[alii ruunt ad portas, alii obsaeptis itineribus super uallum saliunt et ut quisque euaserat protinus ad castra altera fugiunt]* (25.39.5). The Carthaginans do not distinguish between rampart and gate in their eagerness to get away; the ramparts themselves are useless, since the Romans already occupy the inside of the camp. The Carthaginians who do escape from the first camp are killed as they try to make their way to the second by the Romans hidden between the two camps. In fact, the Romans move so quickly from camp to camp that there is no way news of the slaughter can precede them (25.39.7).

Because it is dawn when the Romans approach the second Punic camp, sight now comes into play as well as sound. The Romans once again enter a Punic camp before they make their presence known, and once again the narrative uses space to underscore the contrast between the fighting now and the fighting on the previous day. The Romans, when attacked, ran toward the gates *(ad portas)* and into the enemy *(in hostem . . . incurrunt)*; the Carthaginians run to and fro inside the gates *(intra portas)* and dash out of the camp *(ex castris)*.[35] Noise and confusion cause panic just as they did in the attack on the first Carthaginian camp *(ad primum clamorem et tumultum, 25.39.9)*. But now, since the sun has risen, a visual sign, rather than an aural one, sends the Carthaginians running: "and the fighting would have continued a long time, except that the Romans' bloody shields, a token of the other slaughter, were seen by the Carthaginians and cast panic into them" *[diuque tenuisset, ni cruenta scuta Romanorum uisa indicium alterius cladis Poenis atque inde pauorem iniecissent]* (25.39.10). Although no survivors have come from the first camp, the Carthaginians recognize the meaning of the token *(indicium)* of the recent past, and it panics them. For the reader, the *cruenta scuta* recall the other fear-inspiring sign, the *signum pugnae* set out by Marcius, while the clamor the Romans raise when they attack recalls the news of Hasdrubal's approach and the Punic battle cry. The basic

---

34. On the effect of signs in battle, see Feldherr, "Spectacle and Society," 161.
35. 25.37.11, 39.9.

symmetry of attack and counterattack emphasizes the crucial difference
between them: when the Carthaginians attack the Romans, the signs and
the attack arrive at intervals and come from outside the camp; when the
Romans attack the Carthaginians, the signs and attack appear simultaneously and inside the camp. In sum, the Roman counterattack completely reverses the narrative structure of the Carthaginian attack, and
the narrative uses space to reflect this reversal.

The symmetry of the account is itself evidence for Marcius' complete
and perfect effectiveness as a restorer of the *res perditae*. This restoration
grows primarily from Marcius' historicizing, which confirms the
Romans' identity as one army and convinces them to become the
avengers of the Scipios; it arises only secondarily from his practical strategy.[36] Marcius' speech has several goals: he needs to encourage his men,
to increase by art the confidence they have regained by their spontaneous
attack, and to inspire them to tackle a more ambitious project. While
Marcius' first successful act as a leader in this battle is to stop his men
and lead them back to camp, his first successful act as a speaker is to lead
them back mentally so that they retrieve and reconstruct the memory of
the day's events. His speech falls into two parts: a discussion of the previous day's events and an outline of the plans for the following night.
Only after Marcius' speech has led his listeners back into the past do they
recognize him as *dux*, and it is only after they do so that the Romans take
the initiative and expand their horizons by capturing the Carthaginian
camps.

In the first half of his speech, Marcius analyzes his own memory and
conflicting emotions to show his audience how memory and emotion
influenced his behavior; then he urges his audience to reconstruct its own
experience in the same way. First, Marcius says that the command voted
him has been both an honor and a burden, because the grief he felt for the
dead generals almost incapacitated him at the very time his men needed
him most; fear alone kept him from succumbing to grief.[37] Not even
when he had to contrive a way to save the remnants of two armies could

---

36. Although we came to our conclusions independently, and although Feldherr does
not discuss this passage, my interpretation of Marcius' historicizing agrees with Feldherr's
argument in "Spectacle and Society," 149–70. As Feldherr says (149), "the control over
appearances becomes a crucial, even definitive, aspect of the substance of *imperium*." In
this episode, Marcius grows into his imperium by controlling appearances.

37. *Quo enim tempore, nisi metus maerorem obstupefaceret, uix ita compos mei essem
ut aliqua solacia inuenire aegro animo possem, cogor uestram omnium uicem, quod difficil-
limum in luctu est, unus consulere* (25.38.3).

he turn his attention from his sorrow.[38] For a bitter memory *(acerba memoriae)* was always present, as were the two Scipios, disturbing him by day with concern and by night in dreams, and urging Marcius not to let them, their fellow soldiers, or the state go unavenged.[39] They commanded him to follow their teaching *(et suam disciplinam suaque instituta sequi iubent)* and in every situation to do what he thought they would have done. In Marcius' representation of his experience, the very grief that incapacitated the army reinforced his sense of group identity and compelled him to act when others could not. He had to take counsel as a surrogate for all his men *(uestram omnium uicem),* to save the army for his country *(patria).*

Marcius points out that he acted according to the Scipios' precepts, and he offers his own experience as a paradigm for the army to study. Grief nearly overwhelmed him, but his fear was even worse than his grief. The grief was a result of bitter memory, memory constantly refreshed by the images of the Scipios in dreams. But Marcius' concern for the army overrode both grief and fear, because the specters of the Scipios commanded him and, he says, command him now—as if the Scipios themselves were still alive—to follow their teaching. By taking apart his own emotions, Marcius shows that grief brings with it a desire for revenge, because the very thing that causes grief causes anger as well. Grief turns to anger because the Scipios want it that way. Marcius has presented himself as a model for using memory productively and has turned his experience of bitter memory and strong emotion into a paradigm. Now he superimposes it on his men's experience and urges them to use it as a guide in the future.

Vos quoque uelim, milites, non lamentis lacrimisque tamquam exstinctos prosequi—uiuunt uigentque fama rerum gestarum—sed, quotienscumque occurret memoria illorum, uelut si adhortantes signumque dantes uideatis eos, ita proelia inire. Nec alia profecto species hesterno die oblata oculis animisque uestris memorabile illud edidit proelium, quo documentum dedistis hostibus non cum Scipionibus exstinctum esse nomen Romanum et, cuius populi uis

38. *Et ne tum quidem, ubi quonam modo has reliquias duorum exercituum patriae conseruare possim cogitandum est, auertere animum ab absiduo maerore licet* (25.38.4).

39. *Praesto est enim acerba memoria et Scipiones me ambo dies noctesque curis insomniisque agitant et excitant saepe somno neu se neu inuictos per octo annos in his terris milites suos, commilitones uestros, neu rem publicam patiar inultam* (25.38.5–6).

atque uirtus non obruta sit Cannensi clade, ex omni profecto
saeuitia fortunae emersurum esse. Nunc, qui tantum ausi estis
sponte uestra, experiri libet quantum audeatis duce uestro auctore.
(25.38.8–11)

[I would also wish that you, soldiers, should not follow them with
tears and laments as if they were dead—for they live and will flour-
ish with the fame of their achievements—but, whenever their memory comes to you, that you should see them as if they were encouraging you and giving the signal and thus go into battle. For surely
no other image brought before your eyes and minds yesterday produced that memorable battle, by which you gave evidence to the
enemy that the Roman name did not die out with the Scipios and
that the name of a people whose force and courage were not overwhelmed by the disaster at Cannae would surely emerge from any
ravages of fortune. Now, because you dared so much of your own
accord, I want to see how much you dare with your leader as the
authority.]

Marcius offers his listeners an explanation for their behavior that
removes the trauma and the animal savagery from their past, replaces
them with a call to vengeance, and points the way to success. The trauma
of the double defeat did not destroy his identity as one of Cn. Scipio's soldiers or as a Roman; on the contrary, it reinforced it, and it did so for his
men as well, in spite of themselves. By linking grief to anger, Marcius'
analysis turns the memory of past disasters from a hindrance into a goad.
It is left to the reader to notice how in representing his men's experience
he has changed it.

By pronouncing the Scipios immortal for their reputation *(fama rerum
gestarum)* and by pronouncing the previous day's fight *memorabile,* Marcius takes on the mask of a historian. Livy generally uses the terms *memorabile* or *memoria dignum* in authorial remarks like the preface to the
narrative of the Second Punic War, in death notices, or in the overview of
a year's events. Part of the history's chronological scaffolding, such
phrases mark the annalistic style.[40] In addition, when Marcius uses

---

40. There are many instances throughout the surviving books, but see, e.g., 2.48.4,
3.3.10, 4.57.7, 5.31.4, 7.26.13, 8.37.6, 10.5.13, 21.1.1, 21.57.14, 23.44.4, 25.32.1,
27.2.12, 34.16.9, 36.17.7, 37.58.7, 38.24.2, 40.37.9, 43.1.4, 45.28.4. To appreciate the
degree of deliberate historicizing in this passage, one has only to compare Xen. *An.*

phrases like *quo documentum dedistis* [by which you gave evidence], he speaks through a historian's mask by echoing, for example, such editorial comments as the practical lesson to be learned from the Scipio's deaths: "Roman generals will indeed always have to beware of this and take these examples as evidence that they should not trust foreign auxiliaries so much that they fail to keep a majority of fighting men and forces of their own in the camp" *[id quidem cauendum semper Romanis ducibus erit exemplaque haec uere pro documentis habenda, ne ita externis credant auxiliis ut non plus sui roboris suarumque proprie uirium in castris habeant]* (25.33.6). The references to *documenta* and to *res gestae* in the preface to the entire history also come to mind.

Only after giving his newly unified army a successful past with the historicizing phrase *memorabile illud edidit proelium* does Marcius invoke the most potent and most traumatic memories, those of the dead Scipios and of Cannae (25.38.10). He can do so now because the *memorabile proelium* has distanced the present from the Scipios' deaths. Manlius' repeated references to "yesterday" also help to fix the battle securely in the past (25.38.9, 11, 17, 20). Marcius, then, reinforces his men's sense of themselves as Romans and survivors by placing the new event in the context of Rome's worst disaster. In saying that the fight generated its own epiphenomenon, the teaching of the Carthaginians *(quo documentum dedistis . . .)*, he reinforces the boundary between Romans and Carthaginians by casting the Carthaginians as an audience of outsiders: the previous day's fighting has not only saved Roman skins but has taught the Carthaginians about the Romans. From a more distant vantage point, the reader can see that it has also taught the Romans about themselves.

When he speaks of his critical situation during the fight, Marcius resembles the narrator speaking in the preface. Yet a comparison of the preface and his speech brings to light the contrast between the historian's membership in a community with a past and Marcius' position as leader of a group that has no past and whose history must be mustered up fresh from eyewitness accounts. The author in the Preface says that it will do him good *(iuvabit)* to take counsel for the memory of the Roman people (Pref. 3). Livy, of course, says this after acknowledging that he is one among many writers dealing with the well-worn topic of Roman history. Marcius, however, states that he acted under compulsion: the crisis

---

3.1.4–25, where Xenophon, both author and soldier in an army that has just lost its leaders in a foreign country, dreams and relates his dream.

forced him alone, despite his grief, to think for his men *(cogor vestram omnium vicem . . . unus consulere*, 25.38.3). Livy says that he will find his sure reward for his efforts in distracting himself from present evils while he writes of early Roman history *(ut me a conspectu malorum . . . avertam,* Pref. 5). In contrast, Marcius' dual role as soldier and historian prevents him from turning his attention away from the problems of the present *(et ne tum quidem . . . auertere animum ab adsiduo maerore licet*, 25.38.4). When he begins his speech, Marcius places himself at the starting point of the history of his united army, a place that offers no comfortable or reassuring past in which to retreat. Like the Romans on the citadel during the Gallic invasion, Marcius and his men begin history anew after defending themselves. Their story, however, is designed to expand, and in this it is unlike the short-lived history of the citadel alone, for, unlike Marcus Manlius, Lucius Marcius historicizes his own heroism at the right time.[41]

The immediate rhetorical purpose of Marcius' prosopopoiea is clear: the remnants of two destroyed armies now share a history as one army, a history that Marcius has shaped with an eye to future use. Having taught his men how to interpret their own memory of the past in a way that guarantees future success, Marcius outlines his plans to attack the Carthaginians immediately, before the Carthaginian armies can unite. The most striking points of Marcius' speech are his frequent references to the boldness of his plan and to its very likelihood of succeeding because of that boldness (25.38.11, 14–15, 18), as well as his men's joyous response: "happily they heard the new plan from their new leader, and the more daring it was, the more it pleased them" *[Laeti et audiere ab nouo duce novum consilium et quo audacius erat magis placebat]* (25.38.23). The words *ab nouo duce,* referring to Marcius as the "new leader" at this point, recall the very different reaction of that same audience to the original sign for battle set out *ab nouo duce* at 25.37.8.

Marcius' expansive military strategy is as successful as his rhetoric. His accomplishment becomes part of the canon of Roman experiences preserved in writing and memorialized on the Capitoline. The authors who record it report different numbers of casualties, says Livy, but all of them make much of Marcius.

---

41. See my discussion in chap. 3. For more on the use of historical memory, see Maria-Ruth Morello's 1996 Cornell dissertation "*Ars Imperatoria:* Three Studies of Leadership in Livy's Second Pentad." Since this book was completed before I could consult Morello's dissertation, I can only note here my agreement with her observation that exemplary Roman leaders have a distinctive ability to manipulate historical memory.

Ad triginta septem milia hostium caesa auctor est Claudius, qui annales Acilianos ex Graeco in Latinum sermonem uertit; captos ad mille octingentos triginta, praedam ingentem partam; in ea fuisse clipeum argenteum pondo centum triginta septem cum imagine Barcini Hasdrubalis. Valerius Antias una castra Magonis capta tradit, septem milia caesa hostium; altero proelio eruptione pugnatum cum Hasdrubale, decem milia occisa, quattuor milia trecenta triginta captos. Piso quinque milia hominum, cum Mago cedentes nostros effuse sequeretur, caesa ex insidiis scribit. Apud omnes magnum nomen Marcii ducis est; et uerae gloriae eius etiam miracula addunt flammam ei contionanti fusam e capite sine ipsius sensu cum magno pauore circumstantium militum; monumentumque uictoriae eius de Poenis usque ad incensum Capitolium fuisse in templo clipeum, Marcium appellatum, cum imagine Hasdrubalis. (25.39.12–18)

[About 37,000 of the enemy were slain, according to Claudius, who translated the annals of Acilius from Greek into Latin; 1,830 men were captured, together with a great deal of booty. In it was a silver shield weighing 137 pounds and bearing a likeness of Hasdrubal Barca. Valerius Antias says that only one camp, Mago's, was taken—7,000 of the enemy were slain—and that in another battle there was a breakout and a fight with Hasdrubal, in which 10,000 were killed and 4,330 captured. Piso says that 5,000 men were slain from ambush, when Mago was following in a disorderly manner our men who were withdrawing. All the accounts praise the leader Marcius, and the writers add stories of wonders to his actual glory, that a flame poured from his head while he was addressing the troops, without him feeling it, but to the great fear of the soldiers standing around him. And they say that a memorial of his victory over the Carthaginians was in the temple [of Jupiter] right up until the Capitoline burned, a shield, called the Shield of Marcius, with an image of Hasdrubal on it.]

Livy's long-range motives for Marcius' historicizing become clear when we look back at Marcius' story from this concluding passage. Because of his own ability to exploit memory, Marcius is enshrined in memory as testimony to Roman learning *(doctrina)* and craft *(ars)* preserved in memory. Both subject and object of history, Marcius participates in the first successful battle and creates it as a historical event. He is its *auctor* (25.38.11), monumentalizing it, exploiting its memory, and using it to become *auctor* of yet another, greater event, which memorializes him in turn. The narrative moves from memory, to action, to history, and then to monument, to form a mnemonic loop that increases its dimensions with each cycle.

Marcius received praise in all the written documents, and his name was preserved in a monument on the Capitoline. Livy, in fact, mentions the shield with the image of Hasdrubal on it twice, just as he repeats Marcius' name in the closing passage, to stress that Marcius is in the sources, that the proof is there to see, in books and on the Capitoline— at least it was there until the place burned in 83 B.C. The shield, then, is part of a system that moves from the memory triggered by a sign—in this case the sound of the Punic army—to Roman self-defense and then to Marcius' historicizing speech. The speech itself invoked memory, set immediate experience within a historical framework, and led to a greater action, the attack on the Punic camp. The histories of the annalists, the monumental shield, and most of all Livy's history, which restores the destroyed shield and indicates the key point of consensus in the varying sources *(apud* omnes *magnum nomen Marcii ducis est)*, should inspire Livy's readers to emulation and thus produce more and greater memorable events.

The shield, with its likeness of Hasdrubal, is particularly fitting as the *monumentum* for a fight that involved so many images and reminders. Even before the Scipios' deaths, images fight for the Romans. When, after his initial defeat, Publius Scipio retreats to a small hillock where the ground is too hard to dig, he saves part of his army by using its baggage to create the appearance of a rampart *(imago ualli)*, one that the Carthaginians actually find harder to cross than they anticipated (25.36.7–8). After the Scipios' deaths, they appear to Marcius in dreams that drive him to action, and Marcius' plan works partly because it appears too daring to be true.[42] The Carthaginian soldiers in the second camp panic when they catch sight of the bloody shields, the sign of the previous slaughter. Signs and memory add momentum to events as the reminder of one slaughter causes fear and flight.

---

42. On the strategic use of appearances, see Davidson, "The Gaze in Polybius' Histories."

Livy provides a visual link between the monument that commemo-rates the victory and the signs that helped cause it: the ornamental, for-eign *clipeus* (shield) decorated with a likeness of the Punic general, in contrast to its practical Roman counterpart, the *scutum,* covered with real Punic blood. The Shield of Marcius, with one man's name and another man's *imago,* demands that a story be told, since by itself it leaves gaps between what was heard and seen that provoke questions: Why is the shield named after Marcius? Why does it bear a picture of Hasdrubal Barca?[43] The shield with the *imago* of Hasdrubal Barca also points to something beyond Marcius and his story, to Marcius' own role as an *imitator.* Cn. Scipio, together with his third of the Roman forces and the disloyal Celtiberian mercenaries, was assigned to fight Has-drubal, when he and his brother made the decision to separate that led to their deaths (25.32.8). Even if Hasdrubal himself was never dragged in triumph up to the Capitoline, his likeness was dedicated there.[44] Thus the *imago* on the shield is both a surrogate of Hasdrubal and a reminder of Marcius the surrogate. It commemorates Scipio indirectly for his role as Marcius' commander and teacher, as a persuasive image in Marcius' rhetoric and potent memory. It links Marcius to his lost commander and his lost commander's mission. As a reminder of the bloody Roman *scuta,* themselves a token of slaughter, Marcius' shield reminds the reader, by a roundabout route, of the *disciplina* and *ars* that made possible the restoration of the *res Romanae.* The *monumentum,* then, draws the audi-ence back into Livy's story. Finally, by commemorating at the center of the city the story of Roman identity restored far from Rome, it reaffirms and reinforces a Romanocentric worldview.

By breaking down the boundaries between historical subject and object, between Marcius as soldier and Marcius as student of history, between himself and Marcius, and between himself and the reader, Livy sets in motion a process that moves outward from an initial animal impulse, to the event produced by that impulse, to the memory of that event. Next, the memory leads to a greater event, which leads to written history, with the monuments it commemorates. Finally, history itself leads to another event: whatever the reader chooses to do for himself and for his state (*inde tibi tuaeque rei publicae quod imitere capias, inde foe-*

---

43. On the *fabula/monumentum* dichotomy, see Miles, *Reconstructing Early Rome,* 15–16.

44. For their likenesses accompanying the fates of prominent men, see Vasaly, *Repre-sentations,* 105 n. 27.

dum incepto foedum exitu quod uites, Pref. 10). Such a dissolution of boundaries between reader and writer, soldier and historian, *actor* and *auctor,* resolves the paradox with which the story begins: any one Roman with a memory represents the people and the past that made him. He is not a *vir unus* at all.

The Shield of Marcius and the Spoils from Syracuse

An important feature of Marcius' story in the *Ab Urbe Condita* is its position. While it is part of the extended narrative of the Spanish campaign, it is also embedded in the account of Marcellus' sack of Syracuse. The fall of Syracuse immediately precedes near disaster in Spain (25.23.1–31.15); the arrival of the booty in Rome immediately follows it.

> Quietae deinde aliquamdiu in Hispania res fuere, utrisque post tantas in uicem acceptas inlatasque clades cunctantibus periculum summae rerum facere.
>
> Dum haec in Hispania geruntur, Marcellus captis Syracusis, cum cetera in Sicilia tanta fide atque integritate composuisset ut non modo suam gloriam sed etiam maiestatem populi Romani augeret, ornamenta urbis, signa tabulasque quibus abundabant Syracusae, Romam deuexit, hostium quidem illa spolia et parta belli iure; ceterum inde primum initium mirandi Graecarum artium opera licentiaeque hinc sacra profanaque omnia uolgo spoliandi factum est, quae postremo in Romanos deos, templum id ipsum primum quod a Marcello eximie ornatum est, uertit. Visebantur enim ab externis ad portam Capenam dedicata a M. Marcello templa propter excellentia eius generis ornamenta, quorum perexigua pars comparet. (25.40.1–3)

[After this, things were quiet in Spain for some time, both sides being reluctant to make a supreme effort, since they had each received so much damage and had dealt so much in turn.

While these things were happening in Spain, Marcellus, having captured Syracuse, although he had settled all else in Sicily with such good faith and integrity that he increased both his own repute and the dignity of the Roman people, removed to

Rome the ornaments of Syracuse, the statues and paintings that the city had in abundance. Granted, they were enemy spoils and obtained by right of war, but this was the origin of our marveling at Greek works of art, and from this came the license to despoil everything both sacred and profane, license that in the end turned against the Roman gods and first of all against that very temple that had been so splendidly decorated by Marcellus. For the temples dedicated by M. Marcellus near the Porta Capena used to be visited even by foreigners on account of their outstanding decorations of this kind, of which only the smallest part remains to be seen.]

This transition from one theater of operations to another would be unremarkable, except that in turning from Spain to Sicily the narrative brings together descriptions of spoils that were not juxtaposed in the physical city: the Shield of Marcius in the Temple of Jupiter Optimus Maximus on the Capitoline and the artwork adorning the Temple of Honos and Virtus near the Porta Capena.[45] Livy comments on the quantity of booty taken from Syracuse in the initial account of the sack (25.31.11) and later mentions the outrage felt by the Syracusans on its account (26.32.4–5). According to Burck, he reports the transfer of the spoils at the end of

---

45. On the spoils, see M. Pape, *Griechische Kunstwerke aus Kriegsbeute und ihre öffentlische Ausstellung in Rome* (Hamburg, 1975), 6–7. On this temple and Marius' later Temple of Honos and Virtus, see L. Richardson jr., "Honos et Virtus and the Sacra Via," *AJA* 82 (1978): 240–46; he places it inside the gate. Ziolkowski (*The Temples of Mid-Republican Rome,* 58–59) argues that it was outside. According to Richardson, it was a double temple, possibly founded by Q. Fabius Maximus (later Cunctator) during the Ligurian War as a single temple dedicated to Honos, and built in 234 B.C. It may, however, have been built much earlier, by his great-grandfather, Q. Fabius Maximus Rullianus. In 222 B.C., after the battle of Clastidium, Marcellus vowed a temple to Honos and Virtus, then he renewed the vow after the capture of Syracuse. He attempted to fulfill this vow by refurbishing Maximus' temple and rededicating it to the two deities in 208 B.C., but the pontifices forbade this. Marcellus then restored the Temple of Honos and added a *cella* for Virtus. On the spoils, see, in addition to Livy 26.32.4, Cic. *Rep.* 1.21. Cicero says that Marcellus used none of the booty to decorate private houses, that he dedicated it in the Temple of Honos and Virtus and in other public places, that he left many exceptional items in Syracuse *(Syracusis autem permulta atque egregia reliquit),* and that he profaned no sanctuaries (*Verr.* 2.4.121). Cicero's exaggerations and distortions in *In Verrem* stem, of course, from his desire to make a strong contrast between the restraint of Marcellus and the rapacity of Verres. See Gruen, *Culture and National Identity,* 96.

Book 25 to end the pentad with success in Sicily rather than catastrophe in Spain.[46] Yet two events that soured the victory in Syracuse precede and follow Marcius' story: Archimedes' death and the transfer of the spoils. And, in fact, for members of Livy's audience who saw the Shield of Marcius and the Syracusan art in the mind's eye, it would be clear that Marcius' story was embedded in the account of the sack of Syracuse to salvage what was, when regarded from a distant vantage point, a moral defeat.

Although Livy's contemporary audience could visit both temples, it could see neither the Shield of Marcius nor the Syracusan art, since the shield had been destroyed when the Capitoline burned in 83 B.C. and the artwork had been stolen, possibly during the civil unrest of Livy's own day.[47] Yet Livy's audience, seeing shield and artwork in the mind's eye, and moving through the narrative like an orator through a sequence of mnemonic loci, would imagine these monuments in the space constructed by the text and would be guided by the historian in its impression of them. This raises some questions: How do shield and artwork interact within the space constructed by the text as part of a collection of memory-prompting *imagines*? What lesson does their juxtaposition convey? The issue at hand is not the historical impact of these items on Roman culture but rather Livy's method of weaving them into his narrative and the implications of that technique.[48] The Punic shield and Syracusan art were ornaments, taken as booty and dedicated in sanctuaries. This basic similarity makes all the more striking the difference in the ways in which the narrative represents them.

46. Burck, *Einführung,* 117. On the arrangement of episodes and on 25.30–41, see F. Nicolet-Croizat, *Tite-Live, Histoire romaine,* vol. 15, Budé series (Paris, 1992), xi, xxii–xxiii. On the chronology, see G. De Sanctis, *Storia Dei Romani,* 4 vols. (Turin, 1907–23), 3:365–71.

47. The shield joins Camillus' *paterae* in the set of items Livy says were on the Capitoline when it burned. On the burning, see esp. Tac. *Hist.* 3.71. In Sall. *Cat.* 47.2, the conspirator Lentulus reckons time *ab incenso Capitolio.* Of Livy's comment on the art, Gruen (*Culture and National Identity,* 98) says, "[t]he passage clearly refers to neglect of temples and shrines in Livy's own day, in the turbulence of civil war." P. Gros ("Les statues de Syracuse et les 'dieux' de Tarent," *REL* 57 [1979]: 85–114) also sees the statement as a reference to the author's own time, and observes that the passage was written by a witness to the negligence that temples and sanctuaries suffered during the last century of the Republic (88).

48. On the impact, see Lintott, "Imperial Expansion and Moral Decline," 629; J.J. Pollitt, "The Impact of Greek Art on Rome," *TAPA* 108 (1978): 155–74; Gros, "Les statues de Syracuse"; R. MacMullen, "Hellenizing the Romans (2nd Century B.C.)," *Historia* 40 (1991): 419–38, esp. 424–38; Gruen, *Culture and National Identity,* 84–130.

What does each monument mean in the life story of the man it commemorates? At this point in the narrative, the account describing how
Marcius saved Roman affairs in Spain is over, and his genuine glory *(uera
gloria)* for this accomplishment is guaranteed. His reputation gathers
more glory, by implication false, from the accounts of the annalists, who
add wonders *(miracula)* like the legend of the flame encircling his head.[49]
Yet Marcius' reputation still grows when others (e.g., Africanus) honor
him and invoke him as an exemplum (28.28.13). Thus, for Marcius, who
moves on to other accomplishments in Spain, the description of the shield
brings closure to his story and commemorates the first phase of his
career.[50]

For Marcellus, however, the arrival of the spoils marks the beginning
of the end.[51] References to the Temple of Honos and Virtus punctuate
Marcellus' career: he vowed the temple in 222 B.C., after his victory at
Clastidium; before he set out for his fatal encounter with Hannibal, Marcellus was detained in Rome by scruples concerning their dedication
(27.25.7–10).[52] Marcellus' monuments do not reflect his achievements
precisely. The victory at Clastidium had less impact on the state as a
whole, but from it Marcellus dedicated the *spolia opima* in the Temple of
Jupiter Feretrius on the Capitoline, according to a precedent set by
Romulus (1.10.7). Marcellus' greatest achievement, the capture of Syracuse, was commemorated by a monument that Marcellus himself never
dedicated *(neque tamen ab ipso aedes eae dedicatae sunt, 27.25.9)*; his
son did so in his stead (29.11.13).[53]

How does each monument stimulate memory? At the end of the
account of events in Spain, Livy's audience receives a precise description of the shield; the thought of the shield recalls the story that preserves it in the *Ab Urbe Condita*. As a reward pointing back to a story

---

49. This entire story bears all the signs of an annalistic invention. See DeSanctis, *Storia
Dei Romani*, 3:365–71; F. Münzer, "Marcius," *RE* 14 (1930): 1591–95.

50. The coda to this affair, Marcius' offending the Senate by calling himself propraetor
in the letter that reports these events, appears as a minor event in the following book
(26.2.1–4).

51. E.M. Carawan ("The Tragic History of Marcellus and Livy's Characterization," *CJ*
80 [1984–85]: 131–41) sees Marcellus' life as a tragedy and this episode as its turning point
(138).

52. Cf. 26.29.9: *Rapiente fato Marcellum ad Hannibalem.*

53. Book 20, which contained the account of Marcellus' victory at Clastidinum and his
dedication of the *spolia opima,* may also have included a scene of Marcellus vowing the
temple or at least a reference to it (Livy *Per.* 20.13).

of heroism, this *monumentum* stimulates rivalry *(aemulatio)* for glory in the person who sees it in his or her mind's eye. Marcius' story and his *monumentum* accrue to the *maiestas* of the Roman people, while at the same time they increase it indirectly by inciting Romans to greater accomplishments. Marcius' story, then, generates greater glory and a greater Rome within the period covered by the third decade. As an efficacious exemplum, it continues to do so even in Livy's time. The art from Syracuse, however, although it is legitimate booty, does not commemorate at Rome the *fides* and *integritas* Marcellus displayed in settling Sicilian affairs. While Marcellus' previous temperate behavior increased both his own *gloria* and the Roman people's *maiestas* (note the verb *augere*, "to increase"), the transfer of the art from Syracuse to Rome initiates other processes: those of marveling at Greek artwork and despoiling Roman temples *(inde primum initium . . . hinc)*.[54] There is the suggestion here that, had Marcellus left the art in Syracuse, it would have testified to his *fides* and *integritas* there and would have stimulated the growth of his reputation.[55]

The Greek historian Polybius also discusses these spoils and their impact on Rome. He argues that the Romans acted against their own interests when they took them, and among his arguments is one that involves memory.[56] Polybius points out that spoils attract envy (φθόνος), for the person contemplating the pillaged items is moved by pity for the original owners and envy of the current ones. Polybius goes on to say that when the victor gets more opportunities and gathers to himself all the things that were his neighbors', the things themselves invite those who were robbed of them to come inspect them. The visitors no longer pity their neighbors but instead pity themselves, as they recollect their own calamities (ἀναμιμνῃσκόμενοι). These memories rouse up not only the emotion of envy but that of rage as well, for the viewers' memory (ἀνάμνησις) of their own disasters moves them to hate those who caused them.

---

54. Gruen (*Culture and National Identity,* 101) cites 25.40.1 to support his assertion that "[a]dornment of the city coincided with augmentation of Marcellus' glory." But this does not give due weight to the antithesis of *cetera in Sicilia* and *ornamenta urbis*. On *augere*, see Pinsent, "Livy 6.3.1," 16. I cannot agree with Vasaly, *Representations*, 108: "It was only when statues or monuments had long stood within the city that they gradually acquired a new meaning for the Roman viewers interwoven of associations connected with the origin, subject matter and appearance of the statue, the circumstances of its arrival in Rome, and the 'history' of the statue in its new location." This process can take place quickly, since it requires only one significant event or act of rhetorical or literary interpretation.

55. This is precisely how Cicero talks about the Syracusan artwork in *Verr.* 2.2.4.

56. Polyb. 9.10.3–13. According to Klotz (*Livius und seine Vorgänger,* 170), Polybius

Livy, in contrast, does not say that the artwork provokes memory or envy in this passage. Here the *ornamenta* stimulate only wonder and license. And Livy does not identify the *externi* who visited the temples. Were they Syracusans? He gives no clue. Yet ill will and pity *(inuidia* and *miseratio* or *misericordia)*, while not part of the initial description of the monuments, do play a role in the extended narrative of Sicilian events. The idea that the monuments stimulate memory, pity, and antagonism appears in the next book, when Livy describes the Sicilians' plea for more lenient treatment. Arguing on their behalf, Manlius Torquatus says:

> Si ab inferis exsistat rex Hiero fidissimus imperii Romani cultor, quo ore aut Syracusas aut Romam ei ostendi posse, cum, ubi semi-rutam ac spoliatam patriam respexerit, ingrediens Romam in uestibulo urbis, prope in porta, spolia patriae suae uisurus sit? (26.32.4)

> [If Hiero, that most loyal supporter of Roman might, were to arise from the dead, with what countenance could either Syracuse or Rome be displayed to him, seeing that, after he looked on his fatherland, half ruined and despoiled, he would be going to see the spoils of his own fatherland as he entered Rome, in the entrance hall, as it were, of the city, and almost in its very gate?]

Livy says that the aim of such talk was to generate ill will toward the consul and pity for the Syracusans *(ad inuidiam consulis miserationemque Siculorum,* 26.32.5).[57] The ill will generated by the art, then, is caused not by visitors seeing it but by Marcellus' political enemy raising the specter of one Syracusan visitor seeing it. More important, this ill will is not the hostility felt by a despoiled people toward their robbers but a more pernicious kind aimed at Marcellus by Romans in Rome.

When Livy describes the experience of visitors who come to see the artwork in Marcellus' temple in Book 25, memory does not come into play. Some who see the artwork are transfixed by wonder; others are inspired to steal. Yet even if the artwork itself does not remind, the traces of the vanished spoils do. They become reminders of despoiling, an expe-

---

is Livy's source for this passage. On the parallels in tone in the criticisms of Polybius, Livy, and Plut. *Marc.* 21.1, see Gruen, *Culture and National Identity,* 95. Burck (*Einführung,* 118) points out that nowhere does Polybius discuss the morality of taking the spoils.

57. 26.29.5, 32.4–5. Carawan ("The Tragic History of Marcellus," 136–37) points out the second passage.

rience now common to Syracuse and Rome. The pillaged temple reminds its visitor of Syracuse's fate by itself suffering vandalism that is real and that, at the same time, imitates the original sack of Syracuse. In bringing the spoils of Syracuse to Rome, Marcellus actually brings the act of despoiling to Rome. The less artwork that remains and the less art that remains in other pillaged sanctuaries, the more emphatically the Temple of Honos and Virtus conveys a new message to Livy's audience: the moral integrity of the past has vanished.

Livy, then, compares Marcellus' monument unfavorably to the shield that once adorned Rome's political and religious center. He invites the reader to imagine the two by pinpointing their precise locations in the city: the Shield of Marcius, with its likeness of Hasdrubal, is on the Capitoline; the Temple of Honos and Virtus, decked with artwork, is near the Porta Capena. As Livy presents it, the destroyed shield commemorates a victory achieved through exemplary behavior. But the Syracusan artwork is separated from the great victory that it commemorates. Instead of associating the artwork with victory, Livy uses it to illustrate the rise of wonder, license, and robbery. The Shield of Marcius commemorates the Romans' ability to preserve themselves intact, even against a victorious enemy in a strange land, while the spoils from Syracuse represent the opposite, Romans at Rome falling prey to the influence of a conquered enemy and to internal tensions as well. To do the city any good, spoils cannot simply inspire awe; they need a certain practical value, if not as weapons or as bullion taken from one side to increase the power of the other (cf. Polybius 9.10.11), then as tokens that can be exchanged for other representations—the shield for the story. An artifact that inspires awe without stimulating memory draws attention only to itself, inviting as it does so its own destruction, and generating within the state, as a secondary effect, not healthy *aemulatio* but *inuidia*.

The reader contemplates the juxtaposed monuments from the vantage point of the present, in which little of the artwork remains to be seen *(comparet)*. This allows him or her to see other, slower changes. The date when someone first stole the artwork is unspecified: this was the first temple against which license turned, says Livy, but just when and how this happened is not clear. The theft of the art appears to be another historical first principle, like the Sabine capture of the citadel. Since nothing intervenes to block a direct view from present to past, we can see it as the opening of the narrator's era. In contrast, Livy dates the loss of the Shield of Marcius precisely. Its destruction with the burning of the Capitoline in

83 B.C. becomes a reminder of the civil strife of Sulla's time, while the shield itself commemorates a past that has been irretrievably lost. Livy colors his account of each monument's destruction so that it reflects this perspective. He reports that the shield was destroyed when the Capitoline burned, but in doing so he calls attention to the extent of its duration *(ad incensum Capitolium),* even as he casts the visible remains of the Syracusan artwork in a negative light by stressing their relative paucity *(quorum perexigua pars comparet).* The shield points to the past, the pillaged temple to the present. The reader contemplating them as a compound monument becomes aware of peering through layers of time: the time between the beginning of license and the present; the era introduced by the burning of the Capitoline; the time after the arrival of the shield and before the Capitoline burned; the time before the arrival of the Syracusan art. Marcius' story, that sterling exemplum of Roman *disciplina,* with a hero who represents both one man and everyman, lies far below the surface of the present. It is permanently embedded in the depressing account of the sack of Syracuse, along with the death of that city's unique defender, Archimedes, whose planetarium was dedicated in Marcellus monument.[58] Livy's account teaches the reader who sees the pillaged Temple of Honos and Virtus to remember the Shield of Marcius as well and thus to find the way back from a troubled present to a morally uplifting Roman past.

---

58. *Et habuisse tanto impetu coepta res fortunam, nisi unus homo Syracusis ea tempestate fuisset. Archimedes is erat, unicus spectator caeli siderumque, mirabilior tamen inuentor ac machinator bellicorum tormentorum operumque quibus <si quid> hostes ingenti mole agerent ipse perleui momento ludificaretur* (24.34.1–2). On *unicus,* see E. Dutoit, "*Unicus, unice* chez Tite-Live," *Latomus* 15, no. 4 (1956): 481–88. Cicero (*Rep.* 1.21) says that one of Archimedes' spheres was dedicated in this temple (the other found its way into Marcellus' house).

Chapter 5

The Trials of the Scipios

Quantam statuam faciet populus Romanus,
quantam columnam quae res tuas gestas loquatur.

[How great a statue will the Roman people make,
how great a column to tell of your achievements.]

—Ennius var. 1 Vahlen

For the reader of the *Ab Urbe Condita,* obtaining a clear view of the past involves imagining monuments and features of the landscape no longer visible in Livy's time. It also entails adopting vantage points from which it is possible to see patterns in the landscape and in events. This chapter shows how Livy manipulates points of view in a way that brings out patterns in a body of problematic evidence and how, as a result, the reader gains insight into the nature of one exemplary Roman. Livy's account of Scipio Africanus' trial and departure from political life and of the subsequent trial of his brother is notorious for its incoherence, its repetitions, and its anachronisms. This "nadir of Livian historiography" has found few defenders.[1] One of the strongest presents his defense of it as a salvage operation, and another does not consider it history at all.[2] Generally seen as an unsuccessful attempt at straightforward historical narrative offered by a sincere, if befuddled, author, it has received severe criticism. The last days of Africanus seem to defy Livy's attempts at historical representa-

---

On the epigraph, see the comments of E. Courtney in *The Fragmentary Latin Poets* (Oxford, 1993), 26. Courtney makes several conjectures to complete the lines in a way that points out their trochaic character.

1. The phrase, not the sentiment, is that of Luce (*Livy,* 92).

2. For the salvage operation, see Luce, *Livy,* 104; for an analysis of Livy's account as a rhetorical and dramatic portrait, see R. Adam, *Tite-Live, Histoire romaine,* vol. 28, Budé series (Paris, 1982), lxxxvii–lxxxix. My reading owes a great deal to the introductory essay in Adam's edition, which emphasizes the episode's affinities to tragedy; it is also indebted to Woodman's *Rhetoric in Classical Historiography,* 70–116.

tion. But if, as we have been arguing, the goal of the *Ab Urbe Condita* is to teach its audience to adopt new perspectives on the past rather than simply to reflect the past "as it really happened," it helps if we read the account of Africanus' last days with this goal in mind.[3] When we do so we can see that, for all the story's difficulties, indeed because of its very difficulties, Livy's narrative performs its intended function brilliantly. Faced with problematic materials and a recalcitrant subject, it commemorates Scipio Africanus perfectly by capturing his most memorable and most idiosyncratic traits. And it does so while maintaining the highest standards of classical historiography.

That Livy's account of the trials has received severe criticism is understandable, given the difference between the way modern historians reconstruct the events and the way Livy presents them.[4] According to Scullard, whose brief and lucid reconstruction I follow here, the trials occurred in three phases: an inquiry in the Senate, probably in 187 B.C.; a trial of Lucius Scipio, also probably in 187 B.C.; and a trial of Africanus in 184 B.C., shortly before his death. In the first incident, two men, the Petillii, probably instigated by Cato, requested that Lucius Scipio account for five hundred talents received from Antiochus after Magnesia. Scullard notes that this was not a formal trial at all but simply a request made in the Senate that L. Scipio account for the money. Africanus intervened by tearing up the account books, and the matter was dropped by the Senate, which tolerated Africanus' high-handed behavior through respect for him as princeps senatus. But Cato was not about to let the matter rest. Later that year, the tribune Minucius, backed by Cato, accused L. Scipio of refusing to render accounts when asked. He imposed a fine and asked

---

3. Miles (*Reconstructing Early Rome,* 59–61) has pointed the discussion in the right direction. He argues (60) that in other problematic passages Livy's inconsistencies "suggest an awareness of the limitations of contemporary written sources, limitations that make it impossible for Livy to reach a confident conclusion." This chapter was completed before Miles' book was published, and I have adapted it only to cite his work on points where we make similar observations.

4. For one analysis of the sources, see H. Nissen, *Kritische Untersuchungen,* 213–20. The fullest analysis is that of P. Fraccaro, "I processi degli Scipione," *Studi Storici per l'Antichità Classica* 4 (1911): 217–414 (reprinted in *Opuscula Archaeologica* 1 (Pavia, 1956), 263–392). See the note in Adam, *Tite-Live,* and H.H. Scullard, *Roman Politics, 220–150 B.C.* (Oxford, 1973), 290–303, both with full bibliographies and a convenient list of the sources. The most important primary sources besides Livy are the anecdotes reported by Polybius (23.24) and Gellius (*Noctes Atticae* 4.18 and 6.19, which preserves Nepos).

for surety. L. Scipio refused to pay it.[5] At this point, Africanus asked T. Sempronius Gracchus to intervene; Gracchus vetoed the proceedings, and the attack fell through. The third phase, according to Scullard, did not take place until three years later: Africanus was charged, probably with treason, by one M. Naevius. (The privacy of Africanus' negotiations with Antiochus and his generous foreign policy gave his enemies their means of attack.) Africanus invoked his popularity with the masses one last time and defended himself by reminding them of his victory at Zama.[6] A sick man, he retired from Rome to die at Liternum.

Livy tells the story differently. Drawing on the version of the annalist Valerius Antias, which he follows at the beginning and the end of his own account (38.50.4–55.7 and 38.58–60), he claims that Africanus was the first Scipio charged. Instigating the proceedings were two tribunes, both named Quintus Petilius. Their accusations included the charge that Africanus had embezzled money received for arranging the peace with Antiochus. They bolstered this charge with references to other controversial incidents in Africanus' career, all aimed at generating *inuidia*. They referred to his behavior in the winter quarters at Syracuse, his autocratic bearing, and the conduct of Pleminius. On the first day of his trial, Africanus gave a speech that recounted his service to the state but made no reference to the charges against him; on the second, he reminded the assembly that it was the anniversary of the battle at Zama and led it in an impromptu procession of thanksgiving. After an adjournment had been arranged, Africanus left town and, claiming illness, refused to return on the day appointed for the trial; T. Sempronius Gracchus defended Africanus' decision to stay away. Livy gives the substance of Gracchus' speech, then says that Africanus remained in Liternum and never returned to Rome. He ordered his tomb to be built there, and there he died. Livy sums up Africanus' accomplishments in a standard death notice (38.53.9–10).[7] He was, emphasizes the author, a memorable man.

Livy's version does not end here. Encouraged by Africanus' death, his enemies charged his brother with embezzlement. Cato was behind this attack, and Q. Terentius Culleo was the praetor appointed to the case.

---

5. This is not recorded by Polybius; Gellius preserves a reference to it; as does the better annalistic tradition preserved in Livy.

6. This is the occasion of his remark, reported in Polybius, that the Romans owed it to him that they could speak freely at all (23.14.3); the reference to the "crowning mercy" of Zama in Gellius; and, of course, the coup de théâtre in Livy.

7. On conventions guiding the composition of death notices, see A.. J. Pomeroy, *The Appropriate Comment* (Frankfurt, 1991).

Livy lists the persons charged and says that Lucius Scipio and two others were found guilty of taking bribes to arrange the peace with Antiochus. Then, saying that he does not trust Antias' figures for the amount of money at issue, Livy presents a list of problems with the evidence not just in Antias' account but in all the sources for Africanus' trial, last days, funeral, and place of burial. Livy has seen Africanus' monument at Liternum, but does not know if he was buried there or in the family tomb at Rome. In fact, he says, a speech of Tiberius Gracchus points to a version of the trials that is completely different from the one he has just presented (38.56.8–57.1). In this second version, Lucius Scipio was on trial and had been condemned; Africanus, who was a legate in Etruria at the time, rushed into the city and rescued his brother from the hands of the bailiff. Gracchus criticized Africanus for this act of aggression in a speech that praised his past moderation more than it blamed his present misbehavior. There follows an anecdote telling how Africanus arranged his daughter's marriage to Gracchus (38.57.2–8). All of these stories, says Livy, needed to be put before the public, regardless of the discrepancies in written records and popular talk.

At this point (38.58.1), Livy returns to the original (Antian) account of Lucius Scipio's trial, as if the rift in the evidence that began with Antias' figures did not exist. He reports Scipio Nasica's speech on behalf of the defendant, the praetor's judgment that L. Scipio must pay a fine into the treasury on pain of being imprisoned, and Gracchus' refusal to allow L. Scipio to go to prison. Family, friends, and clients, says Livy, contributed more than enough money to pay the fine, and in the end the inuidia directed toward the Scipios turned against their accusers.

Livy presents as a trial an incident that was probably not a trial at all; he reverses the order in which the brothers' "trials" probably took place and, changing his sources abruptly, embeds an alternate version into his account of the second. His narrative twists and turns, stops, changes directions, and at times appears to be traveling in circles. It is no surprise, then, that critics adduce Livy's handling of the trials as evidence for his failings as a historian. Luce sums up the conclusions about Livy's methodology that are conventionally drawn from this episode: (1) Livy did not read ahead in his sources before he composed his version (in this case, then, since he did not know that the problem with the amount of money would lead him into trouble, he followed Antias blindly into this mare's nest); (2) he checked his secondary sources only when he had already set down a complete adaptation of his main source; (3) when he discovered errors, he did not rewrite but instead added an excursus discussing the problem.[8] Luce has shown convincingly that these conclusions rest on a false assumption, namely, that "if he [Livy] had known of the various conflicting versions at the start, he would have selected a method of composition significantly different from the one he did."[9] This assumption rests on a still more basic one: that Livy's writing reflects his research without distortion, that since his own narrative changes directions when it changes sources, he copied from his sources just as he took them up.

Most striking about Livy's account, however, is not the confusion in the stories but the blanket avowal of ignorance that forms the transition between the two versions. Ironically enough, this admission of ignorance, which has made Livy particularly vulnerable to attack, has defined how others defend him. Luce pronounces the admission a deplorable necessity, while at the same time basing his defense of Livy on it.[10] He gives Livy credit for comparing sources, traveling to the tomb at Liternum, and recognizing when documents have been damaged—in short, he allows Livy precisely the sophistication in handling evidence that Livy explicitly claims. But to assume that Livy the narrator says he did not know which sources to follow only because Livy the historian did not know which sources to follow precludes asking other important questions. Why is Livy's assertion of ignorance so emphatic?[11] Why does it appear between the variant accounts instead of at the end of the book? Is it for the negative reason that Luce suggests, in order not to rob the book of the satisfying ending provided by Nasica's speech? While this is possible, such an explanation assumes that Livy considered the excursus a necessary evil. I do not think that this is so.

Livy's account is, admittedly, incoherent: the narrator appears to waver forever between variants; stories appear to generate more stories. Yet by recognizing the operative metaphors in this narrative, by studying its organization, and by reading the narrator's assertion of ignorance as a

---

8. Luce, *Livy*, 95–96.

9. Luce demonstrates (*Livy*, 96–104) that the arguments made by A. Klotz in *Livius und seine Vorgänger*, 24–78, are untenable. For earlier criticism of this theory, see M.L.W. Laistner, *The Greater Roman Historians* (Berkeley and Los Angeles, 1947), 84–87.

10. About the admission, Luce (*Livy*, 103) writes, "A distasteful business, no doubt, and bound to disfigure the narrative wherever it was placed; but in this case it could not be helped."

11. Miles (*Reconstructing Early Rome*, 59–61) has shown how to approach this problem.

rhetorical stratagem, we can see the system behind an apparently incoherent surface. While this approach does not solve the problems with evidence that Livy says he encountered when he set out to compose his account of the trials, it does help us understand how he attempted to come to grips with them. For, as we shall see, Scipio Africanus' peculiar character requires commemoration other than a straightforward historical account.

A Paradigm

The anecdote that introduces the young Scipio provides a model that helps make the account of his final days more comprehensible, for it displays several features of his characterization in the *Ab Urbe Condita*. During the battle at the Ticinus River, the Roman army's first encounter with Hannibal, the future Africanus saves the life of the wounded consul, who is also his father.

> Is pauor perculit Romanos, auxitque pauorem consulis uolnus periculumque intercursu tum primum pubescentis filii propulsatum. Hic erit iuuenis penes quem perfecti huiusce belli laus est, Africanus ob egregiam uictoriam de Hannibale Poenisque appellatus. Fuga tamen effusa iaculatorum maxime fuit quos primos Numidae inuaserunt; alius confertus equitatus consulem in medium acceptum, non armis modo sed etiam corporibus suis protegens, in castra nusquam trepide neque effuse cedendo reduxit. (21.46.7–9)

> [This fear [of the Numidian cavalry] demoralized the Romans, and the consul's wound increased the fear, as did the danger, although it was averted by the intervention of his son, who was at that time just reaching manhood. This will be the young man who has the glory of completing this war, who is called Africanus on account of his extraordinary victory over Hannibal and the Carthaginians. Nonetheless, there was disorderly flight, especially among the javelin-throwers, whom the Numidians attacked first; the cavalry, however, in close array, having taken the consul into their midst and protecting him with their weapons and even with their bodies, by giving way, but with neither panic nor disorder, led him back to the camp.]

Scipio's deed is extraordinary and laudable in itself, but the narrator's comment that this young man will defeat Hannibal adds luster to the incident. Similarly, when Livy reports Africanus' death in Book 38, Africanus' second consulship, his term as censor, and his service as his brother's legate in the war against Antiochus are anticlimactic after his victories in the Second Punic War.[12] Although both passages set the extremes of Africanus' career against his greatest achievement, they display a shift in authority from author to subject. Livy reports the battle at the Ticenus with complete confidence and situates himself as an omniscient narrator outside the past he relates.[13] In his account of Africanus' last days, however, he engages in a dramatic struggle with Africanus, from which Africanus emerges as the person controlling both the course of events and the nature of their representation.

This anecdote also presents Scipio's arrival on the scene as a movement in the workings of the cosmos. It weaves together a group of apparent coincidences: both father and son are present at what is explicitly labeled the first fight against Hannibal ("this was the first battle with Hannibal" [*hoc primum cum Hannibale proelium fuit*], 21.47.1); the father is consul; the father is wounded; the son is old enough to save him. Africanus' age and his participation in events increase as his father wanes and as the threat posed by Hannibal increases. He reappears after Cannae, when he swears not to abandon Italy (22.53.9–12); then, at the age of twenty-four, he takes over the command in Spain, after his father has died there (26.18.6–11). Livy does not give the young Scipio's age at the Ticenus in years; all he says is that Scipio was "at that time just reaching manhood" [*tum primum pubescentis*].[14] It is Africanus' position relative to events, to places, and to others that signifies, not the abstract standards by which men might measure him.[15] Livy captures the intercon-

---

12. Cf. *hic erit iuuenis penes quem perfecti huiusce belli laus est* (21.46.8) and *Punici tamen belli perpetrati, quo nullum neque maius neque periculosius Romani gessere, unus praecipuam gloriam tulit* (38.53.11).

13. Even the variant that Livy places at the end of the account does not cause undue distress. Livy says that Coelius records a different version of the rescue but that he himself prefers the one he has given, because more authors report it and because the story is generally accepted: *seruati consulis decus Coelius ad seruum natione Ligurem delegat; malim equidem de filio uerum esse, quod et plures tradidere auctores et fama obtinuit* (21.46.10). By discussing the variants, Livy distances himself from the events and situates himself among other writers.

14. *Decem et octo annorum*, according to the author of *De vir. ill.* (49).

15. Livy puts this very argument in Scipio's mouth at 25.2.7: *si me omnes Quirites aedilem facere volunt, satis annorum habeo.* Cf. the concern about his age at 26.18.11. Scipio responds with a speech that restores confidence at 26.19.1–2.

nection of events nicely in the first sentence, which sketches the army's panic, the danger to the consul, and the son's heroics in only fifteen words.[16] The repetition of *pauor . . . pauorem* and the use of the noun *periculum,* which intensifies the impression of danger by reinforcing the idea of risk *(uolnus periculumque)* and then mitigates it through the adversative force of the participle *propulsatum,* together represent the panic, the wounding, and the rescue as a tightly connected sequence of events.[17] One proceeds immediately from another: the collapse in morale is caused by fear; the increase in fear is caused by the consul's wound, and finally the young Scipio's intervention wards off the danger that threatens the wounded man. The order of events implies a causal connection: the father's misfortune brings about the son's entrance into the affairs of history, and danger produces rescue. Time, place, and circumstance together orchestrate the entrance of the man whom Livy later calls the "fated leader of this war" *[dux fatalis huiusce belli]* (22.53.6).

While events proceed sequentially in the first sentence, the second projects the act of rescue onto the plot of the entire war: "this will be the young man who has the glory of completing this war, who is called Africanus on account of his extraordinary victory over Hannibal and the Carthaginians." One last fact concludes the account of the series of events, so that it runs like this: the son, who saved the father, who was endangered by the wound, which increased the fear, which demoralized the Romans—it was he who defeated Hannibal. This prolepsis connects the rescue of the elder Scipio to the victory over Hannibal not in a linear fashion but by analogy: the rescue anticipates the victory *in parvo.* This is the first of a series of analogous actions performed by Africanus, the

---

16. Cf. Polyb. 10.3.3–7, which tells the story at greater length and in far more detail. After citing Laelius as his authority, Polybius gives Scipio's precise age and position in battle as part of the background: Scipio was seventeen (ἑπτακαιδέκατον ἔτος ἔχων), and because this was his first battle, his father had placed him in command of a picked troop of horsemen to ensure his safety. When Scipio saw that his father was wounded and surrounded by the enemy with only a few horsemen defending him, he first urged his men to go with him to the rescue; but when they hung back, he is said to have charged the enemy recklessly, alone. According to Polybius, this forced Scipio's men to attack, and at their rush the enemy fled. Scipio was the first to salute his son as his preserver. Having gained a reputation for physical courage, the young Scipio refrained afterward from risking himself unnecessarily in battle. This, concludes Polybius, is the conduct of an intelligent man who knows how much depends on him. For a list of variants, see Walbank, *A Historical Commentary on Polybius,* 2:198–99.

17. My thanks to C.S. Kraus, for pointing out that this repetition works like *epiploce,* a forward-moving device. See 6.32.8 *(sed eques immissus ordines turbauit; turbatis signa peditum inlata . . .),* with Kraus, *Ab urbe condita Book VI,* 263–64, and W-M ad loc.

effects of which differ only with changes in the scale on which he performs them.

Moreover, Africanus' first recorded action could be considered both an act of *pietas* toward his father and a service to the state.[18] In this case the two coincide—the consul actually is Africanus' father—but such a conflation of public and personal becomes even more pronounced at the end of Africanus' life. This is a result of his idiosyncratic worldview, one that is egocentric, like that of Marcus Manlius, and at the same time all-encompassing, like that of Camillus. A useful illustration of this way of thinking comes from a later text, Hierocles' description of the Stoic wise man and his relationships.

> Each one of us is as it were entirely encompassed by many circles, some smaller, others larger, the latter enclosing the former on the basis of their different and unequal dispositions relative to each other. The first and closest circle is the one which a person has drawn as though around a centre, his own mind. This circle incloses the body and anything taken for the sake of the body. For it is virtually the smallest circle, and almost touches the centre itself. Next, the second one further removed from the centre but enclosing the first circle; this contains parents, siblings, wife, and children. The third one has in it uncles and aunts, grandparent, nephews, nieces, and cousins. The next circle includes the other relatives, and this is followed by the circle of local residents, then the circle of fellow tribesmen, next that of fellow-citizens, and then in the same way the circle of people from neighbouring towns, and the circle of fellow-countrymen. The outermost and largest circle, which encompasses the rest, is that of the whole human race. Once these have all been surveyed, it is the task of the well tempered man, in his proper treatment of each group, to draw the circles together somehow towards the centre, and to keep zealously transferring those from the enclosing circles into the enclosed ones. . . .[19]

Such a model makes it possible for a person to be completely egocentric and, at the same time, concerned for all humankind. It is a matter of

18. On the state as parent, see T.R. Stevenson, "The Ideal Benefactor and the Father Analogy in Greek and Roman Thought," *CQ*, n.s., 42 (1992): 421–36, esp. 429–31.

19. Hierocles *apud* Stobaeus 4.671.7–673.11, trans. Long and Sedley (*The Hellenistic Philosophers,* 1:349–50). I use Hierocles' image only as an illustration. For discussion of Stoic influences on Livy, see P.G. Walsh, "Livy and Stoicism," *AJP* 79 (1958): 355–75.

thinking about human relationships in terms of space and then eliminating the metaphorical distances that separate people by treating them all alike. Livy's Africanus embodies this ideal nicely, for at the end of his life, his actions make no distinctions in time, place, or person. They resemble one another by analogy, just as the large circles in the Stoic model resemble the small ones. Such analogous actions alter the flow of the narrative as, from a linear sequence in which one event leads to another, events come to prefigure subsequent ones. By keeping in mind both the idea of analogous actions and the egocentric model of relationships, we can discern patterns that reflect Africanus' character in the account of the trials.

Africanus' rescue of his father also demonstrates his extraordinary ability to unite people.[20] From the disorderly flight *(fuga effusa)*, there emerges a small, orderly group of horsemen, retreating with their wounded consul and keeping perfect order as they give way *(nusquam trepide neque effuse)*.

Finally, from his first appearance at the Ticinus to his last days in Rome, Africanus demonstrates an uncanny ability to be in the right place at the right time, as well as a knack for turning neutral and even hostile times and places to his advantage. A survey of his activity in the *Ab Urbe Condita* turns up several examples. Africanus' coming-of-age coincides with the year of his father's consulship; he intervenes bodily between his father and danger *(periculumque intercursu . . . filii propulsatum)*. His actions reveal that he understands the importance of place: one of the four military tribunes present at Canusium after Cannae, it is he who most vehemently refuses to flee Italy (22.53.9–12). At Rome he visits the Temple of Jupiter on the Capitoline every morning, thus fostering a close relationship, or at least the impression of a close relationship, with the god (26.19.5–6).[21] In Spain his unerring sense of the importance of one particular part of the country to the whole leads him to attack New Carthage, and his knowledge of topography, winds, and tides helps him

---

20. Africanus, in fact, disappears into the united group: the narrator makes no mention of him after this sentence.

21. The historian reports Africanus' divine birth as a popular fairy tale and interprets Scipio's association with Jupiter, Hercules, and Neptune as so much storytelling. He considers his extraordinary behavior, from meditation in the Temple of Jupiter on the Capitoline to reports of significant dreams, as politically astute stunts, not evidence of divine favor (26.19.3–9). On the "Scipionic Legend," see esp. H.H. Scullard, *Scipio Africanus in the Second Punic War* (Cambridge, 1930), 70–82; idem, *Scipio Africanus: Soldier and Politician* (New York, 1970); R.M. Haywood, *Studies on Scipio Africanus. Johns Hopkins University Studies in Historical and Political Science*, ser. 51, no. 1 (Baltimore, 1933), 9–29; J.M.C. Toynbee, *Hannibal's Legacy*, 2 vols. (Oxford, 1965), 2:500–508; Walbank, *Selected Papers*, 120–37.

capture the city (26.42.2–4, 26.51.14). It is he who insists on carrying the war to Africa (28.43.2–44.18), and the continent gives him a cognomen in turn (30.45.6). His return to Italy at the end of the war is an unbroken triumphal procession beginning with his first step on Italian soil.[22] In addition, Africanus is sensitive to matters of decorum that have to do with time and place. Years later, as one of the Salii and his brother's legate in Asia Minor, he refuses to travel on days the Salii cannot. Thus he preserves the integrity of the Roman religious calender on the very frontiers of the empire (37.33.6–7). The second day of his trial just happens to be the anniversary of the victory at Zama, a coincidence Africanus exploits by leading a procession first to the Capitoline and then to the shrines and temples of all the gods (38.51.7–14). Finally, one report of his death says he died in the same year as Hannibal and Philopoemon, although Livy does not agree (39.52.1–9).

In the light of this interweaving and in the light of Africanus' ability to use time and place to his advantage, it is supremely ironic that Africanus, after he dies, is lost in both time and place. Livy says that he cannot say with confidence when Africanus died or where he was buried (38.56.1–7, 39.52.1). The narrator's ignorance on this point is suggestive, first because he places so much stress on it, and second because he draws attention to the monuments and documents that fail to preserve this information. Livy qua historian cannot account for the death and burial of one of Rome's most memorable men, and he organizes the trial in such a way as to draw attention to this paradox, which is particularly suited to commemorating Africanus. For Africanus embodies another logical contradiction: from the beginning of his public life to its end, it is of supreme importance to Rome that he be in the right place at the right time; yet Africanus himself transends distance, whether it is geographical or metaphorical. The near and the far are the same to him, and when he repeats analogous actions, he collapses distinctions in space and time. This contradiction suggests that we approach the trial narrative as a conflict of perspectives, that we consider events from Africanus' point of view as well as from those of other characters in the story. When we do so, it becomes clear that Africanus is not lost. He has simply and charac-

---

22. The one sentence that conveys his journey all the way to the city illustrates how his procession ties together all of Italy: *inde magna parte militum nauibus missa ipse per laetam pace non minus quam uictoria Italiam effusis non urbibus modo ad habendos honores sed agrestium etiam turba obsidente uias Romam peruenit triumphoque omnium clarissimo urbem est inuectus* (30.45.2).

teristically left tracks that are hard to follow, for they do not mark out a straight line.

Urbs et Orbis

Near the end of Book 38, Livy reports that Gnaius Manlius Vulso was nearly denied a triumph for his Galatian campaign, because his legates opposed it. They argued that in provoking the Galatians to fight Manlius had literally and figuratively stepped out of bounds. Manlius did receive his triumph after lengthy debate, largely because of his friends' efforts and the senior senators' respect for precedent. Having noted this, Livy turns to the trials of the Scipios with the words "after this, a greater struggle, arising from a greater and more illustrious man, buried all talk and memory of this debate" *[oppressit deinde mentionem memoriamque omnem contentionis huius maius et cum maiore et clariore uiro certamen ortum]* (38.50.4). Livy generally presents the history of Rome's internal affairs as a series of debates, but here he assigns the discussion itself a dramatic role by placing the main verb of the sentence, *oppressit,* in the emphatic initial position.[23] The account of the trials thus acquires an ironic tone from the start: Africanus' trial was the talk of the town when it happened, but Livy cannot tell its story in a straightforward manner, although, as one commentator points out, he confidently relates the less important debate about Vulso's triumph.[24]

This initial emphasis on talk should alert us to the images and strategies employed by participants in the debate. Livy calls it a greater struggle *(maius certamen)* not only because it involves a greater man than Vulso but also because the participants bring a more comprehensive worldview to the discussion. It is no surprise that Vulso's story progresses in a straightforward fashion, for his attitude is legalistic and the interpre-

---

23. See Adam, *Tite-Live,* xciv. On the word order, see J.-P. Chausserie-Laprée, *L'Expression narrative chez les historiens latins* (Paris, 1969), 352. Initial verbs in this episode generally have to do with talk: cf., e.g., *dicebantur enim . . .* (38.50.12), and, of Gracchus' speech, *mouit et decretum et adiecta oratio non ceteros modo sed ipsos etiam accusatores . . .* (38.53.5).

24. See Adam, *Tite-Live,* lxxxvii. On Livy's construction of Vulso's campaign, see B. Pagnon, "Le recit de l'expedition de Cn. Manlius Vulso contre les Gallo-Grecs et de ses prolongements dans le livre 38 de Tite-Live," *LEC* 50 (1982): 115–28. Livy introduces the whole account briskly at 38.12.1: *Eadem non aestate solum sed iisdem prope diebus quibus haec a M. Fuluio consule in Aetolia gesta sunt, consul alter Cn. Manlius in Gallograecia bellum gessit quod nunc ordiri pergam.*

tation of custom that results from it is literal. The Senate grants him a triumph for the simple reason that a triumph, according to custom, completes a chain of events: Vulso defeated the enemy, completed his term of office, and brought his army home. There would be no precedent for denying him the traditional finale. (The narrator reports these events in a meticulously historiographical period, whose syntax respects chronology).[25] Vulso's road to honor runs directly from Asia Minor to the Temple of Bellona and from there along the triumphal route to the Temple of Jupiter on the Capitoline.

Vulso's way of thinking and acting is reflected in both the Senate's decision and the historian's straightforward narrative, but Livy, Senate, and city alike face a very different situation when it comes to dealing with Africanus, who thinks and acts in a manner that is neither linear nor legalistic, and who, like Vulso, ignores boundaries, though he does so to reconcile rather than provoke. The problems that this narrative presents have their origins in the very conflict between Africanus and his detractors, and the conflict itself arises from conflicting worldviews. Africanus' supporters, his detractors (the tribunes who accuse him), and Tiberius Gracchus (the enemy who comes to his aid)—indeed all who engage in the debate about the Scipios—wield rhetorically the idea of the *orbis terrarum*, the image of the known world divided into regions. The people on both sides of the conflict also project a model of Rome onto their image of the *orbis terrarum*. But they perceive boundaries within it differently, look on the city from different vantage points, and disagree about the exact location of its center.[26] By expressing their positions on the Scipios as a matter of general principle and by presenting their principles in terms of space, they turn the inquiry concerning the Scipios' finances into a general debate about the location of the center of the Roman world and movements of power and authority around it.[27] The various conceptions of city and

---

25. *Postero die et cognati amicique Cn. Manli summis opibus adnisi sunt, et auctoritas seniorum ualuit, negantium exemplum proditum memoriae esse ut imperator, qui deuictis perduellibus, confecta provincia exercitum reportasset, sine curru et laurea priuatus inhonoratusque urbem iniret* (38.50.2–3). I am grateful to C.S. Kraus for pointing this out to me.

On the use of precedent in this debate, see Chaplin, "Livy's Use of Exempla," 131–43.

26. On the concept of the *orbis terrarum* in the Augustan Age, see esp. Nicolet, *Space, Geography, and Politics*, chaps. 1–5.

27. On the importance of the center, see Kraus, "No Second Troy," 281.

orbis terrarum, which at first appear to explain and substantiate opinions about Africanus and his trial, themselves become objects of contention. As Africanus' egocentric worldview clashes with and remains unreconciled to those of his opponents, the reader has the impression of suffering from double vision, and the many contradictions in the narrative enhance this disturbing phenomenon.[28] It is a natural reaction to a narrative that is less interested in relating events than in presenting different points of view.

Livy continues to weave together abstract and specific views of the world by combining plot structures and historically significant places, as he did in the stories of the Sabine women, Marcus Manlius, and Lucius Marcius. Here, however, the undertaking is more elaborate, since events take place in several settings: on the Capitoline, in the Forum, at the rostra, around the circuit of the city's shrines and temples, in Africanus' house, and in that of his brother Lucius. (Livy also refers to the Scipio family tomb at the Porta Capena and to Africanus' villa at Liternum.) In addition, the participants in the debate refer to places in Rome, and their references convey to us their mental models of the city. In Book 5, after the departure of the Gauls, new buildings and property boundaries covered the ruins of the old city, a physical change that commemorated the transition from one era to the next.[29] Livy introduces Africanus' story in a similar way, only here it is a matter of the conceptual cities that people wield, so that the narrative conveys the impression not of buildings covering buildings but of models covering models as talk buries talk.

The first version of Africanus' trial (38.50.4–55.7) falls into three stages, each of which uses space to present the division of opinion. First is the anticipatory stage, with its abstract discussion of principle. Then comes the trial itself, a dramatic performance involving both speech and movement. And last is the discussion after the trial, with its rhetorical deployment of specific places.

In the first stage, after the Petillii have indicted Scipio and the trial has become the talk of the town, people disagree about the justice of the charge.

---

28. According to Tuan (*Topophilia,* 30–44), this typifies the spatial organization of primitive ethnocentric worldviews.

29. On the refounding and rebuilding, see Kraus, "No Second Troy," 282–87. On rebuilding, see also Jaeger, "*Custodia Fidelis Memoriae,*" 350–53.

Alii non tribunos plebis, sed uniuersam ciuitatem quae id pati pos-
set incusabant: duas maximas orbis terrarum urbes ingratas uno
prope tempore in principes inuentas, Romam ingratiorem, si quidem uicta Carthago uictum Hannibalem in exsilium expulisset,
Roma uictrix uictorem Africanum expellat. Alii neminem unum
tantum eminere ciuem debere ut legibus interrogari non possit; nihil
tam aequandae libertatis esse quam potentissimum quemque posse
dicere causam; quid autem tuto cuiquam, nedum summam rem
publicam, permitti, si ratio non sit reddenda? qui ius aequum pati
non possit, in eum uim haud iniustam esse. (38.50.6–9)

[Some were reproaching not the tribunes of the people but the
entire state that could allow this: the two greatest cities in the
world, they said, had been found ungrateful toward their chief citizen at almost the same time—Rome the more so, inasmuch as,
when conquered, Carthage had exiled the conquered Hannibal,
whereas victorious Rome was driving out the conquering
Africanus. Others said that no one citizen should stand out to such
a degree that he could not be called to question by the laws; nothing made freedom so equal as when every man, no matter how
powerful, could be brought to trial; could anything now, much less
the supreme authority of the state, be safely entrusted to anyone, if
there were no necessity of rendering an account? Against a person
who could not endure the equality of the law, the use of force was
hardly unfair.]

Both sides see the indictment as a matter of principle. Their interpretations fall out according to whether they see Rome as one part of the
world or see only the city and look toward its interior (*alii . . . alii* marks
the division in the Latin). The first group, whose vision of Rome encompasses the entire *orbis terrarum*, is willing to spread the blame for the trials among the entire community *(uniuersam ciuitatem)*. From its point of
view, Rome is part of the larger whole that includes its rival Carthage.
Since this group arranges states in a hierarchy, setting *uicta Carthago*
against *Roma uictrix,* the fact of material importance is not individual
prestige but Rome's position relative to that of the enemy. Africanus' critics, in contrast, recognize a hierarchy of citizens within the state and portray the outstanding individual within the city as a hill that must be leveled by law *(neminem unum tantum eminere ciuem debere;* aequandae

libertatis), a worldview similar to Marcus Manlius' in Book 6.[30] Looking inward and contracting their vision of the *orbis terrarum* to encompass only the *urbs,* Africanus' critics consider power relations among citizens to be governed by the principles of *lex* and *ius,* rather than by gratitude for the leadership that has secured Rome's international standing. This first part of the narrative, then, focalizes Africanus' indictment in two incompatible ways. In doing so it divides those who look outward to the edges of the known world from those who look inward toward an eminence inside the city. To look outward in space is analogous to looking outward in time, to seeing that events throughout the inhabited world are connected on a large scale *(duas maximas orbis terrarum urbes; uno prope tempore),* while to look inward is to forget about the past and to focus attention on the debate at hand.

Yet Africanus also resolves the conflict that he creates among his fellow citizens. The second stage of the narrative, the trial itself, relates his transformation from a cause of factional strife into a locus of concord. The trial occurs in two phases; one emphasizes talk and the other movement. On the first day of the trial, Africanus unites opposing points of view by changing the focus of the debate. On the second, he turns the ritualized strife of a trial into consensus that finds ritual expression in a procession all around the town.

On the first day, Africanus draws the debate away from the legal question and toward himself in a way that produces one shared point of view in his audience. He ignores the charges against him and instead recounts his accomplishments on behalf of the state. The narrator's fulsome description implies that Africanus' words mirror perfectly his *res gestae:* his speech *de rebus ab se gestis* is so magnificent that everyone agrees no one was better or more truly praised, all the more so because Africanus speaks of his achievements just as he accomplished them, with the same spirit and courage.[31] The narrator underscores Africanus' honesty by saying that he speaks "in a manner corresponding to the danger" *[pro periculo]* and not "for the sake of glory" *[in gloriam].*[32] There are no discrepancies between Africanus and his reputation or even between his present self and his past self that might lessen the verisimilitude of this repre-

---

30. See 6.11.4, 18.14.

31. *Dicebantur enim ab eodem animo ingenioque a quo gesta erant* (38.50.12).

32. Africanus has added nothing for the sake of increasing his reputation. Cf. Livy's remarks on this kind of embellishment at 8.40; see also Woodman's comments on Cicero, in *Rhetoric in Classical Historiography,* 91.

sented past. Africanus can look to the present like his opponents, but his speech makes the present meaningful as a repetition of the past. By relating his deeds in the same manner in which he performed them, Africanus unites past and present, and nullifies the distance between city center and periphery of the empire. Thus he collapses the very distinctions between Rome and abroad and between then and now that divided the city after his indictment.

In contrast, his accusers, who shape the inhabited world to their ends, draw a marked distinction between space inside the city and space outside. Their view of the *orbis terrarum* is hierarchical.

> . . . dictatorem eum consuli, non legatum, in prouincia fuisse; nec ad aliam rem eo profectum quam ut id quod Hispaniae, Galliae, Siciliae, Africae iam pridem persuasum esset, hoc Graeciae Asiaque et omnibus ad orientem uersis regibus gentibusque appareret, unum hominem caput columenque imperii Romani esse, sub umbra Scipionis ciuitatem dominam orbis terrarum latere, nutum eius pro decretis patrum, pro populi iussis esse. (38.51.3–4)

> [. . . [They argued that] he had been in the province as a dictator for the consul, not as legate, and that he went there for no other purpose than to make clear to Greece and Asia and all the kings and peoples of the east what Spain, Gaul, Sicily, and Africa had long since been persuaded: one man was the head and bulwark of Rome's dominion; the state that was mistress of the world hid in Scipio's shadow; and his nod stood for the decrees of the Senate and the orders of the people.]

The tribunes' view of the *orbis terrarum* places the city in the center of its entire empire by listing subdued peoples to the west *(Hispaniae),* to the north *(Galliae),* to the south *(Siciliae, Africae),* and to the east *(Graeciae Asiaque).*[33] The tribunes speak of these regions as identical, equal in status, and equidistant from Rome, because in their minds a place's rela-

---

33. Note that Livy's version puts in the mouths of the tribunes the comprehensive picture of the empire that Polybius puts in the mouth of Africanus himself (23.14): "Then he asked the Senate how it could demand an account of three thousand talents—how the money had been spent and by whom—and not ask by whose agency the fifteen thousand talents that they were receiving from Antiochus had come into the treasury or how they had become masters of Asia, Africa, and Spain."

tionship to the center gives that place its significance. When they look to the inside of the city, the tribunes continue to stress hierarchy by using metaphors that draw attention to the vertical *(unum hominem caput columenque. . . . ; sub umbra Scipionis)*. They sketch a picture of an *orbis terrarum* divided into four regions, all subordinated to a Rome rising in the center; in the center of that Rome is a peak, and at the pinnacle of that Olympian height is Africanus, whom they assimilate to Jupiter with the expression *nutum eius*.[34] By juxtaposing these antithetical conceptions of Roman space—the tribunes' differentiated and hierarchical model and Africanus' uniform and level one—Livy locates the source of Africanus' liberal foreign policy in his mental embrace of the entire *orbis terrarum*. But he also finds there the source of Africanus' political problems in Rome. Africanus views the world as space radiating outward from himself and containing a series of orbiting personal relationships that he draws constantly closer to himself. This all-embracing egocentrism means that from Africanus' point of view, space in the city is no different than space outside it. It is simply space around him. His opponents, however, arrange lands and peoples hierarchically around a center of political power. They are afraid that Africanus has appropriated this center to himself and that he takes it along with him even when he leaves the city.

The second day of the trial sees more action than talk, as Livy moves prosecutors and defendant about the city in ways that demonstrate both their assumptions about centers of power and authority in the state and the directions in which they think these forces travel. At dawn the tribunes take up their places on the rostra (38.51.5). The defendant and his crowd of supporters approach the speaking platform from below. Once again Africanus refuses to answer to the charges against him, this time by pointing out that it is the anniversary of Zama.[35] Having done so, he turns away.

Ab rostris in Capitolium ascendit; simul se uniuersa contio auertit et secuta Scipionem est, adeo ut postremo scribae uiatoresque tribunos relinquerent nec cum iis, praeter seruilem comitatum et praeconem qui reum ex rostris citabat, quisquam esset. Scipio non in

---

34. W-M ad loc.

35. Feldherr ("Spectacle and Society," 14) points out that "one way of ensuring a collective response to a spectacle was to provide a shared historical association." Africanus shows that he understands this tactic well.

Capitolio modo, sed per totam urbem omnia templa deum cum
populo Romano circumiit. (38.51.12–13)

[From the rostra, he climbed the Capitoline. At the same time, the
entire assembly turned away and followed Scipio, so that finally
even the scribes and bailiffs left the tribunes, and no one was left
with them besides their servile gang and the herald who summoned
the defendant from the rostra. Scipio made the rounds of all the
temples of the gods not only on the Capitoline but also throughout
the entire city, with the Roman people accompanying him.]

The rostra is the focal point of movement in this passage: the tribunes
take their places on the rostra (*in rostris,* 38.51.5); Africanus moves
toward the rostra (*ad rostra,* 38.51.7) then away from it *(ab rostris);* and
the herald left behind summons defendants from the rostra *(ex rostris)*—
a gratuitous detail that shows Livy playing up the role of the place. The
trial, then, begins with a dance around the center of tribunician power,
but Africanus undermines the tribunes' lofty and central position by
pointing out that even they belong to a city that is subordinate to the
Capitoline gods. The episode ends with a procession to the divine and
aristocratic center of power and from there to all the shrines and temples
in the city. Africanus has turned a hostile place and time to his own
advantage by substituting ritual for argument. He repeats the triumph for
Zama on the day of the battle of Zama, thus destroying the distance in
space and time between Zama and Rome and between then and now.
Livy is emphatic about Africanus' thoroughness. Processing through the
entire city *(per totam urbem),* he visits all the sanctuaries *(omnia templa).*
Save for the tribunes and their followers, the entire assembly *(uniuersa
contio)* follows.

Africanus unites his fellow citizens around him by showing the people
that his relationship with them is one of reciprocity. As he says before
turning toward the Capitoline, "if from my seventeenth year up until my
old age you have anticipated my coming-of-age by awarding me offices,
I, on my part, have anticipated your honors by my achievements" *[ita, si
ab annis septemdecim ad senectutem semper uos aetatem meam honoribus uestris anteistis, ego uestros honores rebus gerendis praecessi]*
(38.51.11). The elaborately entwined interlocking cases and chiastic
word order *(aetatem meam honoribus uestris . . . uestros honores rebus
gerendis)* help convey the impression of a state of equilibrium in relations

between Africanus and his fellow citizens. Africanus, however, presents this reciprocity in the context of Rome's relations with the gods, who, according to him, are responsible for his victory: "and to them I shall give thanks for granting me, on this very day, and often at other times, the ability to render my country exceptional service" [*iisque gratias agam quod mihi et hoc ipso die et saepe alias egregie gerendae rei publicae mentem facultatemque dederunt*] (38.51.9). Africanus' call to prayer links him, the people, and the gods in a network of reciprocal obligations: the people have voted Africanus offices; he has given them service; the gods have given him the opportunity to render service.[36] The only obligation left unfulfilled is to thank the gods and enlist their future support: "and you too Romans, whoever finds it convenient, come along with me, and pray to the gods that you have leaders like me" [*uestrum quoque quibus commodum est, Quirites, ite mecum, et orate deos ut mei similes principes habeatis*] (38.51.10). In the two days of the trial, then, through speeches and movements that invoke past times and distant places, Africanus demonstrates that, although there is a hierarchy of authority in Rome and in the provinces, it is the same hierarchy throughout the *orbis terrarum:* the gods are on top, and men are below them. Thus the narrative links Africanus' ability to create concord among citizens to his leading them away from the center of civic power to the center of aristocratic and divine power instead.

The unified point of view produced by invoking the past through ritual cannot last; Africanus must re-create it anew whenever his political enemies harass him. Anticipating more trouble, he withdraws to Liternum.[37] Rome supplies topographical metaphors to the debate that follows, as Africanus' supporters and opponents argue about the significance of his trial and departure. Both sides make clear their assumptions about the center of Roman power and the directions in which they think power and privilege move in relation to it, only this time they do so through topographical figures of speech that vary according to one's point of view.

The tribunes' model of space is just as egocentric as Africanus' and differs from his only in that it arranges people hierarchically. The tribunes represent Africanus' impromptu thanksgiving procession first as a triumph over the Roman people and then as a secession of the plebs from

---

36. On the reciprocity in relations between benefactor and beneficiary, see Stevenson, "The Ideal Benefactor," 424.

37. See 38.52.1.

the tribunes to the Capitoline: ". . . and accompanied by the very people from whom he had taken both the right of pronouncing judgment on him and their freedom, and dragging them like captives, he had celebrated a triumph over the Roman people and had brought about a secession on that day to the Capitoline away from the tribunes of the people" [. . . *et quibus ius sententiae de se dicendae et libertatem ademisset, iis comitatus, uelut captos trahens, triumphum de populo Romano egisset secessionemque eo die in Capitolium a tribunis plebis fecisset]* (38.52.5). Richard Adam points out that a secession of the plebs not to the Aventine or the Sacred Mount but to the center of aristocratic power, and indeed to the center of the city, is a paradox, as is the idea of a triumph over the Roman people being celebrated on the Capitoline.[38]

Yet the apparent lapse of logic that produces such a paradox indicates the high degree to which the tribunes have differentiated space within the city and have placed themselves at its center. The rostra is the focal point of tribunician power; the Capitoline lies entirely outside the tribunes' conception of the city.[39] They see Africanus' procession from the rostra to the Capitoline as a departure from Rome or, if it is to be considered a return, as a return from their Rome to his and a triumph over the Roman people, who in following Africanus up the Capitoline are prisoners in a foreign city. The tribunes have defined the Roman world as a narrow and vertically oriented space, just as Marcus Manlius did in Book 6. Africanus' procession on the day of the trial united the competing centers of power *(a rostris in Capitolinum ascendit),* but the tribunes interpret his act as a political gesture directed against them. For although the tribunes, like Africanus' original critics, claim that the law should set everyone on level ground, their model of the city places the rostra at its center and them on the rostra, which they summon Africanus to approach from below (ad rostra subiit 38.51.7). Theirs are not the first insincere calls for equality in the *Ab Urbe Condita,* but this episode dramatizes the familiar metaphors in a way that illustrates clearly how one city has become two.[40]

From the tribunes' point of view, power and authority radiate outward and downward from the rostra. In turning from it, the people have abandoned their champions.

---

38. See Adam, *Tite-Live,* 193.

39. Cf. the motif of two cities in one at 2.33, 34; see also Cic. *Rep.* 131.

40. Cf., e.g., 3.65.11: *adeo moderatio tuendae libertatis, dum aequari uelle simulando ita se quisque extollit ut deprimat alium, in difficili est . . . et iniuriam ab nobis repulsam tamquam aut facere aut pati neccesse sit iniungimus aliis.*

Habetis ergo temeritatis illius mercedem; quo duce et auctore nos reliquistis, ab eo ipso relicti estis, et tantum animorum in dies nobis decrescit ut ad quem, ante annos septemdecim, exercitum et classem habentem, tribunos plebis aedilemque mittere in Siciliam ausi sumus qui prenderent eum et Romam reducerent, ad eum, priuatum, ex uilla sua extrahendum ad causam dicendam mittere non audeamus. (38.52.6–7)

[You have, then, your reward for that rashness. The leader you followed when you abandoned us has himself left you, and our courage decreases so much every day that we, who dared seventeen years ago, when he had a fleet and an army, to send the tribunes of the people and an aedile to Sicily to arrest him and bring him to Rome, we do not dare to send anyone to extract him from his country house, although he is a private citizen, and bring him to Rome to stand trial.]

Unlike Africanus, who united his fellow citizens by reminding them of the network of reciprocal relationships between himself, the people, and the gods, the tribunes speak of reciprocal relationships between themselves, the people, and Africanus. They argue that the community has disintegrated into isolated groups, that the people have abandoned the tribunes and that Africanus has abandoned the people. Their own authority over Africanus has dissolved, since they do not dare even to recall him from Liternum.

Tiberius Gracchus' unexpected defense of Africanus ends the discussion by reconciling both sides. He uses an image of Rome that is both a paradox and a compromise. It adapts Africanus' practice of conflating space outside the city and space within, and it accepts Africanus' assumption that accomplishments at the periphery should at least earn a man security at the center, if not privilege. Yet it also accommodates these points to the tribunes' highly differentiated and hierarchical model of the world.

Adiecit decreto indignationem: "Sub pedibus uestris stabit, tribuni, domitor ille Africae Scipio? Ideo quattuor nobilissimos duces Poenorum in Hispania, quattuor exercitus fudit fugauit, ideo Syphacem cepit, Hannibalem deiecit, Carthaginiem uectigalem nobis fecit, Antiochum (recepit enim fratrem consortem huius gloriae L. Scipio) ultra iuga Tauri emouit, ut duobus Petiliis succumberet, uos de P. Africano palmam peteretis? Nullisne meritis suis, nullis uestris honoribus, umquam in arcem tutam et uelut sanctam clari uiri peruenient, ubi si non uenerabilis, inuiolata saltem senectus eorum considat?" (38.53.1–4)

[He added an indignant outburst to his decree: "Will Scipio, the master of Africa, stand at your feet, tribunes? Did he rout and put to flight four most noble Carthaginian generals in Spain, and four armies, did he capture Syphax, conquer Hannibal, make Carthage our tributary, push Antiochus beyond the Taurus Mountains (for Lucius Scipio admits his brother as his partner in glory), so that he might succumb to two Petilii? So that you might seek the palm of victory over Publius Africanus? Will great men never by their own service or by the honor you bestow reach a safe and, as it were, sacred citadel, where their old age can rest, if not venerated, at least undisturbed?"]

By setting a list of conquered foreign lands against the Forum and the Capitoline, Gracchus presents Africanus' situation in terms of periphery and center, just as Africanus' opponents did in their talk before the trial (38.50.8–9), and just as the tribunes did in their original accusations. Like the tribunes, Gracchus describes a world that is subject to Africanus. But he neutralizes the force of this worldview by changing the nature of the center and of Africanus' relationship to it. The citadel to which Gracchus refers is not the center of Roman aristocratic power but a refuge granted men of accomplishment. Africanus' withdrawal to the country is the flight of a sick old man.

Gracchus' indignant outburst, while raising Africanus above the position in which the tribunes want to see him, places him below the lofty situation his enemies claim he occupies. While Africanus does not belong beneath the tribunes' feet *(sub pedibus . . .)*, he will not be, even if left unmolested, a Jove-like figure at the pinnacle of Rome. Africanus reaches the citadel, only to settle there *(considat)*. The verb *considere* can mean simply to come to rest, but it can also mean to sink, subside, or collapse into ruins, as a building does.[41] It recalls the metaphor

---

41. Livy uses the verb topographically at 30.38.8: *terra ingentibus cauernis consedit.* Tacitus uses it of buildings collapsing in flames: *cum omnia sacra profanaque in igne considerent (Hist.* 3.33). See the *OLD,* s.v. *considere,* 5, 6.

Africanus' critics used when they called him the ridgepole or pinnacle *(columen)* at the city's peak.[42] According to Gracchus, Africanus is neither a permanent center of power nor Jupiter incarnate but a deteriorating reminder of his past self. The passage of time makes his return neither a victor's triumph over Romans nor the return of an outlaw dragged from his villa at the tribunes' bidding. Instead it is a refugee's flight to a sanctuary inviolate. Gracchus, then, by emphasizing Africanus' age and impotence, plays down any threat to tribunician authority that Africanus' absence might pose. His model of Rome shows how Africanus' enemies can accommodate Africanus in their worldview. It reconciles the opposing sides, not by making them forget their differences, but by exacting concessions from both.

When Gracchus draws attention to Africanus' age, he brings into play a new type of reciprocity between Africanus and Rome, one that appeases Africanus' enemies as well as his supporters.[43] Since Africanus has served Rome well, Rome should anticipate him once more, not by selecting him for office or command before the usual age, but by offering him protection of its own accord. Africanus may be permitted to remain in his citadel partly because old age itself is a privileged position. In allowing him to do so, the community, including the tribunes, will be displaying its magnanimity to a pensioner, rather than acceding to the demands of a powerful aristocrat. Better yet, this metaphorical citadel is one that Africanus cannot leave; it is not a center from which Africanus will radiate political power but a vanishing point into which he will disappear. Gracchus defends Africanus, but the world that his speech creates allows Africanus no role in public life.[44] After the speech, the narrative resumes, quite appropriately, with the words "From that time on there was silence about Africanus" *[silentium deinde de Africano fuit]* (38.53.7). No longer the subject of debate, Africanus lapses into obscurity. He lives out his life at Liternum with no longing for the city (*sine desiderio urbis,* 38.53.8), has his tomb built at Liternum, and dies there.

---

42. The word *columen* refers to the roof or summit of a building (see the *OLD*, s.v. *columen*) or to a ridgepole (Vitr. 4.7.5). Other figurative uses occur at 6.37.10 (where the consulship is called the *arx libertatis*, as well as a *columen*); Hor. *Carm.* 2.17.4 *(Maecenas, mearum grande decus columenque rerum);* and Cic. *Sest.* 19 *(columen rei publicae).*

43. See also 38.52.11, where Gracchus is reported to have said that it was a disgrace for such a man to have to stand below the rostra, but a particular disgrace for him to have to listen to the insults of adolescents.

44. Cf. Adam's discussion of this story as a reworking of the Oedipus myth, in *Tite-Live,* lxxxix.

After reporting his death, the narrator pronounces his obituary and, it seems, concludes the account of Africanus' life.

But Africanus' *animus maior* does not allow him to endure silence, especially from Livy. The narrative continues: after Africanus' death, his enemies' courage grows; the Petilii attack Lucius Scipio, and Africanus returns to the narrative, if only courtesy of a variant version of his brother's trial. This alternate account of the trial, in which Africanus defends his brother and Gracchus criticizes this defense, reverses both the sequence of events related in the first trial (Africanus') and the direction in which Africanus moves through Rome. To a reader imagining the Roman cityscape as a set of mnemonic loci, the second account represents a memory that runs counter to the first, for instead of leaving the city for the south to die at Liternum, Africanus, alive and well, abandons his post as legate in Etruria *(relicta legatione),* rushes into the Roman Forum, and assaults the bailiff and tribunes who have seized his brother. In this story, Africanus leads no unifying procession around the city. Instead he moves directly from Etruria to the city gate, then straight to the Forum and his brother's side *(cucurrise eum [Africanum] Romam, et cum a porta recte ad forum se contulisset . . . ,* 38.56.9). This invasion of the city by a man acting more loyally than civilly *(magis pie quam ciuiliter,* 38.56.9) stands in sharp contrast with the speech and ritual that united Rome in the previous account. Africanus does not evoke past glory, as he did when he spoke at his trial in the first version, nor does he triumph metaphorically, as he did when he led the tour of shrines. He intervenes physically, as he did when he saved his father at the Ticinus.

The two versions of the trials leave the reader with two images of Africanus, each supported by a different view of the city. The first shows Africanus uniting Rome and leaving when it becomes clear that his career is over. He convinces Romans to adopt, for a day, a worldview in which places have meaning only in relation to the gods. He leads a procession all around the city. The second tradition shows him valuing a family connection over the rules of civic life and rushing straight into the Forum to do so. When, in the second version, Gracchus rebukes Africanus for assaulting the tribunes (38.56.10–13), his words imply that Africanus has transgressed the boundaries of permissible behavior, because he can only transform the world so much. Africanus can conflate Forum and battlefield only metaphorically and only for an audience that is willing to accept his metaphors and look at the world, including Rome, from his point of view.[45] But this time Africanus has not erased distinctions in time and space by means of rhetoric and ritual; instead, as Gracchus points out, he has fallen away from his earlier standards of civil behavior *(quod degenerauerit tantum a se ipse,* 38.56.11). When Gracchus compares Africanus' previous moderate behavior to his present arrogance, he points to the statues Africanus refused, *in comitio, in rostris, in Capitolino, in cella Iouis,* as evidence of previous moderation (38.56.12–13). By referring to the absent monuments, Gracchus places Africanus' former *ciuilis habitus* in a historicized and monumentalized past.[46] The story of an Africanus so debased that he uses force against a magistrate temporarily disfigures the narrative, muddling the sequence of events.

Yet we can see patterns in these contradictory accounts. On the one hand, Africanus' worldview collapses distinctions in time or place. This works nicely in the first version, where it is limited to representation and metaphor: Africanus defends himself by speaking of his achievements as courageously as he accomplished them; the day of the trial happens to be the anniversary of Zama, so the past can live again in ritual. It does not work in the second version, where Africanus intervenes physically as if the Forum really were a battlefield. Gracchus' model of the Roman world, on the other hand, recognizes these distinctions, assumes that time brings permanent change (even Africanus will die, eventually), and includes compromise. As his worldview supersedes that of Africanus, one era ends and another begins. Perhaps the significant chronological question raised by the Scipios' trials is not about the year the trial took place,

---

45. This analysis of competing worldviews owes much in a general way to recent developments in discussions of Augustan art, architecture, and literature and of their impact on their audience (e.g., Zanker, *The Power of Images;* Wallace-Hadrill, *"Civilis Princeps";* and, most recently, K. Galinsky, *Augustan Culture: An Interpretive Approach* [Princeton, 1996]). The idea of planned "propaganda" imposed from above is gradually giving way to that of a more spontaneous dialogue between Augustus and the artists, writers, and architects of his era. Reviewing Zanker's study, Wallace-Hadrill ("Rome's Cultural Revolution," *JRS* 79 [1989]: 160) puts it nicely: "The ruler acts, restoring the *res publica* and adopting the pose of simple citizen, . . . injecting a new morality and religiosity. . . . Subject and artist respond spontaneously, answering modest restraint with veneration and imitation. Augustan values are absorbed without the full awareness of the participants as to what is going on." In the first account of the trial, Africanus behaves in an appropriate manner, announcing that he owes a debt of gratitude to the gods, and thus performing an act to which the people can respond "with veneration and imitation"; in this second version, however, he acts without even moderate restraint; consequently, Gracchus must correct him by pointing to his previous civility.

46. On denying commemoration as part of the *ciuilis habitus* of a *princeps,* see Wallace-Hadrill, *"Ciuilis Princeps,"* esp. his remarks about Africanus on 43.

nor about the year Africanus died, but about the moment when Tiberius Gracchus' model of Roman space took precedence over that of Africanus. Did it happen before or after Africanus left Rome?

At the end, the final anecdote about his daughter's engagement restores to the narrative an Africanus who acts recognizably but on a circumscribed scale.[47] The story of Cornelia's engagement transforms the variant version of the trials into a drama of succession (38.57.2–8). Richard Adam suggests that Gracchus is a double for Africanus and that Livy presents this story as recapitulation of the Oedipus myth.[48] Rome's various centers, personal, political, and topographical, all come together in this final anecdote. Africanus, who erases distinctions in his relationships by moving people from outer circles toward the center, does more than bring an outsider into the inner circle occupied by his immediate family. By marrying Gracchus to his daughter, he superimposes the great man of the next generation on himself. At the same time, Africanus, who is linked closely to the aristocratic center, the Capitoline, draws Gracchus to the center publicly as well as personally, by performing the engagement on the Capitoline at the Senate's request: *quibus ita inter publicum sollemne sponsalibus rite factis cum se domum recepisset . . .* (38.57.7). By describing the circumstances of the event in detail and mentioning Africanus' subsequent return to house and wife, Livy pointedly identifies the engagement as a public arrangement made in a public place.[49] The public nature of the event is confirmed by Aemilia's complaint that she was not consulted about her daughter's engagement. According to Aemilia, the marriage was arranged in the wrong sphere and by the wrong people: a decision traditionally made by both parents should not be made at a dinner of the Senate. Aemilia complains that Africanus has excluded her, that he has treated his daughter as if she were only his, not *communis* (shared) between mother and father. But Africanus' action makes sense from his idiosyncratic point of view: he actually has treated his daughter as if she were *communis*, but *communis* to him and the Senate. He has not excluded his wife from the decision; he has included the

47. See Adam, *Tite-Live*, 205–6, on the authenticity of this anecdote. He points out that it is a doublet for Plutarch's story about the younger Tiberius Gracchus.

48. See Adam, *Tite-Live*, lxxxviii–lxxxix.

49. *Quibus ita inter publicum sollemne sponsalibus rite factis cum se domum recepisset, Scipionem Aemiliae uxori dixisse filiam se minorem despondisse. Cum illa muliebriter indignabunda nihil de communi filia secum consultatum, adiecisset non si Ti. Graccho daret expertem consilii debuisse matrem esse, laetum Scipionem tam concordi iudicio ei ipsi desponsam respondisse* (38.57.7–8).

Senate. By engaging his daughter to Gracchus, Africanus has drawn together all his associations, personal, political, and topographical. He has made his political opponent into his future son-in-law; he has brought the entire political body into the domestic orbit occupied by his wife; he has even drawn together his house and the political and religious center of Rome.

Finally, this anecdote produces the narrative's third and most intimate expression of *concordia*. During his trial, Africanus united the Roman people in his own support. At that time, Gracchus' praise showed sympathy that was unexpected, coming as it did from a political opponent. The story of the engagement brings the account of Africanus' life to a close with one last expression of unexpected concord, this time between husband and wife. Like Africanus' procession to the Capitoline, which made the day of his trial almost more illustrious than that of his triumph, and like Gracchus' unexpected defense of Africanus and refusal to have his name put to the decree adjourning Africanus' trial, this example of unexpected concord is marked by hyperbole. Aemilia reproaches her husband: he should not have excluded her from the decision about their daughter's engagement, not even if he were to engage her to Tiberius Gracchus himself. Thus a third paradox marks a third example of Scipionic transcendence: on trial, Africanus triumphs; blamed, he is praised; having acted against his wife's wishes, he fulfills them perfectly. After this final example of concord arising from initial discord, Livy closes his account of Africanus' life.[50] The parallel progression of time and narrative resumes, Livy returns to Antias' version of the trials as if nothing has happened, and all signs of conflict in the sources have disappeared, not to resurface until the opening of Book 39.[51]

In the final segment of the trial narrative, Scipio Nasica and Gracchus use images of the Roman world to defend L. Scipio. They describe it in terms of center and periphery, but its center is no longer the Capitoline; it is the *carcer,* the prison below the hill. Scipio Nasica's speech presents L. Scipio's accomplishments as the capstone of an edifice of family achievement. It contrasts the vast, rich, and varied territory under Rome's control, whose boundaries the Scipios have expanded, with the narrow

---

50. *Haec de tanto uiro, quamquam et opinionibus et monumentis litterarum uariarent, proponenda erant* (38.57.8).

51. *Dum haec, si modo hoc anno acta sunt, Romae aguntur, consules ambo in Liguribus gerebant bellum* (39.1.1).

confines of the Roman prison.[52] Without indicating the reaction it pro-
voked, thus perhaps implying that it drew no response, Livy turns immediately from Nasica's speech to the praetor's verdict: L. Scipio must produce the money in question or go to prison. In his response to the verdict,
Gracchus uses Nasica's image of the Roman world selectively. Taking his
cue from both sides, he says that he will not prevent the collection of the
money from L. Scipio. But he also says that he will not allow the imprisonment, together with enemies of the Roman people, of a man who has
extended the limits of the empire and triumphed. Livy says that the audience was so pleased and approved of Gracchus' position so wholeheart-
edly that the judgment appeared scarcely to have been made in the same
state.[53] Although the concluding episode of L. Scipio's trial repeats the
familiar motif of discord transformed into concord, and although it is a
Scipio, Scipio Nasica, who speaks at length, it is once again Gracchus
who brings about the final settlement. He does so in his characteristic
manner, by reconciling claims of gratitude to those of accountability, and
by persuading his audience through compromise instead of charisma. It
is now Gracchus' skill at extending concessions to those on both sides of
the issue, rather than Africanus' knack for pulling them inward toward
himself, that holds the city together.

As one version of the trials follows the other (and despite the variant
version that obscures a clear picture of any unitary truth behind the stories), the reader experiences the repetition and the suspension of time that
characterized Africanus' temporary transformations of the city. Had
Africanus stayed in Rome, however, he would have found himself obliged
to wrangle with the tribunes and respond repeatedly to their trumped-up
charges. To defend himself, he would have had to invoke Zama over and
over, endlessly repeating and ultimately parodying himself, much as Marcus Manlius repeatedly invoked his rescue of the Capitoline. The narrative seems to suggest that in the end Africanus' burial place and the date
of his trial and death are not as meaningful as the replacement of his egocentric and transforming worldview with that of Gracchus the mediator.
At the end of Book 38, significant chronology resides in this sea change,
not in the transition to a new set of magistrates that marks out the annalist's years.

---

52. See 38.58.4–8. The text at 38.58.4 reads, *parentes suos et P. Africani ac L. Scipionis, qui in carcerem duceretur, fuisse Cn. et P. Scipiones, clarissimos uiros.* See also
38.59.10, 11: *in carcere . . . ante carcerem.*

53. *Tanto assensu auditum est decretum, adeo dimissum Scipionem laeti homines
viderunt, ut vix in eadem civitate uideretur factum iudicium* (38.60.7).

Rationem reddere

In what may be part of Africanus' epitaph, the poet Ennius writes:

> Hic est ille situs, cui nemo ciuis neque hostis
>   Quibit pro factis reddere opis pretium.
>
> (Epigrammata 3 Vahlen)

[Here he is buried, to whom no one, neither citizen nor foreigner, can give the value of his aid in recompense for his deeds.]

Whether or not Livy read these words on the tomb at Liternum, his account of the last days of Scipio Africanus is an ironic comment on the couplet, for unlike Ennius, Livy cannot with any confidence write of Africanus, "Here he is buried."[54] Although he might agree with Ennius that no one could fully repay Africanus for his service to the state, he might well add that this was because no one had any way of reckoning precisely how much Rome owed him. Livy's discussion of Africanus' death and possible burial sites may seem only loosely to associate the idea of burial with that of recompense, but, in fact, the metaphor of balancing accounts aptly symbolizes a narrative that begins with a request to render a fiscal account and constantly emphasizes the narrator's difficulty with rendering a historical account. As we have seen, any attempt to present a coherent narrative of Africanus' last days suffers from a surfeit of records that are flawed. Confronted with that paradoxical subject—the most memorable of Romans who is nonetheless the most difficult to preserve in a clear record—Livy demonstrates how the multiplication of monuments alters their bearing on historical facts. He also shows that Africanus himself is responsible for the problems with the material evidence. Livy orchestrates the confusion in his sources so as to make them illustrate just how difficult it is to account for Africanus, except on Africanus' own terms. In doing so, he rejects a straightforward presentation of the facts—he does not have them anyway—in favor of making his audience share his quandary by enlisting it as a companion in a direct encounter with Africanus' extraordinary behavior.

Livy's discussion of the problematic evidence lies between the two versions of the trials and falls into three parts: (1) previous histories with

---

54. On the tomb and Ennius' lines, see F. Coarelli, "Sepolcro degli Scipioni," *Dialoghi di archeologia* 6 (1972): 36–106, esp. 76.

attendant anecdotes; (2) previous histories, material evidence, and oral tradition; (3) original documents with the attendant written tradition. In the first, when Livy suggests that Valerius Antias has reported incorrect figures for the amounts of silver and gold received from Antiochus, he supports this point with a pair of anecdotes about Africanus.

> Has ego summas auri et argenti relatas apud Antiatem inueni. in L. Scipione malim equidem librarii mendum quam mendacium scriptoris esse in summa auri atque argenti: similius enim ueri est argenti quam auri maius pondus fuisse, et potius quadragiens quam ducentiens quadragiens litem aestimatam, eo magis quod tantae summae rationem etiam ab ipso P. Scipione requisitam esse in senatu tradunt, librumque rationis eius cum Lucium fratrem adferre iussisset, inspectante senatu suis ipsum manibus concerpsisse, indignantem quod cum bis milliens in aerarium intulisset, quadragiens ratio ab se posceretur. ab eadem fiducia animi, cum quaestores pecuniam ex aerario contra legem promere non auderent, claues poposcisse et se aperturum aerarium dixisse, qui ut clauderetur effecisset. (38.55.8–13)

> [These are the sums of gold and silver I found reported in Antias. In Lucius Scipio's case I should prefer to think it a mistake of the scribe rather than a falsehood of the writer. For it is more likely that the weight of silver was greater than that of gold and that the suit was for four million sesterces rather than twenty-four million. This is all the more likely because they say that an accounting for that very quantity was requested from Publius Scipio [Africanus] himself in the Senate and that when he had ordered his brother Lucius to bring the account book, with the Senate looking on, he tore it to pieces with his own hands, complaining that when he had brought two hundred million into the treasury, an account for four million was demanded of him. Because of this same self-confidence, when the clerks did not dare to take money from the treasury, since it was against the law, he demanded keys and said that he would open it, seeing that it was due to him that it was locked.]

Either Valerius Antias has reported an incorrect figure for the relative weights of gold and silver at issue in L. Scipio's trial, or a scribe has written the wrong numbers. As Luce has pointed out, Livy is kinder to Antias here than he is elsewhere.[55] He looks for other places to assign blame and considers scribal error more likely than deliberate falsification. Yet the anecdotes that follow include the one original reason for the problem: the destruction of the evidence by Africanus himself. Africanus tore apart the record books when asked to account for the very sum that Livy thinks is correct *(tantae summae)*. This anecdote, then, begins as evidence for a specific amount of money but changes in its course into a demonstration of Africanus' impatience at being held to the letter of the law, an attitude he feels is justified because of his tremendous service to the state. The anecdote concerning the keys to the treasury follows, not as additional evidence supporting or contradicting Antias' figures, but as a second illustration of Africanus' impatience with legalistic details. Emphasis moves from the precise sum of money *(eo magis quod* tantae summae . . .*)* to the same boldness of character *(ab* eadem fiducia *animi . . .).* In destroying the account books, Africanus changes the topic in question from compliance with specific laws to personal character. The piece of evidence Livy invokes to show that he is writing history more carefully than Antias shows Africanus tearing up the records for that very piece of evidence. The reader comes away from Livy's account with no better knowledge of the numbers but with two vivid illustrations of Africanus' indestructible *fiducia animi*. Hence Livy's uncharacteristic sympathy with Antias. The destruction of the evidence at the source, at the very point where, as information requested in the Senate, it becomes historical evidence, places both Livy and Antias in the same position. Even if Livy can overcome the problems posed by Antias and the hypothetical erring scribe, he will encounter an intransigent object of study, one who works at cross-purposes with anyone wanting a numerically precise account of numbers or an objective recital of the facts.[56] A perfectly accurate scribe

---

55. Cf. Polybius' criticism of Timaeus, who falsely accused Ephorus of a mistake in arithmetic when, according to Polybius, the problem was quite certainly one of scribal error (12.4a). On Polybius' polemics against Timaeus, see Sacks, *Polybius*, 21–78, esp. 66–78; Miles, *Reconstructing Early Rome*, 10–11.

56. Cf. Scipio's response to accusations in Polyb. 23.14.3: "he said that he ought not be criticized before the people, since it was to him they owed their freedom to speak at all." Polybius reports that when someone in the Senate demanded that Africanus give an account of money received from Antiochus, "Africanus answered that he had the account book but that he was not obliged to render an account to anyone." Polybius continues: "When the questioner pressed the issue and ordered him to bring it, he requested his brother to do so. When it was brought to him, he held it out and tore it to pieces as all [the Senate] looked on, then told the questioner to seek the account among the fragments. Then, he asked the Senate how it could demand an account of three thousand talents—how the money had

and a scrupulously honest annalist cannot compensate for Africanus' destruction of the documents.

In the second section of his discussion of problematic sources, Livy claims complete ignorance about the facts pertaining to Africanus' trial, death, and burial, and he calls on the duplicate grave monuments to support his claim. According to Livy, two places, Rome and Liternum, display Africanus' tomb. Accurate knowledge about the matter is impossible to come by, because the evidence has both multiplied and deteriorated: the statue at Liternum has toppled from its base, while the trio in Rome is only said to represent Africanus, his brother, and Ennius.[57]

> Multa alia in Scipionis exitu maxime uitae, dieque dicta, morte, funere, sepulcro, in diuersum trahunt, ut cui famae, quibus scriptis adsentiar non habeam. Non de accusatore conuenit: alii M. Naeuium, alii Petilios diem dixisse scribunt; non de tempore quo dicta dies sit, non de anno quo mortuus sit, non ubi mortuus aut elatus sit; alii Romae, alii Literni et mortuum et sepultum; utrobique monumenta ostenduntur et statuae; nam et Literni monumentum (monumentoque statua superimposita fuit, quam tempestate disiectam nuper uidimus ipsi), et Romae extra portam Capenam in Scipionum monumento tres statuae sunt, quarum duae P. et L. Scipionum dicuntur esse, tertia poetae Q. Ennii. (38.56.1–4)

> [Many other things, especially about the end of Scipio's life—his indictment, death, funeral, and tomb—contradict each other, so that I don't have any report or any written sources with which I might agree. There is no agreement about the accuser: some say that M. Naevius indicted him, others that it was the Petilii. And there is no agreement about the time when he was indicted, the year he died, or where he died or was carried out. Some say he died and was buried at Rome; others say Liternum. Monuments are pointed out in both places, and statues too, for at Liternum there is a mon-

---

been spent and by whom—and not ask by whose agency the fifteen thousand talents that they were receiving from Antiochus had come into the treasury or how they had become masters of Asia, Africa, and Spain" (23.14.7–11).

57. This was already tradition in Cicero's time: *carus fuit Africano superiori noster Ennius; itaque etiam in sepulcro Scipionum putatur is esse constitutus ex marmore* (*Arch.* 22).

ument, and there was a statue placed on top of the monument, which I myself recently saw, toppled over by a storm; and at Rome, outside the Porta Capena, in the tomb of the Scipios, there are three statues, two of which are said to be of P. and L. Scipio, the third of the poet Ennius.]

The breadth of uncertainty that Livy claims and the structure of the sentences in which he claims it distinguish this central passage from the first and third. With the words *multa alia,* Livy turns from questioning one detail, the numbers in Antias, to saying that he has no idea what sources he can believe for any of the basic facts about Africanus' trial, death, and burial. Livy lists the contested issues in the first sentence, then treats them one at a time, under their separate headings. His evidence falls into three categories, written documents *(scriptis),* oral tradition *(famae)* and first-hand experience *(uidimus ipsi).*

There is no point on which the sources agree. Livy says first that they draw the issues in opposite directions *(in diuersum trahunt).* The sentence that follows, with its antithetical cadence, aptly reflects this metaphor. Its many repetitions—for example, the repetition of *non de* and *alii;* the repetition of forms of the words *mortuus* (three times), *monumentum* (four times), and *statua* (three times); and the repetition of forms of *monumenta* and *statua* together (three times)—leave the reader with the impression that Livy is moving back and forth between sources placed before him. Moreover, by combining partial ignorance about separate events into one cumulative and striking expression of complete ignorance, Livy gives the impression that he does not know any of the basic facts of this episode; he does not know the "hard core," as A.J. Woodman calls it, the infrastructure of written history.[58] As far as the historian is concerned, the variant versions have diverged so much that they leave no trustworthy *monumenta* at all. The statuary *monumenta* that decorate Africanus' duplicate tombs do not provide the factual *monumenta* that the historian needs as the foundation of his account. They do not even represent such a "hard core" symbolically; rather they rep-

58. See the discussion of *De oratore* in Woodman, *Rhetoric in Classical Historiography,* 76–101. Livy may have in mind Cicero's comments on the bare-bones history of early Roman writers who followed the pattern of the *Annales Maximi: hanc similitudinem scribendi multi secuti sunt, qui sine ullis ornamentis monumenta solum temporum, hominum, locorum gestarumque rerum reliquerunt (De or. 2.53).*

resent the *absence* of such *monumenta,* for although the conflicting evidence suggests that Africanus is either here or there, there is no way to choose between them. And, as in the case of the figures for silver and gold, this dilemma too can be traced to an action of Africanus reported in the account of the trials: Livy says that Africanus, after leaving Rome, ordered his *monumentum* to be built at Liternum.[59]

In the third section of his excursus on evidence, Livy complains about contradictions in documentary sources. Discussion of these problems leads into the alternate version of the trials and then into the story of Cornelia's engagement.

> Nec inter scriptores rerum discrepat solum, sed orationes quoque, si modo ipsorum sunt quae feruntur, P. Scipionis et Ti. Gracchi abhorrent inter se. index orationis P. Scipionis nomen M. Naeui tribuni plebis habet, ipsa oratio sine nomine est accusatoris; modo nebulonem modo nugatorem appellat. ne Gracchi quidem oratio aut Petilliorum accusatorum Africani aut diei dicti Africano ullam mentionem habet. alia tota serenda fabula est Gracchi orationi conueniens, et illi auctores sequendi sunt qui cum L. Scipio et accusatus et damnatus sit pecuniae captae ab rege legatum in Etruria fuisse Africanum tradunt. . . . (38.56.5–8)

> [Not only is there a difference in what the writers say, but the speeches of Publius Scipio and Tiberius Gracchus contradict one another, if they are even genuine. The label of Publius Scipio's speech has the name of Marcus Naevius as the tribune of the plebs, but the speech itself does not name the accuser, instead calling him now "trifler" now "idler." Not even Gracchus' speech refers either to the Petilli, Africanus' accusers, or to the indictment of Africanus. Another story entirely must be stitched together to fit the speech of Gracchus, and those authorities are to be followed who say that when Lucius Scipio was both accused and condemned for money taken from the king, Africanus was a legate in Etruria. . . .]

Not only do the speeches of Africanus and Gracchus contradict each other, but their very authenticity is dubious. The *monumenta litterarum,*

---

59. *Vitam Literni egit sine desiderio urbis; morientem ruri eo ipso loco sepeliri se iussisse ferunt monumentumque ibi aedificari, ne funus sibi in ingrata patria fieret* (38.53.8).

like the statues, fail to provide the basic facts: the *oratio* of Africanus, if genuine, would have helped Livy assign a date to the trial, but it never mentions the accuser's name; the *index* to the speech has the name of the tribune M. Naevius, but it could be attached to the wrong speech. The only trustworthy information, then, is contained in the speech itself, and it too presents problems that can be traced to Africanus' actions elsewhere in the account of the trials. Livy says here that Africanus calls his opponent simply "trifler" *[nugatorem]* or "idler" *[nebulonem]*. In the first, Antian account, Livy describes Africanus' speech in defense of himself as one of the highlights of the trial, an *oratio magnifica,* whose particularly laudable feature was that Africanus made no mention of the charges against him (*sine ulla criminum mentione,* 38.50.11). Yet the very feature of Africanus' speech that Livy the narrator singles out for praise becomes a problem when Livy the historian consults the speech as a source for the trial. If, as Luce suggests, Livy added the first day of the trial to the account he found in Antias, he may have added the reference to Africanus giving such a speech on that first day. In fact, he may have added the first day for the sake of adding the speech.[60] For the speech allows Livy to illustrate more pointedly how Africanus' confidence in his past service to the state makes it impossible to write transparent narrative history about him: one finds unproblematic records of facts only in the lives of people who allow themselves to be held accountable. Once again Livy's statement of ignorance offers positive evidence for Africanus' willful behavior.

As we have seen, the extant speeches lead to completely different versions of the trial. In the first, Africanus enters the Forum, proceeds to the Capitoline, visits all the shrines and temples, then afterward leaves for the south to die at Liternum; according to the second, he returns to Rome from Etruria and rushes straight to the Forum to save his brother. Next, the anecdote about his daughter's engagement finds him back in his own house. The specific and familiar topographical references that provide such a vivid background for Africanus' actions lead the reader's imagination in opposite directions. In doing so they contribute to the impression that confusion entered into the events when they first occurred and that the original *auctor* of this confusion was the dramatic actor in this landscape, Africanus himself.

In sum, Livy's excursus on sources directs his audience's attention to

---

60. See Luce, *Livy,* 92 n. 30.

problems in the evidence that can be traced back to the actions of Africanus himself. The excursus shows clearly that the past can resist attempts to represent it. Livy compels his audience to share his frustration with this baffling evidence by making it share his vantage point in time and space *(nuper uidimus ipsi).* The sources are considered from the point of view of the investigating historian, a narrator who is therefore a traveler—at least to Liternum—and, for the moment, a character in the narrative. The shift in perspective, from that of an omniscient narrator telling of the distant past to that of the investigating historian reporting a recent firsthand experience, diminishes the distance in space and time that divides this narrator and his reader. The reader sees the tomb at Liternum with the narrator, and they waver together between the two *monumenta.* As reader and narrator see the monuments, both ask which is the real burial site.

Let us take a closer look at the monuments. Although not syntactically parallel, both relative clauses that describe the statues end with a writer at a grave, the historian in the first clause *(uidimus ipsi),* and the poet Ennius in the second *(tertia poetae Q. Ennii).* The description of the monuments, then, juxtaposes two images, that of the tomb at Liternum, with its sole statue knocked over and the historian contemplating it, and that of the tomb outside the Porta Capena at Rome, with its three standing figures. The picture appears slightly unbalanced, but not just because of the different numbers of statues. The phrase *uidimus ipsi,* which emphasizes the writer's role as eyewitness at Liternum, is more vivid than the verb *dicuntur,* by which Livy indicates that he is passing on information he has heard. *Vidimus ipsi* invites the reader to be an eyewitness too, to see in the mind's eye what the narrator saw. The scene before the tomb at Rome, in contrast, removes both reader and historian; it replaces eyewitness with oral tradition and includes the poet Ennius and both Scipio brothers instead. For the reader, then, the difference between the two tombs is the difference between seeing one toppled statue and hearing oral tradition about three. In addition, the tradition concerning the statues at Rome suggests that they commemorate the relationship between Ennius and the Scipios. According to Cicero, Ennius wrote the epic *Scipio* and received in turn a statue on the family tomb.[61] The monuments

---

61. Cic. *Arch.* 22. On Ennius, see E. Badian, "Ennius and His Friends," in *Ennius,* ed. O. Skutsch, *Entretiens Fondation Hardt,* vol. 17 (Geneva, 1971), 151–99; Skutsch, *The Annals of Quintus Ennius,* 1–7. The tomb of the Scipios is a particularly apt monument on which to focus a discussion of poetry. The *elogia* on the tomb (not attributed to Ennius)

as they appear in the text illustrate the contrast between Livy's immediate and present relationships with both reader and Africanus, on the one hand, and Ennius' past relationships with his patron and audience, on the other. Livy portrays Ennius in a static situation (as a statue on a monument) and himself in one that is in flux (as a visitor to a tomb), for he is still struggling with Africanus and the Africanus narrative even as the reader reads. The monument that commemorates Livy's relation with the Scipios is, appropriately enough, a *tableau vivant* composed of damaged evidence, investigating historian, and his companion, the reader.

Livy's emphasis on his role as a historian and his many references to the process of writing history suggest that we see these contrasting images—the historian standing before a broken piece of evidence, the poet monumentalized together with the subjects of his poetry—as a reminder of the difference between history and poetry. This is not the first time that Livy has defined his project by its relationship to epic.[62] Livy opens his preface with a partial hexameter, and at its end he talks of beginning his enterprise with a prayer, as poets do, although his comparison also draws attention to the difference between historians and poets: "we would invoke the gods *if it were* our practice, as it is for the poets *[si, ut poetis, nobis quoque mos esset]* . . ." (Pref. 13). Livy also says that he will neither defend nor refute the truth of stories about events that happened before the founding of the city, events "glorious because of poetic stories rather than intact reminders of achievements" *[poeticis magis decora fabulis quam incorruptis rerum gestarum monumentis]* (Pref. 6). As Ogilvie has observed, this statement does not mean simply that Livy will use the poets as sources; rather, it means that his attitude toward poetic sources will be neutral until he enters a period that offers him others.[63] Poetry is a natural precursor to history: not only did Homer precede Herodotus, but the historian uses poetic sources when he is writing about a period for which he has not yet got secure accounts—ideally, eyewitness reports—to use as evidence. In the early books, Livy's undertaking more closely resembles that of a poet, or, to define it negatively, it does not yet resemble that of a historian, which is to argue and refute.

Livy uses the two tombs of Africanus to define precisely the relation-

---

transformed Hellenistic epigram into a specifically Roman genre. See J. Van Sickle, "The Elogia of the Cornelii Scipiones and the Origins of Epigram at Rome," *AJP* 108 (1987): 41–55; idem, "The First Hellenistic Epigrams at Rome," *BICS* suppl. 51 (1988): 143–56.

62. On the ambiguity of historians' references to epic poetry and truth, see Moles, "Livy's Preface."

63. Ogilvie, 7.

ship to poetry and history of what he is accomplishing through his strange account of the Scipios' trials. The narrative places an extraordinary amount of emphasis on the narrator's identity as a historian, yet the very markers that label his activity as generically historical—the consideration of the numbers presented by the previous historian Antias, the visit to the tomb, the consultation of the speeches—all show that in this case the *monumenta* of history have failed to provide credible information; they are no longer *incorrupta rerum gestarum monumenta*. Here, as in the preface, poetry, represented by the statue of Ennius, serves as a marker for the absence of history, since the problematic evidence for Africanus' final days provides Livy with examples of deeds that are "glorious because of poetic stories rather than intact reminders of achievements." While Africanus has two monuments, neither points unequivocally to an independently existing past. One of the tombs must be empty, but no one knows which. Each has lost its ability to represent a solid fact, because there is an alternate tomb, because one has deteriorated physically, and because only oral tradition links the other to Africanus. The fragmented and multiplied *monumenta*, although they fail to give a clear picture of the past, show very clearly what the data look like without interpretation. If Livy did not follow one line of evidence, however skeptically, for a time, then he would have to write the entire account as he began it, using the construction *alii . . . alii*. The convoluted narrative relating the Scipios' trials represents not events as they happened but the confusion and superfluity of sources that exists before the historian sets out events in a straightforward, if selective, narrative. The two funerary *monumenta* stand for history that Livy has not yet written, or rather for what exists when the historian is not yet writing history, for they show him forever weighing the variant accounts but never deciding in favor of one or the other.[64] Africanus' willful behavior has an effect on the historian's research and composition that is as direct as his impact on his fellow Romans during his lifetime. He has overcome distinctions in space and time once again, for from a distance of two centuries he holds the narrating historian in suspense.

According to Livy's arguments, because one statue of Africanus has been knocked over by a storm, the historical evidence has deteriorated irreparably; and when the number of places that claim to hold a great man's tomb multiply, the tombs commemorate not a fact ("Africanus is

---

64. Luce (*Livy*, 102) writes, "History required a narrative of events, not an analysis of problems."

buried here") but a reputation. As Livy relates it, the body of literature, monuments, and rumor surrounding Africanus is a living and expanding tradition in which one anecdote leads to another and then another. Stories about Africanus may be of dubious facticity, but what is important is that they are recognizable by a set of generic features. All the stories about Africanus' last days generally lead to the Capitoline. In addition, the competing versions of the trial and their attendant anecdotes are variations of one plot: Africanus produces *concordia* between opposing forces, whether they are the popular and aristocratic factions in Rome, himself and Gracchus, or himself and his wife. Moreover, stories about Africanus consistently show him redefining a situation: he speaks of his accomplishments rather than of the charges against him; he leads a procession from the rostra to the Capitoline instead of pleading his case; he tears up the account books, and in doing so focuses attention on his service to the state; he treats his daughter's engagement as a public affair. Finally, Africanus provides the standard against which others are measured or measure themselves and against which he himself, finally, is measured.[65]

The two tombs, then, should not be considered simply as nutshells, one of which hides a fact. They are reminders that there are different ways to represent the past. When too many physical monuments testify to competing versions of the truth, the historian does not know which way to turn. The funerary *monumenta* demonstrate what happens when reminders fail, when one can't recognize Africanus in the monument at Rome and when the one at Liternum is broken. When *fabulae* and *opiniones* multiply, even if they vary, they preserve through their generic qualities the important features by which one can recognize Africanus. Yet, as Livy relates this story, he emphatically shows himself traveling, checking variants, and weighing two existing versions of the trial in his head. In citing the variants, in bringing all his problems with the evidence out into the open, in setting himself against Ennius and at a distance from him, in invoking poetry as a marker for the absence of history, Livy uses Africanus' two tombs to mark out the limits and the limitations of the historian's task.[66] The poet and the historian stand apart, with different

---

65. Aemilia's remark about T. Gracchus (*an si Ti. Graccho daret expertem consilii debuisse matrem esse*, 38.57.7) is the exception that proves the rule. Since, as Adam points out (*Tite-Live*, lxxxiv), this is a story of succession, the point where Gracchus receives Africanus' daughter is the one place where Africanus cannot be invoked as the best man at Rome.

66. For a similar opinion, see Miles, *Reconstructing Early Rome*, 59–61.

statues commemorating them: the statue that tradition said Africanus set up to Ennius, who was dear to him because of his commemorative poetry; and the toppled statue seen recently by the historian, who by the nature of his undertaking—annalistic, not contemporary, history—always arrives on the scene too late.

Stabiliora quaedam et uiridiora praemiorum genera

I have been arguing that the story of Africanus' last days is an account of Livy's attempt to treat a recalcitrant subject rather than a conventional historical narrative. As such it demonstrates a cunning way of compensating for Africanus' refusal to be measured by traditional standards and commemorated by traditional methods. A pair of metaphors associated with the Scipio family comes to mind. In the sixth book of Cicero's *De republica,* when Laelius complains that there are no statues in public places honoring Scipio Nasica for killing a tyrant, Scipio Aemilianus answers that the excellence of exceptional men seeks rewards more lasting and more eternal than statues and triumphs. He associates each of the impermanent awards with laurel or lead, materials subject to decay, then describes the preferred awards as greener and more stable than laurel wreaths or statues anchored in lead.[67] Thus begins the famous *Somnium Scipionis,* in which young Scipio Aemilianus confers with the ghost of Africanus, who is enjoying an afterlife in the Milky Way.

Thematic echoes of this passage are fairly obvious in Livy's account. Livy relates Africanus' downfall, not his triumph, but Africanus triumphs repeatedly in the narrative. When he reminds the assembled crowd that it is the anniversary of Zama, Africanus says, "on this day I fought well and with good results *[bene ac feliciter pugnaui]*" (38.51.7). These are the words with which a returning *imperator* introduces his request for a tri-

---

67. *Cum enim Laelius quereretur nullas Nasicae statuas in publico in interfecti tyranni remunerationem locatas, respondit Scipio post alia in haec verba: "Sed quamquam sapientibus conscientia ipsa factorum egregiorum amplissimum virtutis est praemium, tamen illa diuina uirtus non statuas plumbo inhaerentes nec triumphos arescentibus laureis, sed stabiliora quaedam et uiridiora praemiorum genera desiderat." Quae tandem ista sunt?" inquit Laelius. Tum Scipio: "Patimini me" inquit, "quoniam tertium iam diem feriati sumus, et cetera quibus ad narrationem somnii venit, docens illa esse stabiliora et viridiora praemiorum genera, quae ipse uidisset in caelo bonis rerum publicarum servata rectoribus.* (Macr. *in Somn. Scip.* 1.4.2).

umph.[68] That Manlius Vulso made this very point in the previous episode, when he argued for his own triumph, will not have escaped Livy's readers.[69] Africanus' impromptu procession to the Capitoline is a virtual triumph celebrated on the anniversary of Zama, and Livy takes care to see that this is not lost on his readers: "so far as the favor of men and the true measure of his greatness was concerned, that day was almost more celebrated than the day on which he entered the city triumphing over Syphax the king and the Carthaginians." The hostile tribunes claim that Scipio has celebrated a triumph over the Roman people. Even after Gracchus has pronounced his opinion, the idea of a triumph is still in the air: the Senate criticizes the Petilii for attempting to triumph over Africanus.[70]

Africanus' impromptu procession of thanksgiving (recast repeatedly as a metaphorical triumph), the toppled statue at the tomb, and the statues that were never set up all around the city suggest that the same metaphors that introduced the *Somnium* are operating here as well. Livy calls attention to his ignorance about the location of Africanus' mortal remains not only to show that it is hard to account for his trial and burial but also to argue that standard forms of commemoration are inadequate rewards for a man who in memorability can be compared only to himself.[71] Whatever Africanus does, including his actions in self-defense, becomes a virtual triumph. Even Gracchus' criticism of him is the eulogy, the *laudatio*, that we are told he did not receive after death (38.54.9). The very nonexistent statues of himself that he forbade to be set up on the

---

68. See H.S. Versnel, *Triumphus: An Inquiry into the Origin, Development, and Meaning of the Roman Triumph* (Leiden, 1970), 361. Africanus' metaphorical "triumph" is all the more meaningful because the years between Zama and Pydna are filled with frequent and ostentatious triumphs, some for quite dubious achievements, and several, like Manlius Vulso's, hotly contested. On the frequency of triumphs in this period, see J.S. Richardson "The Triumph, the Praetors, and the Senate in the Early Second Century B.C.," *JRS* 65 (1975): 50–63.

69. For Manlius' speech, see 38.48.14–16. Manlius speaks at such length that he apologizes for it, and the next day his relatives and friends exert the political pressure that secures him his triumph (38.49.13–50.3). On the debate, see Chaplin, "Livy's Use of Exempla," 113–14.

70. See 38.51.13, 52.5, 53.1–7.

71. *Uir memorabilis, bellicis tamen quam pacis artibus memorabilior. < . . . > prima pars uitae quam postrema fuit, quia in iuuenta bella adsidua gesta, cum senecta res quoque defloruere, nec praebita materia ingenio* (38.53.9). This is Livy's only use of *memorabilis* in the comparative degree. Cf. Livy on Cicero, who needed a Cicero to praise him (Sen. *Suas.* 6.21–22).

rostra and on the Capitoline are even more enduring, as reminders of his *civilis habitus,* than are the statues at his tombs.[72] Not meticulously kept accounts but the destruction of the account books, not a tomb but the confusion between two burial sites, not a story but the proliferation of anecdotes—all these problems for the historian ensure the continuation of Africanus' fame. The reader of this narrative, then, witnesses at firsthand the generation of a legend, with the suspension of *logos* and *ratio,* and with the growth of *mythos* and *fabula* in their place.

As a writer of history, Livy cannot create his *monumenta,* his "hard core" of fact; yet, working within the laws of his genre and pointing out that he upholds its standards, he can show how variant stories belong to the same genus and point to the same man. While specific *monumenta* commemorating particular events can deteriorate or point in the wrong direction, a consistently repeated motif can disclose a familiar general truth masquerading in an unfamiliar guise. Livy proposes such *ornamenta* as a solution to a problem intrinsic to ancient historiography, that of extracting general truths about the human condition from a mass of particulars.[73]

Livy intends his history to stimulate recognition of what is lost to Rome, both general and specific, through contemplation of what can be seen or, if not seen, then heard or felt. Standing in front of the tomb at Liternum, weighing the evidence, Livy abdicates responsibility for the *monumentum illustre* his reader must construct with his or her own *cognitio.* Since the *monumenta* fail, it falls to the reader to perceive how the *ornamenta* compensate, how they prove not that Africanus was tried but that the event was the talk of the town, not that he gave a speech but that everyone agreed that no one was ever more truly or better praised, not that he led a procession in thanksgiving but that tribunes and historians alike recast it as a triumph, not the date of the engagement but Aemilia's rebuke and Africanus' happiness at family concord. The narrative offers the reader the duplicate monuments, duplicate traditions, and duplicate speeches and leaves him or her to recognize the unchanging patterns in the anecdotes. Simply to see an *inlustre monumentum* occasionally does not suffice. One must move around the monument, viewing it from sev-

---

72. See Wallace-Hadrill, "*Civilis Princeps,*" 43.

73. On *ornamenta/monumenta,* see Woodman, *Rhetoric in Classical Historiography,* 83–95. Woodman (111 n. 106) illustrates the contrast with the Arch of Constantine as a *monumentum* and its reused reliefs and sculptures as *ornamenta.* Moles ("Truth and Untruth," 104) discusses this topic in relation to Thucydides.

eral angles. Africanus is best remembered for puzzles and paradoxes, for a comprehensive model of the *orbis terrarum,* and for his transformation of past and absent times and places into the here and now. The reader sees Africanus from several different perspectives, from that of Africanus himself, from those of his supporters and opponents, and from that of the investigating historian. Livy invites the reader to share several points of view as a way of ensuring that he or she does not forget the most extraordinary features of Africanus' character.[74]

In telling this obscure and convoluted story, Livy models his narrative on the response of another tactician who found a novel way of admitting defeat at Africanus' hands. When Africanus met Hannibal at Ephesus, he asked him who was the greatest general ever. "Alexander of Macedon," Hannibal replied. Asked who was the second greatest, he said, "Pyrrhus." In third place Hannibal unhesitatingly named himself. Africanus laughed at this and asked Hannibal what he would say if he (Hannibal) had beaten him. "Then," said Hannibal, "I would be greater than Alexander and Pyrrhus and all other generals." Africanus, says Livy, was pleased by the cleverness of the answer and by the unexpected praise, since Hannibal had removed him from the ordinary run of generals as if he were unmeasurable *(inaestimabilis).* Livy calls the answer "a response muddled with Punic wit" *[perplexum Punico astu responsum]* and an "unforeseen kind of affirmation" *[improuisum adsententionis genus].*[75]

The reader will recognize that the puzzling account of the trials is also an "unforeseen kind of affirmation," for it bears a generic resemblance to this anecdote. The trial narrative—an account of unexpected admiration from hostile sources, paradoxical conclusions, and commemoration and praise that appear in disguise—emphasizes the impossibility of measur-

---

74. Livy's vivid, if confusing, portrait of Africanus may be an attempt to avoid what T.P. Wiseman ("Lying Historians: Seven Types of Mendacity," in *Lies and Fiction in the Ancient World,* ed. C. Gill and T.P. Wiseman [Austin, Tex., 1993], 146) categorizes as the seventh kind of mendacity found in ancient historians, the absence of elaboration: "In rhetoric, *evidentia* meant 'vivid illustration'; in philosophical discourse, it meant 'self-evidence.' With *evidentia* there was no need for argument: you could simply *see* the thing was true. And you achieved that end by making explicit 'all the circumstances which it is reasonable to imagine must have occurred.' That is, the invention of circumstantial detail was a way to reach the truth."

75. *Et perplexum Punico astu responsum et improuisum adsentationis genus Scipionem mouisse, quod e grege se imperatorum uelut inaestimabilem secreuisset* (35.14.12). The entire episode is related in 35.14.5–12.

On *aestimare,* see Kraus, *Ab urbe condita Book VI,* 150. Kraus points out that it is a historian's word.

ing Africanus by ordinary means. Like Hannibal's, Livy's response to Africanus is *perplexum* (muddled), because Livy, like Hannibal, wants to show that it is impossible to account factually and logically for Africanus. Livy does not treat Africanus as a static object of historical study but instead answers the question of Africanus' memorability as if Africanus were posing it in person. Like Hannibal, Livy shows that he understands Africanus by presenting an image of the world that shows a paradoxical kind of concord despite its many and conflicting points of view. It is no wonder that the account of Africanus' last days, a narrative of events that Livy considered unimportant compared to those of Africanus' youth, is so irksome to the reader. Livy composed it as a response calculated to please an interlocutor who did not want a straight answer.

Conclusion

Facturusne operae pretium sim si a primordio urbis res populi
Romani perscripserim, nec satis scio nec, si sciam, dicere ausim
quippe qui cum ueterem tum uolgatam esse rem uideam, dum noui
semper scriptores aut in rebus certius aliquid allaturos se aut
scribendi arte rudem uetustatem superaturos credunt.

[Whether I shall accomplish anything worthwhile if I set down in
writing the achievements of the Roman people from the origin of
the city, I do not know, nor if I knew would I dare say, since I perceive that the matter is both old and well worn, while new writers
constantly believe that they will either bring more certainty in
regard to the facts or surpass crude antiquity with their skill in
writing.]

—Livy Pref. 1–2

In a famous passage at the beginning of the *Academica,* Cicero compli-
ments Varro on his *Antiquitates,* saying, "for your books have, as it were,
led us home, we who were strangers in our city and straying about like
foreigners, so that we might finally recognize who and where we are"
[*nam nos in nostra urbe peregrinantis errantisque tamquam hospites tui
libri quasi domum duxerunt, ut possemus aliquando qui et ubi essemus
agnoscere*] (1.9). Varro's aetiologies guide his readers to a greater understanding of their city by leading them to the explanations behind obscure
customs, institutions, and place-names. The reverse might be said of
Livy's history: the *Ab Urbe Condita* draws its audience away from the
objective world by making it an observer of and, to a degree, a partici-
pant in the world created by the text.[1]

---

1. Livy's creation of views "from the edge" and from outside may reflect the moral
advantages attributed to this position by other writers. On this idea in the *Timaeus,* see C.
Osborne, "Topography in the Timaeus: Plato and Augustine on Mankind's Place in the
Natural World," *PCPS,* n.s., 34 (1988): 104–14.

Livy presents episodes of Roman history in such a way that two things happen: first, the dynamic narrative produces a new perspective on events and on their sometimes familiar but usually abstracted setting; then, each reader's act of reading makes the meaning of the story complete. The account of the battle between the Romans and Sabines, for example, brings together the Temple of Jupiter Stator and the Lacus Curtius in the Forum valley. The monuments commemorate the episode by marking turning points in both the battle and the narrative. The reader's active attention to the movement in the account of the battle allows him or her to see what the Sabine women see, a clear picture of civil war, and to retain an impression of being drawn into this striking and memorable tableau. The story of Marcus Manlius encourages the reader to adopt increasingly distant points of view, even as Marcus Manlius presents the city more and more narrowly. This effect occurs also at the end of Book 25, where the narrative juxtaposes the Shield of Marcius and the artwork from Syracuse. The reader contemplating them is less aware of the distance between their locations in the objective city than of the differences in their representation. The exemplary account of Roman courage commemorated by the shield appears through the filter of the plundered art and allows the reader to see the morally intact past even from the vantage point of a troubled present. Finally, Livy causes the reader to share his perspective on the two tombs of Scipio Africanus and their broken, unidentifiable statues, in a way that conveys his own sense of futility in searching for factual truth among the variants.

We have seen that representations of particular places and monuments in Rome have social and political effects when they produce points of view or shifts in points of view, and that these points of view, in turn, influence the actions of various audiences within the narrative. Viewing the entire history as a metaphorical monument produces yet another set of vantage points, as the narrator and reader move together through, past, and around the history. From the very beginning of the *Ab Urbe Condita,* the narrator indicates that he occupies an ambiguous position in regard to his project. The indirect question that begins the preface, "whether I shall accomplish anything worthwhile," is contingent on his successfully carrying out the action of the conditional clause that follows, "if I set down in writing the achievements of the Roman people from the

On Livy's engagement of the reader, see J. Solodow, "Livy and the Story of Horatius," esp. 258–59.

origin of the city." *Perscribere,* "to set down in writing," is what the narrator must do before any reckoning of his accomplishment can be made. This verb, on which so much depends, deserves a closer look.

Livy uses it elsewhere in two ways. It describes the action of a person taking testimony or transcribing legal documents when that person merely records material for which he takes no authorial responsibility.[2] If we read the opening sentence with an eye to this act of simple transcription, then Livy stands outside his work. He intends merely to set down the *res gestae populi Romani* as he finds them in his sources, from the beginning of the history to the last event and the last word on the last papyrus roll.[3] This is the external point of view that Livy adopts when relating, for example, the account of the young Scipio saving his father. But the other uses of *perscribere* appear in passages where the narrator refers to his own act of writing, and they suggest a second way to interpret the sentence in the preface.[4] In these passages, Livy links the idea of recording Rome's history to the idea of traveling through that history: the author who has dared to say that he will record all Roman history *(perscribere)* is happy to have arrived at *(peruenisse)* the end of the Second Punic War (31.1.1); Greek affairs, which were not in themselves worth the narrator's while to record *(perscribere),* led him off course, as it were *(abstulere me uelut de spatio . . . ,* 35.40.1); the narrator says, in a passage that recalls the preface, that he cannot follow up *(persequi)* foreign wars, because to relate *(perscribere)* Roman achievements is enough of a burden for him to uphold (41.25.8).

The spatial connotations of *perscribere* in these passages suggest that the narrator intends to make his way through the *res gestae* of the Roman people to a time and place somewhere outside of and beyond them. Indeed, the verb puts a nice spin on Herodotus' definition of historiogra-

---

2. See Livy 21.49.6, 24.18.15, 27.5.10.

3. Moles ("Livy's Preface," 160) sees the use of *perscribere* as a challenge to Sallust's plan in the *Catilina* "to write the achievements of the Roman people selectively" *[res gestas populi Romani carptim perscribere]* (*Cat.* 4.2). According to Livy's usage, *carptim perscribere* would be an oxymoron.

4. Cf. *exitu aestatis eius qua haec gesta* perscripsimus. . . . (23.48.4); *me . . . iuuat* peruenisse. *nam etsi profiteri ausum* perscripturum *res omnes . . .* (31.1.2); *abstulere me uelut de spatio Graecae res immixtae Romanis, non quia ipsas operae pretium esset* perscribere . . . (35.40.1); *sed externorum inter se bella, qua quaeque modo gesta sint,* persequi *non operae satis est superque oneri sustinenti res a populo Romano gestas* perscribere (41.25.8).

On the parallel between the growth in the narrative and Rome's expansion, see Jaeger, "*Custodia Fidelis Memoriae,*" 352–53 n. 13; Kraus, "No Second Troy," 267–69. On movement in the preface, see Moles, "Livy's Preface," 148.

phy, which divides the craft into investigation *(historia)*—ideally through extensive travel—and the setting forth of what the historian has found *(apodeixis)*.[5] Livy's use of the verb *perscribere* encompasses both his personal inquiry as a metaphorical traveler through Roman history and his exposition of his research. The narrator stands outside the events he narrates; yet he also moves through the records of Roman history and sometimes loses his way among them. He is, in fact, exposing the history from the inside.[6] This double perspective is an important facet of the narrator's patriotic and hesitant persona. Livy intends to act on behalf of the state by writing his way from beginning to end and from end to beginning, from past to present and from present to past, from the city center to the frontiers of the Roman world and from the frontiers to the Capitoline. And he will do this for an empire that is always expanding.

In the preface, Livy speaks as a historian from a position somewhere between a lost past and an unknown future. It is an isolated position outside the narrative proper. In it, the historian speaks in his own present time. He directly confronts the reader, who is addressed in the second person *(te . . . intueri, inde tibi tuaeque rei publicae . . . ,* Pref. 10).[7] When Book 1 opens, the anticipation of the beginning *(ab initio . . . ordiendae rei; libentius inciperemus; orsis tantum operis . . . ,* Pref. 13) gives way to a declaration that the beginning is at hand *(iam primum omnium constat . . . ,* 1.1.1). First and second person give way to third, except in speeches and the occasional authorial aside. According to the historian, the here and now of the preface is not a desirable place to be, for the present is a time of crisis, a temporal dystopia as it were, both diseased and structurally unsound (Pref. 9).[8] Rome's resources cannot support its bulk *(eo creuerit ut iam magnitudine laboret sua,* Pref. 4); its past lies in shambles, and its future is bleak. Indeed, the historian, as he introduces a narrative that he has not yet begun and speaks from a vantage point that is inside

---

5. See Fornara, *The Nature of History,* 47.

6. According to Kraus ("No Second Troy," 268), the text is an object that "Livy simultaneously builds and traverses." On the monumental qualities suggested by the preface, see M.J. Wheeldon, " 'True Stories': The Reception of Historiography in Antiquity," in *History as Text,* ed. A. Cameron (London, 1989), 56. See also Moles, "Livy's Preface," 153–55, with references to earlier work.

7. On the attention Livy draws to himself in the first sentence, see Wheeldon, "True Stories," 56. Wheeldon points out that of the fourteen uses of first-person verbs in the preface, six are in the first sentence.

8. Moles ("Livy's Preface," 149) suggests that *incorruptis . . . monumentis* in Pref. 6 "anticipates both the medical imagery and the crucial historical and historiographical claims of sections 9–10."

the text yet still outside the story of Rome's past, occupies a position comparable to that of the Romans enclosed in their citadel during the Gallic sack. He too is *interclusus,* "shut away," within a limited situation. Past and future are lost territory that he hopes to reclaim by writing. His pessimism and alienation are understandable.[9]

Why is it so important to write on straight to the end? If we continue using the analogy between the preface and the besieged citadel, we can see that writing to the end is important for much the same reason that it was important to maintain contact between the besieged Capitoline and Veii in Book 5: to bring help from outside.[10] We have seen that in times of crisis, help comes from a person who treats the emergency with a degree of detachment. Sometimes this person is able to do so because he or she, like Camillus at Ardea or the Sabine women, is physically on the margins of events and enters the fray only at the critical moment (1.13.1, 5.49.1). But not everyone who acts with such detachment comes from a physically external position. Romulus, when he fights the Sabines, and Marcius, when he fends off the Carthaginians in Spain, find themselves at the very heart of a critical situation. Both men avert disaster, however, by setting the present, critical moment in a broader context and, at the same time, invoking outside help. Romulus' prayer joins past, present, and future as it calls on Jupiter's aid, while Marcius' speech gives the remnants of two armies a shared past and future by conjuring up the *imagines* of their dead generals. Both men construct their external rescuers: Romulus prays and acts as if *(uelut)* his prayers were answered; Marcius represents the soldiers' impulsive attack as a response to the goading of the dead Scipios (25.38.9). The *Ab Urbe Condita* thus schools its audience in the best way to meet a crisis: exemplary Romans view such situations with detachment, place events in context, and summon outside help even if they have to invent it. Adopting or creating detached and external points of view helps Romans recapture space and expand their territory.

The *Ab Urbe Condita* uses monuments, especially the missing, lost, or broken ones, to make its reader into a helpful viewer, one who looks on

---

9. On Livy's pessimism, see Moles, "Livy's Preface," 149; A.D. Leeman, *Orationis Ratio: The Stylistic Theories and Practice of the Roman Orators, Historians, and Philosophers,* 2 vols. (Amsterdam, 1963), 1:190–97; Solodow, "Livy and the Story of Horatius," 252 n. 3.

10. See 5.46.4–11. Moles ("Livy's Preface," 145) points out the analogy between the historian and the warriors about whom he writes: "Instead of achieving immortality through his immortal work, Livy runs the risk of achieving complete annihiliation through failure."

Roman history from the outside, but from a position on the very margin of events. The monuments offer direct but focalized views from present to past and draw the reader into the dynamic action of the story's plot, even as they make him or her acutely aware of the act of observing. The monuments, particularly the ones presented as troublesome, allow each reader to contribute to the meaning of the text through his or her own reconstructive effort, and they permit the narrator to step outside the narrative into the present to adjust the reader's point of view. The narrator and reader meet in a space created jointly by the papyrus roll, the structure of the narrative, and the references to the objective world.

By restoring lost, ruined, or decayed monuments within the text, Livy displays his own authority. He did not invent this practice: Cicero is adept at manipulating monuments in limited contexts.[11] Livy, however, is unique in that he incorporates them into a comprehensive history of the city. Livy shapes Rome's past as he shapes space, by altering the received tradition to fit a grand design. Where monuments break down and are restored, they lose authority as markers that point back to one authentic past, but they gain authority as witnesses to the irretrievable loss of the past as well as to the author's act of reconstruction. The reader who sees the monuments recognizes not just specific historical events and names but significant patterns as well, from which he or she gains insight into ways of thinking about the past. The famous incident concerning Cossus and the *spolia opima* is a case in point. The idea that those who restore *monumenta* reinterpret them is as much the point of the passage as is the technical argument concerning Cassius' eligibility for the honor. The narrative makes it clear that three *auctores* stand behind the *Ab Urbe Condita*'s story of Cossus: first Cossus himself, who is the *auctor pugnae;* then Augustus, who restored the Temple of Jupiter Feretrius, where the *spolia* were stored, and who is the *auctor templi;* and finally Livy himself, with his carefully expressed doubts and acknowledgments.[12] The reader sees clearly that reclaiming facts is impossible in this situation, for the person who restores has license to reinterpret. Livy grants authority to Augustus' reconstruction of the past yet makes it clear that it is a reconstruction and that he can claim the same authority in his written Rome.

---

11. E.g., he uses his destroyed house as a reminder of his distress and of Clodius' wrongdoing in *Dom.* 61–62, 100, 136, 146.

12. For a detailed analysis of the passage, see, most recently, Miles, *Reconstructing Early Rome,* 38–54; see also Fornara, *The Nature of History,* 74–75.

Livy's grand scheme runs parallel to developments in the physical city, for restoring and reconstructing monuments became one of Augustus' favored means of presenting important political ideas. We cannot know to what degree Livy drew his inspiration from the Augustan building program. The extent to which Augustus would alter the urban landscape using a coherent program of images was probably not apparent when Livy first began writing, and the loss of Livy's later books, especially those dealing with the first century B.C., leaves us with little indication of how he represented the city during the Augustan Age. We are left to speculate, for example, about whether or not Livy responded to the changing role of the Capitoline, as the Temple of Mars Ultor and the Augustan Forum took over its functions.[13]

Any discussion of Livy's attitude toward Augustus himself is also necessarily subject to debate, given the loss of the later books and the lack of concrete evidence about the relationship between the two men.[14] We are left to infer what Livy thought about Augustus from what Livy wrote about other great Romans.[15] From the portraits of Romulus, Camillus, Marcus Manlius, Lucius Marcius, and Africanus, it appears that Livy welcomes Augustus as the *uir unus* who can restore the state; but the entire surviving narrative also makes it clear that in the crises of Roman history, whether the city is under attack or a camp is surrounded, the *uir unus* is a paradox, for he does not act alone except at the moment when he flares forth in contrast to those around him. Seen from the detached and comprehensive point of view that Livy encourages his reader to take, the man who saves the state always does so with help from outside. Marcus Manlius and Camillus complement each other spatially. The story of

13. T.J. Luce ("Livy, Augustus, and the Forum Augustum," in *Between Republic and Empire: Interpretations of Augustus and His Principate,* ed. K.A. Raaflaub and M. Toher [Berkeley and Los Angeles, 1990], 123–38) discusses the possible influence of the *Ab Urbe Condita* on the *elogia* of the Augustan Forum. He concludes (137–38) that Livy's history probably did not suggest the figures represented in the Forum and that the marked differences between Livy and the information on the fragments suggests that Livy's version of history was treated by the composers of the *elogia* "with calculated indifference."

14. J. Deininger ("Livius und der Prinzipat," *Klio* 67 [1985], 265–66) sums up the positions taken by previous scholars and points out the difficulty of assessing Livy's view of the principate.

15. Camillus and Romulus supply the most parallels. For discussion, see J. Hellegouarc'h, "Le Principat de Camille," *REL* 48 (1970): 112–32; R. Syme, "Livy and Augustus," *HSCP* 64 (1959): 27–87, esp. 48 and 55. Miles (*Reconstructing Early Rome,* 75–109) explores this line of interpretation fruitfully in his discussion of Camillus and cycles of Roman history in the first pentad.

Marcus Manlius offers a negative exemplum of the *uir unus* who refuses to place himself in a larger context. And even Camillus, who qualifies to be titled *uir unus* if anyone does, directs attention away from himself toward the city he saved, discourages emigration to Veii, the *monumentum gloriae suae,* and involves himself in wars of expansion outside of Rome. Lucius Marcius could not have saved affairs in Spain without the training and the examples of the Scipios. Africanus may have received the most glory for winning the Second Punic War, but Livy emphasizes the specificity of this accomplishment both when he introduces Africanus and when he makes his final assessment of his life.

As Livy says, his *monumentum* is a context for exempla (Pref. 10). His understanding of the historicized past as significant space influences the way he reconstructs it in narrative. The history calls out for the help of the *uir unus,* but anyone who stands back from the *monumentum* can see that the *uir unus,* paradoxically, is the product of others and is most influential for his effect on the people around him.

The narrator of the preface intends to write Roman history from its beginning to the present and at the same time to overcome the intermediary nature of the *monumentum* that typically recalls the absent dead to the passerby. The *monumenta* in the narrative demonstrate with particular clarity how well Livy achieves this goal. They engage the reader in reconstructing the past, so that he or she receives the impression not of viewing an inert statue but of encountering Africanus directly, not of passing figures and words carved in static stone but of witnessing in person the shaping of the inchoate city by the Forum battle. The various *monumenta* make the *Ab Urbe Condita* the most attractive of all the *monumenta* that compete for attention by summoning the traveler to "stop and read me" *[asta ac pellege].*[16] And they persuade the reader hurrying toward contemporary times (*festinantes ad haec noua,* Pref. 4) to move slowly through this written city and to learn from its stories.

---

16. *CIL* 1.2.1211. Cf. the throng of *monumenta* outside the gates at Syracuse (Cic. *Tusc.* 5.65.1). On the attention-getting devices of inscriptions, see Lattimore, *Themes in Greek and Latin Epitaphs,* 230–37; Häusle, *Das Denkmal als Garant des Nachruhms,* 41–63; Davis, "Epitaphs and the Memory."

Bibliography

Citations of Livy are from the Oxford Classical Text series for Books 1–10 and 21–30, and from the Teubner series for Books 30–45.

T. Livius, *Ab Urbe Condita.* Vol. 1. Ed. R.S. Conway and C.F. Walters. Oxford, 1914.

Titi Livi Ab Urbe Condita: Libri I–V. Ed. R.M. Ogilvie. Oxford, 1974.

Titi Livi Ab Urbe Condita: Libri VI–X. Ed. C.F. Walters and R.S. Conway. Oxford, 1919.

Titi Livi Ab Urbe Condita: Libri, XXI–XXV. Ed. C.F. Walters and R.S. Conway. Oxford, 1929.

Titi Livi Ab Urbe Condita: Libri XXVI–XXX. Ed.. R.S. Conway and S.K. Johnson. Oxford, 1935.

Titi Livi Ab Urbe Condita: Libri XXXI–XL. 2 vols. Ed. J. Briscoe. Stuttgart, 1991.

Titi Livi Ab Urbe Condita: Libri XLI–XLV. Ed. J. Briscoe. Stuttgart, 1986.

Adam, R., ed. *Tite-Live, Histoire romaine.* Vol. 28. Budé series. Paris, 1982.

Badian, E. "The Early Historians." In *Latin Historians,* ed. T.A. Dorey, 1–38. New York, 1966.

———. "Ennius and His Friends." In *Ennius,* ed. O. Skutsch, *Entretiens Fondation Hardt,* vol. 17, 151–99. Geneva, 1971.

———. "Livy and Augustus." *Xenia* 31 (1993): 9–38.

Bal, M. "The Narrating and the Focalizing: A Theory of the Agents in Narrative." *Style* 17 (1983): 234–69. Originally published as "Narration et focalisation," in *Narratologie: Essais sur la signification narrative dans quatre romans modernes,* 21–55 (Paris, 1977).

Bann, S. "Analysing the Discourse of History." *Dalhousie Review* 64, no. 2 (1984): 376–400.

Bayet, J., ed. *Tite-Live, Histoire romaine.* 2d ed. Vol. 1. Budé series. Paris, 1985.

———. *Tite-Live, Histoire romaine.* 2d ed. Vol. 6. Budé series. Paris, 1989.

Béranger, J. *Recherches sur l'aspect idéologique du Principat.* Basel, 1953.

Bettini, M. *Anthropology and Roman Culture.* Trans. J. Van Sickle. Baltimore, 1991.

Blum, H. *Antike Mnemotechnik.* Hildesheim and New York, 1969.

Borgeaud, P. "Du mythe à l'idéologie: La tête du Capitole." *MH* 44 (1987): 86–100.

Bourdieu, P. *Language and Symbolic Power.* Trans. G. Raymond and M. Adamson. Cambridge, Mass., 1991.

Bréguet, E. "*Urbi et orbi:* Un cliché et un thème." In *Hommages à Marcel Renard,* ed. J. Bibauw, 1:140–52. Brussels, 1969.

Briscoe, J. "The First Decade." In *Livy,* ed. T.A. Dorey, 1–20. London, 1971.

———. *A Commentary on Livy Books XXXIV–XXXVII.* Oxford, 1989.

———. *A Commentary on Livy Books XXXI–XXXIII.* Oxford, 1981.

———. "Livy and Polybius." *Xenia* 31 (1993): 39–52.

———, ed. *Titi Livi Ab urbe condita libri XLI–XLV.* Stuttgart, 1986.

Burck, E. *Einführung in die Dritte Dekade des Livius.* Heidelberg, 1950.

———. *Die Erzählungskunst des T. Livius.* Berlin, 1934. Reprint, Berlin and Zurich, 1964.

———. "Aktuelle Probleme der Livius-Interpretationen." *Gymnasium* 4 (1964): 22–30, 41–45. Reprinted as "Die Gestalt des Camillus," in *Wege zu Livius,* ed. E. Burck (Darmstadt, 1967), 310–28.

———. "Das Bild der Revolution bei römischen Historikern." *Gymnasium* 73 (1966): 86–109.

———. *Vom Menschenbild in der romischen Literatur: Ausgewahlte Schriften.* Ed. Eckard Lefevre. 2 vols. Heidelberg, 1966, 1981.

———. "The Third Decade." In *Livy,* ed. T.A. Dorey, 21–46. London, 1971.

Cameron, A., ed. *History as Text.* London, 1989.

Cancik, H. "Rome as Sacred Landscape and the End of Republican Religion in Rome." *Visible Religion: Annual for Religious Iconography* 4 (1985): 250–65.

Carawan, E.M. "The Tragic History of Marcellus and Livy's Characterization." *CJ* 80 (1984–85): 131–41.

Ceauşescu, P. "*Altera Roma:* Histoire d'une folie politique." *Historia* 25 (1976): 79–108.

Chaplin, J.D. "Livy's Use of Exempla and the Lessons of the Past." Ph.D. diss., Princeton University, 1993.

Chausserie-Laprée, J.-P. *L'Expression narrative chez les historiens latins.* Paris, 1969.

Coarelli, F. "Sepolcro degli Scipioni." *Dialoghi di archeologia* 6 (1972): 36–106.

———. "Public Building in Rome between the Second Punic War and Sulla." *PBSR* 45 (1977): 1–23.

———. *Il Foro Romano.* 2 vols. Rome, 1983, 1985.

Cobet, J. "Herodotus and Thucydides on War." In *Past Perspectives: Studies in Greek and Roman Historical Writing,* ed. I.S. Moxon, J.D. Smart, and A.J. Woodman, 1–18. Cambridge, 1986.

Cornell, T.J. "The Annals of Quintus Ennius." *JRS* 76 (1986): 244–50.

Courtney, E. *The Fragmentary Latin Poets.* Oxford, 1993.

Daube, D. "Withdrawal: Five Verbs." *CA* 7 (1974): 93–112.

David, J.-M. "Du *Comitium* à la roche Tarpéienne." In *Du Chatiment dans la Cité,* 131–75. Rome, 1984.

Davidson, J. "The Gaze in Polybius' Histories." *JRS* 81 (1991): 10–24.

Davis, H.H. "Epitaphs and the Memory." *CQ* 53 (1958): 169–76.

Deininger, J. "Livius und der Prinzipat." *Klio* 67 (1985): 265–72.

de Romilly, J. *The Rise and Fall of States according to Greek Authors.* Ann Arbor, 1977.

De Sanctis, G. *Storia Dei Romani.* 4 vols. Turin, 1907–23.

Dorey, T.A. *Latin Historians.* New York, 1966.

———, ed. *Livy.* London, 1971.

Ducos, M. "Les passions, les hommes et l'histoire dans l'oeuvre de Tite-Live." *REL* 65 (1987): 132–47.

Dunkle, J.R. "The Rhetorical Tyrant in Roman Historiography." *CW* 65 (1971): 12–20.

Dutoit, E. "Tite-Live s'est-il intéressé à la médicine?" *MH* 5 (1948): 116–23

———. "*Unicus, unice* chez Tite-Live." *Latomus* 15, no. 4 (1956): 481–88.

Eder, W. "Augustus and the Power of Tradition: The Augustan Principate as Binding Link between Republic and Empire." In *Between Republic and Empire: Interpretations of Augustus and His Principate,* ed. K.A. Raaflaub and M. Toher, 71–122. Berkeley and Los Angeles, 1990.

Encyclopedia of Contemporary Literary Theory. Ed. Irena R. Makaryk. Toronto, 1993.

Fabre, P. "'*Minime Romano sacro*': Note sur un passage de Tite-Live et les sacrifices humains dans la religion romaine." *REA* 42 (1942): 419–24.

Favro, D. "Reading the Augustan City." In *Narrative and Event in Ancient Art,* ed. Peter J. Holliday, 230–57. Cambridge, 1993.

Feldherr, A.M. "Spectacle and Society in Livy's History." Ph.D. diss., University of California, Berkeley, 1991.

———. "*Caeci Avaritia*: Avarice, History, and Vision in Livy V." Paper presented at the annual meeting of the American Philological Association, Atlanta, Ga., 1994.

Fentress, J., and C. Wickham. *Social Memory.* Oxford and Cambridge, Mass., 1992.

Fornara, C.W. *The Nature of History in Ancient Greece and Rome.* Berkeley and Los Angeles, 1983.

Fraccaro, P. "I processi degli Scipione." *Studi Storici per l'Antichità Classica* 4 (1911): 217–414. Reprinted in *Opuscula Archaeologica* 1 (Pavia, 1956), 263–392.

Frier, B. *Libri Annales Pontificum Maximorum: The Origins of the Annalistic Tradition.* Papers and Monographs of the American Academy in Rome, vol. 27. Rome, 1979.

Fussell, P. *The Great War and Modern Memory.* Oxford, 1975.

Gabba, E. "True History and False History in Classical Antiquity." *JRS* 71 (1981): 50–62.

Galinsky, K. *Augustan Culture: An Interpretive Approach.* Princeton, 1996.

Genette, G. "Boundaries of Narrative." Trans. A. Levonas. *New Literary History* 8 (1976): 1–13.

———. *Narrative Discourse: An Essay in Method.* Trans. J.E. Lewin. Ithaca, 1980. Originally published as *Figures III* (Paris, 1972).

Gerschel, L. "Saliens de Mars et Saliens de Quirinus." *RHR* 138 (1950): 145–51.

Girod, M.R. "La Géographie de Tite-Live." *ANRW* II.30.2 (1982): 1190–1229.

Griffe, M. "L'Espace de Rome dans le Livre I de l'Histoire de Tite-Live." In *Arts et Légendes d'Espaces: Figures du Voyage et rhétoriques du Monde. Communications Réunies et Présentées par Christian Jacob et Frank Lestringant*, 111–22. Paris, 1981.

Gros, P. *Aurea Templa: Recherches sur l'architecture religieuse de Rome à l'époque d'Auguste*. Rome, 1976.

———. *Architecture et société à Rome et en Italie centro-méridionale aux deux derniers siècles de la République*. Brussels, 1978.

———. "Les statues de Syracuse et les 'dieux' de Tarent." *REL* 57 (1979): 85–114.

Gruen, E.S. *Culture and National Identity in Republican Rome*. Ithaca, 1992.

Habinek, T. "Seneca's Circles: *Ep.* 12.6–9." *CA* 1 (1982): 66–69.

Haehling, R. von. *Zeitbezuge des T. Livius in der ersten Dekade seines Geschischtswerkes: Nec vitia nostra nec remedia pati possumus*. Stuttgart, 1989.

Häusle, H. *Das Denkmal als Garant des Nachruhms: Eine Studie zu einem Motiv in lateinischer Inschriften*. Zetemata no. 75. Munich, 1980.

Haywood, R.M. *Studies on Scipio Africanus*. Johns Hopkins University Studies in Historical and Political Science, vol. 51, no. 1, 1–114. Baltimore, 1933.

Hellegouarc'h, J. *Le vocabulaire latin des relations et des partis politiques sous la Republique*. Paris, 1963.

———. "Le Principat de Camille." *REL* 48 (1970): 112–32.

Hemker, J. "Rape and the Founding of Rome." *Helios,* n.s., 12 (1985): 41–47.

Henderson, J. "Livy and the Invention of History." In *History as Text,* ed. Averil Cameron, 64–85. London, 1989.

Hoffmann, W. *Livius und der zweite punische Krieg*. Leipzig, 1942.

Horsfall, N. "From History to Legend: M. Manlius and the Geese." *CJ* 76 (1980–81): 298–311.

———. "Illusion and Reality in Latin Topographical Writing." *G&R* 32, no. 2 (1985): 197–208.

Immerwahr, H. "*Ergon:* History as a Monument in Herodotus and Thucydides." *AJP* 81 (1960): 261–90.

Jaeger, M. "*Custodia Fidelis Memoriae:* Livy's Story of M. Manlius Capitolinus." *Latomus* 52, no. 2 (1993): 350–63.

———. "Reconstructing Rome: The Campus Martius and Horace, *Ode* 1.8." *Arethusa* 28, nos. 2–3 (1995): 177–91.

Joshel, S.R. "The Body Female and the Body Politic: Livy's Lucretia and Verginia." In *Pornography and Representation in Greece and Rome,* ed. A. Richlin, 112–30. Oxford, 1992.

Kahn, M. "Stone-Faced Ancestors: The Spatial Anchoring of Myth in Wamira, Papua New Guinea." *Ethnology* 29 (1990): 50–66.

Kajanto, I. *God and Fate in Livy*. Annales Universitatis Turkensis, vol. 64. Turku, 1957.

Kissel, W. "Livius, 1933–1978: Eine Gesamtbibliographie." *ANRW* II.30.2 (1982): 899–997.

Klotz, A. *Livius und seine Vorgänger.* Leipzig and Berlin, 1941. Reprint, Amsterdam, 1964.

Konstan, D. "Narrative and Ideology in Livy: Book I." *CA* 5 (1986): 198–215.

Kraus, C.S. *Ab urbe condita Book VI.* Cambridge, 1994.

———. "No Second Troy: Topoi and Refoundation in Livy, Book V." *TAPA* 124 (1994): 267–89.

Kuttner, A. "Some New Grounds for Narrative." In *Narrative and Event in Ancient Art,* ed. Peter J. Holliday, 198–229. Cambridge, 1993.

Laistner, M.L.W. *The Greater Roman Historians.* Berkeley and Los Angeles, 1947.

Lajar-Burcharth, E. "David's Sabine Women: Body, Gender, and Republican Culture under the Directory." *Art History* 14, no. 3 (1991): 397–430.

Lattimore, R. *Themes in Greek and Latin Epitaphs.* Urbana, 1948.

Leach, E.W. *The Rhetoric of Space: Literary and Artistic Representations of Landscape in Republican and Augustan Rome.* Princeton, 1988.

Leeman, A.D. *Orationis Ratio: The Stylistic Theories and Practice of the Roman Orators, Historians, and Philosophers.* 2 vols. Amsterdam, 1963.

Le Gall, J. *Le Tibre, fleuve de Rome dans l'antiquité.* Paris, 1953.

Levene, D.S. *Religion in Livy.* Leiden, 1993.

Liebeschuetz, W. "The Religious Position of Livy's History." *JRS* 57 (1967): 45–55.

———. *Continuity and Change in Roman Religion.* Oxford, 1979.

Linderski, J. "Roman Religion in Livy." *Xenia* 31 (1993): 53–70.

Lintott, A.W. "The Tradition of Violence in the Annals of the Early Roman Republic." *Historia* 19 (1968): 12–29.

———. "Imperial Expansion and Moral Decline in the Roman Republic." *Historia* 21 (1972): 626–38.

Lipovsky, J. *A Historiographical Study of Livy: Books IV–X.* New York, 1981.

Long, A.A., and D.N. Sedley, eds. *The Hellenistic Philosophers.* 2 vols. Cambridge, 1987.

Lowenthal, D. "Past Time, Present Place: Landscape and Memory." *Geographical Review* 65 (1975): 1–36.

———. *The Past Is a Foreign Country.* Cambridge, 1985.

Luce, T.J. "The Dating of Livy's First Decade." *TAPA* 96 (1965): 209–40.

———. "Design and Structure in Livy: 5.32–55." *TAPA* 102 (1971): 265–302.

———. *Livy: The Composition of His History.* Princeton, 1977.

———. "Livy, Augustus, and the Forum Augustum." In *Between Republic and Empire: Interpretations of Augustus and His Principate,* ed. K.A. Raaflaub and M. Toher, 123–38. Berkeley and Los Angeles, 1990

———. "Structure in Livy's Speeches." *Xenia.* 31 (1993): 71–88.

MacCormack, S. "*Loca Sancta:* The Organization of Sacred Topography in Late Antiquity." In *The Blessings of Pilgrimage,* ed. R. Ousterhout, 7–40. Urbana, 1990.

MacMullen, R. "Hellenizing the Romans (2nd Century B.C.)." *Historia* 40 (1991): 419–38.

Magdelain, A. "Le Pomerium Archaïque et le Mundus." *REL* 54 (1976): 71–109.

McDonald, A.H. "The Style of Livy." *JRS* 47 (1957): 155–72.

Mette, H.J. "Livius und Augustus." *Gymnasium* 68 (1961): 269–85.

Miles, G. "The Cycle of Roman History in Livy's First Pentad." *AJP* 107 (1986): 1–33.

———. "*Maiores, Conditores,* and Livy's Perspective on the Past." *TAPA* 118 (1988): 185–208.

———. "The First Roman Marriage and the Theft of the Sabine Women." In *Innovations of Antiquity,* ed. Ralph Hexter and Daniel Selden, 161–96. New York, 1992.

———. *Reconstructing Early Rome.* Ithaca, 1995.

Miller, J.F. "Ovidian Allusion and the Vocabulary of Memory." *MD* 30 (1993): 153–64.

Moles, J.L. "Livy's Preface. " *PCPS,* n.s., 39 (1993): 141–68.

———. "Truth and Untruth in Herodotus and Thucydides." In *Lies and Fiction in the Ancient World,* ed. C. Gill and T.P. Wiseman, 88–121. Austin, Tex., 1993.

Momigliano, A. "Camillus and Concord." *CQ* 36 (1942): 111–20.

Mommsen, T. "Sp. Cassius, M. Manlius, Sp. Maelius, die drei Demagogen der älteren republikanischen Zeit." In *Römische Forschungen* 2:153–220. Berlin, 1879.

Monmonier, M. *How to Lie with Maps.* Chicago, 1991.

Moore, T. *Artistry and Ideology: Livy's Vocabulary of Virtue.* Frankfurt, 1989.

Morello, M-R. "*Ars Imperatoria:* Three Studies of Leadership in Livy's Second Pentad." Ph.D. diss., Cornell University, Ithaca, 1996.

Nash, E. *Pictorial Dictionary of Ancient Rome.* 2 vols. London, 1968.

Nicolet, C. *Space, Geography, and Politics in the Early Roman Empire.* Ann Arbor, 1991.

Nicolet-Croizat, F., ed. *Tite-Live, Histoire romaine.* Vol. 15. Budé series. Paris, 1992.

Nissen, H. *Kritische Untersuchungen über die Quellen der vierten und fünften Dekade des Livius.* Berlin, 1863.

Ogilvie, R.M., ed. *A Commentary on Livy, Books I–V.* Oxford, 1965.

———. "Livy." In *The Cambridge History of Classical Literature,* ed. E.J. Kenney and W.V. Clausen, 2:162–70. Cambridge, 1982.

Osborne, C. "Topography in the *Timaeus:* Plato and Augustine on Mankind's Place in the Natural World." *PCPS,* n.s., 34 (1988): 104–14.

Packard, D.W. *A Concordance to Livy.* 4 vols. Cambridge, Mass., 1968.

Pagnon, B. "Le recit de l'expedition de Cn. Manlius Vulso contre les Gallo-Grecs et de ses prolongements dans le livre 38 de Tite-Live." *LEC* 50 (1982): 115–28.

Panitschek, P. "Sp. Cassius, Sp. Maelius, M. Manlius als *exempla maiorum.*" *Philologus* 133 (1989): 231–45.

Pape, M. *Griechische Kunstwerke aus Kriegsbeute und ihre öffentliche Augstellung in Rome.* Hamburg, 1975.

Paschoud, F. "Refléxions sur quelques aspects de l'idéologie patriotique romaine de Tite-Live." *Xenia* 31 (1993): 125–49.

Patterson, J. "The City of Rome: From Republic to Empire." *JRS* 82 (1992): 186–215.

Paul, G.M. "*Urbs Capta:* Sketch of an Ancient Literary Motif." *Phoenix* 36 (1982): 144–55.

Pauw, D.A. "The Dramatic Elements in Livy's History." *Acta Classica* 34 (1991): 33–49.

Peter, H. *Die Quellen Plutarch in den Biographieen der Romer.* Amsterdam, 1965.

Petzold, K. "Zur Geschichte der römischen Annalistik." *Xenia* 31 (1993): 151–88.

Phillips, J.E. "Form and Language in Livy's Triumph Notices." *CP* 69, no. 4 (1974): 265–73.

———. "Current Research in Livy's First Decade, 1959–1979." *ANRW* II.30.2 (1982): 998–1057.

Pinsent, J. "Livy 6.3.1 *(caput rei Romanae):* Some Ennian Echoes in Livy." *LCM* 2 (1977): 13–18.

Platner, S.B., and T. Ashby. *A Topographical Dictionary of Rome.* Oxford, 1929.

Pollitt, J.J. "The Impact of Greek Art on Rome." *TAPA* 108 (1978): 155–74.

Pomeroy, A.J. "Livy's Death Notices." *G&R* 35, no. 2 (1988): 172–83.

———. *The Appropriate Comment.* Frankfurt, 1991.

Poucet, J. *Recherches sur la légende sabine des origines de Rome.* Kinshasa, 1967.

———. "Le premier livre de Tite-Live et l'histoire." *LEC* 43 (1975): 327–49.

Purcell, N. "Rediscovering the Roman Forum." *JRA* 2 (1989): 156–66.

Quint, D. *Epic and Empire.* Princeton, 1993.

Raaflaub, K.A., and M. Toher, eds. *Between Republic and Empire: Interpretations of Augustus and His Principate.* Berkeley and Los Angeles, 1990.

Reiter, W. *Aemilius Paullus: Conquerer of Greece.* New York, 1988.

Richardson, J.S. "The Triumph, the Praetors, and the Senate in the Early Second Century B.C." *JRS* 65 (1975): 50–63.

Richardson, L., jr. "Honos et Virtus and the Sacra Via." *AJA* 82 (1978): 240–46.

———. *A New Topographical Dictionary of Ancient Rome.* Baltimore, 1992.

Romm, J. *The Edges of the Earth in Ancient Thought.* Princeton, 1992.

Russel, D.A. *Greek Declamation.* Cambridge, 1983.

Russel, D.A., and N.G. Wilson, eds. *Menander Rhetor.* Oxford, 1981.

Rykwert, J. *The Idea of a Town: The Anthropology of Urban Form in Rome, Italy, and the Ancient World.* Princeton, 1976.

Sacks, K. *Polybius on the Writing of History.* Classical Studies 24. Berkeley and Los Angeles, 1981.

Santoro L'Hoir, F. "Heroic Epithets and Recurrent Themes in *Ab Urbe Condita.*" *TAPA* 120 (1990): 221–42.

Scullard, H.H. *Scipio Africanus in the Second Punic War.* Cambridge, 1930.

———. *Scipio Africanus: Soldier and Politician.* New York, 1970.

———. *Roman Politics, 220–150 B.C.* Oxford, 1973.

Shatzman, I. "The Roman General's Authority over Booty." *Historia* 21 (1972): 177–205.

Shipley, F.W. "Chronology of the Building Operations in Rome from the Death of Caesar to the Death of Augustus." *MAAR* 9 (1931): 7–60.

———. *Agrippa's Building Activities in Rome*. St. Louis, 1933.

Skutsch, O., ed. *The Annals of Quintus Ennius*. Oxford, 1985.

Solodow, J.B. "Livy and the Story of Horatius I.24–26." *TAPA* 109 (1979): 251–68.

Spengel L., and A. Spengel, eds. *M. Terenti Varronis de lingua latina libri*. New York, 1885. Reprint, 1979.

Stadter, P.A. "The Structure of Livy's History." *Historia* 21 (1972): 287–307.

Stanton, G.R. "*Cunctando Restituit Rem:* The Tradition about Fabius." *Antichthon* 5 (1971): 49–56.

Stevenson, T.R. "The Ideal Benefactor and the Father Analogy in Greek and Roman Thought." *CQ*, n.s., 42 (1992): 421–36.

Strong, E.S. *Roman Sculpture from Augustus to Constantine*. New York, 1907. Reprint, 1969.

Syme, R. *The Roman Revolution*. Oxford, 1939.

———. "Livy and Augustus." *HSCP* 64 (1959): 27–87.

Thomas, R. *Lands and Peoples in Roman Poetry: The Ethnographical Tradition*. Cambridge, 1982.

Toher, M. "Augustus and the Evolution of Roman Historiography." In *Between Republic and Empire: Interpretations of Augustus and His Principate,* ed. K.A. Raaflaub and M. Toher, 139–54. Berkeley and Los Angeles, 1990.

Toynbee, J.M.C. *Hannibal's Legacy*. 2 vols. Oxford, 1965.

Trankle, H. *Livius und Polybius*. Basel, 1977.

Tuan, Y. *Topophilia: A Study of Environmental Perception, Attitudes, and Values*. Englewood Cliffs, N.J., 1974.

Ullman, B.L. "History and Tragedy." *TAPA* 73 (1942): 25–53.

Vahlen, J., ed. *Ennianae poesis reliquiae*. Amsterdam, 1963.

Valvo, A. *La Sedizione di Manlio Capitolino in Tito Livio*. Memorie dell'instituto Lombardo, Accademia di Scienze e Lettere, vol. 38, no. 1. Milan, 1983.

Van Sickle, J. "The Elogia of the Cornelii Scipiones and the Origin of Epigram at Rome." *AJP* 108 (1987): 41–55.

———. "The First Hellenistic Epigrams at Rome." *BICS* suppl. 51 (1988): 143–56.

Vasaly, A. *Representations: Images of the World in Ciceronian Oratory*. Berkeley and Los Angeles, 1993.

Versnel, H.S. *Triumphus: An Inquiry into the Origin, Development, and Meaning of the Roman Triumph*. Leiden, 1970.

Walbank, F.W. *A Historical Commentary on Polybius*. 3 vols. Oxford, 1957–79.

———. "The Fourth and Fifth Decades." In *Livy,* ed. T.A. Dorey, 47–72. London, 1971.

———. *Selected Papers: Studies in Greek and Roman History and Historiography*. Cambridge, 1985.

Wallace-Hadrill, A. "*Civilis Princeps:* Between Citizen and King." *JRS* 72 (1982): 32–48.

———. "The Social Structure of the Roman House." *PBSR* 56 (1988): 43–97.

———. "Rome's Cultural Revolution." Review of *The Power of Images in the Age of Augustus,* by P. Zanker. *JRS* 79 (1989): 157–64.

———. *Houses and Society in Pompeii and Herculaneum.* Princeton, 1994.

Walsh, P.G. "The Literary Techniques of Livy." *RhM* 97 (1954): 97–114.

———. "Livy and Stoicism." *AJP* 79 (1958): 355–75.

———. *Livy, His Historical Aims and Methods.* Cambridge, 1961.

———. *Livy, Greece, and Rome.* New Surveys in the Classics, no. 8. Oxford, 1974.

———. "Livy and the Aims of 'Historia': An Analysis of the Third Decade." *ANRW* II.30.2 (1982): 1058–74.

Wankenne, J. "Le chapitre 1.13 de Tite-Live." *LEC* 43 (1975): 350–66.

Weinstock, S. *Divus Julius.* Oxford, 1971.

Wheeldon, M.J. " 'True Stories': The Reception of Historiography in Antiquity." In *History as Text,* ed. A. Cameron, 33–63. London, 1989.

White, H. "Rhetoric and History." In *Theories of History: Papers Read at a Clark Library Seminar, March 6, 1976,* by H. White and F.E. Manuel, 3–25. Los Angeles, 1978.

———. *The Content of the Form: Narrative Discourse and Historical Representation.* Baltimore, 1987.

Wirszubski, C. *Libertas as a Political Idea at Rome.* Cambridge, 1950.

Wiseman, T.P. *Clio's Cosmetics.* Leicester, 1979.

———. "Monuments and the Roman Annalists." In *Past Perspectives: Studies in Greek and Roman Historical Writing,* ed. I.S. Moxon, J.D. Smart, and A.J. Woodman, 87–100. Cambridge, 1986.

———. "*Conspicui Postes Tectaque Digna Deo:* The Public Image of Aristocratic and Imperial Houses in the Late Republic and Early Empire." In *Urbs: Éspace Urbain et Histoire,* Coll. de L'École Française de Rome, vol. 98, 393–413 (Rome, 1987).

———. *Roman Studies.* Liverpool, 1987.

———. "Lying Historians: Seven Types of Mendacity." In *Lies and Fiction in the Ancient World,* ed. C. Gill and T.P. Wiseman, 122–46. Austin, Tex., 1993.

———. *Remus: A Roman Myth.* Cambridge, 1995.

Witte, K. "Über die Form der Darstellung in Livius' Geschichtswerk." *RhM* 65 (1910): 270–305, 359–419. Reprinted as a monograph, Darmstadt, 1969.

Woodman, A.J. *Rhetoric in Classical Historiography.* London, 1988.

Yates, F. *The Art of Memory.* Chicago, 1966.

Young, J.E. *The Texture of Memory: Holocaust Memorials and Meaning.* New Haven, 1993.

Zanker, P. *The Power of Images in the Age of Augustus.* Trans. A. Shapiro. Ann Arbor, 1988. Originally published as *Augustus und die Macht der Bilder* (Munich, 1987).

Ziolkowski, A. *The Temples of Mid-Republican Rome and Their Historical and Topographical Context.* Rome, 1992.

———. "Between Geese and the Auguraculum: The Origins of the Cult of Juno on the Arx." *CP* 88, no. 3 (1993): 206–19.

General Index

Actors in historical narrative, 27, 57–58, 124, 167
Aedes Libertatis, 106
Aemilia (wife of Scipio Africanus), 158–59
L. Aemilius Paullus, 1–4, 9, 11
Aemulatio, 130
Aetiology
  of Lacus Curtius, 31–32, 32n. 6, 51
  of Tarpeian Rock, 36
  of Temple of Jupiter Stator, 31–32, 32n. 6, 51
Africa, 142, 148
Africanus. *See* Cornelius
Allia, 60
Analepsis, 40
Analogy, 139–42
Animus magnus, animus maior, 98, 98n. 11, 109–10
Annals, annalistic style, annalists, 6, 8, 118
Antithesis, "one vs. all," 73, 79
Apodeixis, 180
Archimedes, 126, 131
Ardea, 63
Ars, 108–9, 121–22
Ars memoriae, 19, 22
Arx, 10. *See also* Capitoline; Citadel
Asia, 148
Auctor, 122, 167–68, 182
Audax, 120
Audience, 27–28, 33, 34, 46, 47–50. *See also* Reader
Augustus, Augustan, 13–14, 183–84
Author, 13. *See also* Narrator

Autopsy, 21–22, 161, 168
Avarice, 62
Aventine, 7, 89, 152

Basilica Julia, 106
Bellona, Temple of, 144
Beneventum, 106
Boundaries, 27, 48–49, 84, 110–12, 123
Burck, 96, 102, 125–26

Calpurnius Piso, 34–35, 42–44, 51, 121
Camillus. *See* M. Furius Camillus
Campus Martius, 7, 86
Cannae, 96–99, 99n. 14, 100n. 16, 141
Capitoline, 7, 75, 83, 90, 125, 152
  as boundary of Forum, 34–35, 38–40
  burned in 83 B.C., 76, 122, 126, 126n. 47
  as center of Roman religion, 3, 4
  as center of Roman world, 4–5, 76, 92–93
  as epitome of Rome, 10, 74
  as focal point of narrative, 59, 76, 145
  as "head" of Rome, 60, 63, 79, 90
  monumentum of M. Manlius, 59, 77
  as refuge from Gauls, 60–63
  rhetorical use of, 81–83, 85, 89–90, 149–50, 152

Index of Ancient Authors

Aeneas Tacticus
  1.1–3.6, 5.1, 6.1–6.7:
    101n. 19

Cato
  Orig. (*HRR* 83.10): 17n. 9
Catullus
  95: 17n. 9
Cicero
  Academica 1.9: 177
  De off.
    1.55: 30
    3.4.3: 17n. 9
  De orat.
    2.53: 165n. 58
    2.86.351–87.360: 19n. 13
  De rep.
    1.21: 125n. 45, 131n. 58
    1.31: 152n. 39
    2.12–14: 30n. 1
CIL 1.2.1211: 17, 184, 184n.16

Dio Cassius
  7.24.1: 88
  7.26.2: 84n. 56
Dionysius of Halicarnassus
  2.30–47: 30n. 1
  2.37.5–38.1: 35n. 15
  2.41–46: 34n. 13
  2.41.2: 35n. 15
  2.42.1: 35n. 15
  2.42.1–5: 44n. 28
  2.43.1–5: 31n. 5
  2.50.3: 31n. 5
  13.8.1: 65n. 21, 71n. 30

Ennius
  Ann. 370 (Skutsch): 109n. 32
  Epigr. 3 (Vahl): 161
  Var. 1 (Vahl): 132

Ad Her.
  3.30: 20
  3.31: 33n. 11
  3.30–31: 20–21
  3.37: 19
  3.16–40: 19n. 13
Herodotus
  1.1–5: 36
  1.6: 37n. 20
Hierocles (Stobaeus)
  4.671–673: 140–41
Horace
  Odes 3.30.1–2: 17n. 9, 23

ILLRP 323: 1n. 2

Livy
  Pref.
    1–2: 177
    3: 12, 20, 119–20
    4: 20, 180, 184
    5: 120
    6: 169
    9: 6n. 15, 23, 180
    10: 6n. 15, 23, 124, 180, 184
    13: 169, 180

    1.1.1: 180
    1.3.8, 9: 7n. 20
    1.4.4: 7n. 20

Livy *(continued)*
  25.37.1–3: 108–9
  25.37.4, 5, 6, 7, 8–11: 110
  25.37.8: 120
  25.37.15, 16: 113
  25.38.3: 116n. 37
  25.38.4: 117n. 38, 120
  25.38.5–6: 117n. 39, 119–20
  25.38.8–11: 117–18
  25.38.11, 14–15, 23: 120
  25.38.18: 107n. 32, 120
  25.39.2, 3, 4: 114
  25.39.5, 7, 9, 10: 115
  25.39.12–18: 121
  25.39.17: 4
  25.40.1–3: 124–25

  26.2.10–11: 106n. 26
  26.7.3: 99n. 14
  26.8.3–4: 100n. 16
  26.18.6–11: 138
  26.19.1–2: 138n. 15
  26.19.5–6: 141
  26.29.5: 128n. 57
  26.29.9: 127n. 52
  26.32.5: 125, 129
  25.41.10–13: 100n. 16
  26.41.11: 17n. 9
  26.41.13: 99n. 14
  26.42.2–4: 142
  26.51.11–14: 95n. 3
  26.51.14: 142

  27.1.4: 99n. 14
  27.2.2: 99n. 14
  27.25.7–10: 127
  27.49.5: 96n. 6
  27.51.11–12: 94
  27.51.13: 95n. 4
  28.28.10–14: 107n. 29
  28.28.13: 127
  28.43.2–44.8: 142

  29.11.13: 127

  30.45.2: 142n. 22

  30.45.6: 142
  31.1.1: 179
  31.1.5: 20

  35.14.5–12: 174–75
  35.40.1: 20, 179

  37.15–16: 32n. 7
  37.33.6–7: 142

  38.12.1: 143n. 24
  38.48.14–16: 173n. 69
  38.50.2–3: 144n. 25
  38.50.4: 143
  38.50.4–55.7: 145–56
  38.50.6–9: 146–47
  38.50.11: 167
  38.50.12: 143n. 23
  38.51.5: 149–50
  38.51.7–14: 142, 149–52
  38.52.5: 152
  38.52.6–7: 153
  38.52.11: 155n. 43
  38.53.1–4: 153–54
  38.53.5: 143n. 23
  38.53.7: 155
  38.53.8: 155, 166
  38.53.9: 173n. 71
  38.53.11: 138n. 12
  38.54.9: 173
  38.55.8–13: 162–64
  38.56.1–7: 142
  38.56.1–4: 164–66
  38.56.5–8: 166–67
  38.56.9, 10–13: 156–57
  38.57.2–8: 158–59
  38.57.8: 23, 159n. 50
  38.58.4–8: 160
  38.59.10, 11: 160n. 52

  39.1.1: 159n. 51
  39.52.1–9: 142

  41.25.8: 179

  42.49.16: 4, 5n. 12

45.27.5–28.6: 1
45.27.10: 1–2, 2n. 3
45.28.4: 2n. 5
45.28.5: 3
45.39.10–11: 4

Macrobius
1.4.1: 172n. 67
Menander Rhetor
350.26–29: 33n. 11
351.1–3: 49n. 38

Ovid
Ars Am. 1.101–34: 30n. 1
Fasti 3.167–258: 30n. 1
6.403–4: 32n. 7
6.793–94: 31n. 5
Tristia
3.3.71–84: 18n. 11
3.1.31–32: 31n. 5

Plautus
Curc. 140–41: 17n. 9
Plutarch
Aem. 28: 2n. 5
Cam.
27: 65n. 21, 71n. 30
38.6: 86
Cic. 16: 31n .5
Rom. 18–19: 34n.13
Polybius
9.10: 128n. 56, 130
10.3: 139n. 16
12.4: 22, 163n. 55

12.24, 25: 22
23.14: 134n. 6, 148n. 33,
163n. 56
Propertius
1.21, 22: 18n. 11
2.11: 18n. 11

Quintilian
Inst.
11.2.19: 19
11.2.1–52: 19n. 13

Sallust
Cat. 47.2: 126n. 47

Tacitus
Ann. 12.24: 50n. 42
Hist. 3.71: 62n. 16, 126n. 47
Thucydides
1.10.1–4: 2n. 5

Varro
De lingua latina
5.148–50: 32n. 6
5.149: 34
6.49: 15
Vergil
Aen.
6.24–27: 17n. 8
6.512: 17n. 9
Aen. 12.945–49: 111n. 33

Xenophon
Anabasis 3.1.4–25: 118n. 40